The Naked Truth About Self-Publishing

Jana DeLeon

Tina Folsom

Colleen Gleason

Jane Graves

Denise Grover Swank

Liliana Hart

Debra Holland

Dorien Kelly

Theresa Ragan

Jasinda Wilder

CONTENTS

TIPS FOR VIRGINS

(HOW TO GET STARTED SELF-PUBLISHING)

THERESA RAGAN

Since self-publishing in March 2011, many exciting things have happened to me. If you take the time to learn your craft and then put in the hard work, I believe exciting things can happen for you, too.

After writing a great book and then self-publishing and releasing your story for the world to enjoy, I recommend spending the majority of your time writing your next book. It's by far the best promotion you can do.

If you write romance, I suggest you join Indie Romance Ink:

Indie Romance Ink
http://groups.yahoo.com/group/IndieRomanceInk/

PLEASE NOTE MEMBERSHIP REQUIREMENTS: New members must be ***ROMANCE WRITERS*** who have self-published or are indie-curious. They are a genre-focused group by and for romance authors, and they do not allow self-promo. Author service providers and other industry professionals are welcome as long as they are ALSO romance writers.

If you are NOT a romance writer, no worries. There are many helpful sites, including the following:

The Writer's Guide to E-Publishing (WG2E) is your destination site for practical and real information about E-Publishing in any genre. "We share what we've learned -- including the good, the bad, and the ugly – as well as "real numbers" stats. WG2E's goal is to do a lot of the legwork for you, to keep you informed, and empower you as you embark or continue on your own publishing journey."

The Writer's Guide to E-Publishing (WG2E)
http://thewritersguidetoepublishing.com/

Author E.M.S. Business Resources for Authors. Authors today are faced with a changing industry, evolving technology and growing competition. Tired of trying to find all the answers on your own? We're here to help. Author E.M.S. is a growing online community designed to help you streamline your business time without sacrificing the creative artist within.

Author E.M.S.
http://www.authorems.com/

These are only a few of the resources available to you. Just do a quick internet search for "self-publishing" to see what I mean. If you're new to self-publishing, you have a lot of reading to do.

For the first three months of my journey, I was learning everything I could. I spent hours reading blogs and soaking in any and all information I could find. I suggest you do the same.

***

Once you have published your book, you'll have many decisions to make. Use your instincts. Whether you're trying to decide where or when to advertise or what to price your book, the ultimate decision is yours. Nobody knows your product like you do. If ten people tell you not to go FREE, you should try it for yourself before you decide. You'll never know if something will work until you experiment and try it yourself. There is no one-step process to self-publishing. I know plenty of successful Indie authors who have never spent a dime on advertising, or who never priced their book for $.99, or free for that matter. Every writer will have their own journey.

When it comes to self-publishing, what do you have to lose? Maybe you won't sell hundreds or even a dozen books right away. There are no guarantees in this business. You need to be patient. If you're passionate about writing, write another book while you let readers discover your first book. Nobody is going to believe in your stories more than YOU.

Becoming an independent author has been life-changing for me. For the first time in twenty years, I am making money doing what I love best. If you want to succeed, you must work hard. Never stop learning and growing.

The industry is changing fast, but listed below are the steps I took when I self-published in March, 2011. This should help you get started.

1. Write a great book.

2. Find Beta Readers. Beta readers consist of anyone who is willing to read your book and let you know if your story is working. They can give you feedback on character development or continuity. I have family and friends who are willing to read my book and everyone tends to find something to fix, even if it's a missing word or two.

Tips from Belinda Pollard - What Makes a Good Beta Reader?
http://www.smallbluedog.com/what-makes-a-good-beta-reader.html

3. Hire a proofreader. I use Faith Williams at The Atwater Group. Send her an email to get a quote and to find out when you can get your book scheduled. Proofreading and copy editing needs to be set up weeks, if not months in advance, so make sure you contact her before your project is finished so you can get on her calendar. More editors and proofreaders are listed later in the chapter.

The Atwater Group
http://www.theatwatergroup.com/Meet Faith.html

4. Find a cover artist. Dara at LFD Designs for Authors has created all of my covers. She offers premade covers from $20 to $60 and custom covers now start at $100 (subject to change). More cover artists are listed later in the chapter.

LFD Designs for Authors
http://mycoverart.wordpress.com/

5. Hire a formatter. Lucinda Campbell at LK-E-Book Formatting Services is fast and affordable. "I am an author, so I know first-hand the formatting/publishing issues that can keep a book from being accepted by e-book retailers. I strive to give my clients a finished format that will view in the best possible way on all e-reading devices. I specialize in fiction (novels, novellas and short stories). Professional-quality formatting for Smashwords, Amazon KDP, Nook, Kobo, Apple iTunes and Sony."

Go to LK-E-Book Formatting Services website and email Lucinda if you have questions. Get a quote and get started. Depending on her schedule, she can have your manuscript ready for download within 3 to 4 weeks.

LK-E-Book Formatting Services
http://design.lkcampbell.com

6. Register at Amazon (KDP) by going to kdp.amazon.com and upload the prc file that your formatter sends you. KDP = Kindle Direct Publishing

kdp.amazon.com
https://kdp.amazon.com/self-publishing/signin

7. Register at Barnes & Noble (Nook Press - used to be PubIt) by going to nookpress.com and upload the epub file that your formatter sends you. Before the end of 2013, PubIt will become Nook Press, so you might as well register on nookpress.com to download your books to Barnes & Noble.

Nookpress.com
https://www.nookpress.com/

8. Register at smashwords.com and upload the word doc file that your formatter sends you.

Smashwords.com
http://www.smashwords.com/

9. Register at kobowritinglife.com and upload the ePub file that your formatter sends you.

Kobo Writing Life
http://www.kobo.com/writinglife

10. To upload directly to Apple iTunes you must have a Mac. You will need an Apple ID and then you will need to sign up at iTunes Connect:

iTunes Connect
https://itunesconnect.apple.com/WebObjects/iTunesConnect.woa/wa/bookSignup

If you do not own a Mac, you can hire Author E.M.S. to upload your file for you. For pricing and upload information go to:

Author E.M.S.
http://www.authorems.com/apple-upload-info-pricing/

11. Once you have published, you can copyright your book for a fee of $35 at the U.S. Copyright Office.

U.S. Copyright Office
http://www.copyright.gov/

12. You can buy ISBN's from Bowker (Identifier Services). I let Barnes and Noble and Amazon assign my book an ISIN #. When I used CreateSpace for my print on demand books, I used their FREE ISBN.

Bowker
http://www.bowker.com/en-US/products/servident_myid.shtml

To learn about International ISBN's
http://www.isbn-international.org/faqs

13. If you want a print book, it's free if you do it yourself. Register at CreateSpace.com. Use CreateSpace to help you with book covers, formatting, and editing for a fee, or you can go to the site, register for free, download a FREE template and then copy and paste your manuscript into the template one chapter at a time. CreateSpace will provide you with a FREE ISBN number.

CreateSpace.com
https://www.createspace.com/

TIPS FOR PUBLISHING A PRINT BOOK by Dana Delamar
http://danadelamar.blogspot.com/p/createspace-
tips.html?zx=6f42a62989252d3

Createspace Ins and Outs Explained by Bob Sanchez
http://bloodredpencil.blogspot.com/2012/01/createspace-ins-and-outs-
explained-by.html

14. Start a newsletter. Subscribe to a few newsletters to find out which newsletter service you prefer. A newsletter is something I did not do right away, but I wish I had. A newsletter is one of the best ways to reach readers

and let your fans know when your next book is available. Get started as soon as possible.

15. Start a Twitter Account. https://twitter.com/

16. Start a Facebook account. https://facebook.com/

17. Make a FREE website using Blogger or WordPress. Talk about whatever makes you happy.

18.Once I began making money, I used the following online sites to advertise:

Pixel of Ink
http://www.pixelofink.com/authors-corner/

The Romance Reviews
http://www.theromancereviews.com/

The Frugal eReaders
http://thefrugalereader.com/

Digital Book Today
http://digitalbooktoday.com/

Eye on Romance
http://www.eyeonromance.com/

Just Romantic Suspense to advertise.
http://www.justromanticsuspense.com/

To see more about how I spent my advertising dollars visit WG2E to read an article I wrote in 2012.

http://thewritersguidetoepublishing.com/how-i-spend-my-advertising-dollars

That's it. Those are the basic steps I took to self-publish.

Need more help? There are plenty of helpful tips to be found on the internet, but here are few of my favorites:

MORE HELPFUL ONLINE SITES

Susan Kay Quinn's Self Pub Basics (4 parts)

http://thewritersguidetoepublishing.com/susan-kaye-quinns-self-pub-basics-part-one-of-four-where-to-publish

Author E.M.S. offers a wonderful list of websites where you can promote your work.

http://www.authorems.com/promotion/online-promotion/

Kimberly Killion- Writer Resources - she offers a great list of reviewers, places to advertise, contests you might want to enter, where to find royalty free music for book trailers, etc.

http://www.kimberlykillion.com/writers.asp

Brenda Hiatt - Show Me the Money - Brenda Hiatt has been taking surveys for years and collecting data on what authors are earning. Lots of interesting information on what's possible when it comes to making money writing books. If you're an author who has already published a book, feel free to share your numbers with Brenda. All information is kept confidential.

http://brendahiatt.com/show-me-the-money/indie-earnings/

The Book Deal - An inside view on publishing - lots of great articles

http://www.alanrinzler.com/blog/2011/03/20/strategic-tweeting-for-authors/

Joe Konrath's A Newbie's Guide to Publishing - Read the archives, read everything.

http://jakonrath.blogspot.com/

EDITORS, PROOFREADERS, COPY EDITORS
(Don't forget to schedule in advance!)

iProofread and More - affordable proofreading and editing - Alicia Street
http://iproofreadandmore.com/

Proofreader, Faith Williams @ The Atwater Group
http://www.theatwatergroup.com/Meet Faith.html

Freelance Editor, Pat Thomas
http://patthomaseditor.webs.com

Freelance Editor - Glen Krisch
http://glenkrisch.wordpress.com/editing/

Victory Editing
http://www.victoryediting.com/services.html

Adela Brito of Four Eyes Editing
foureyesedit@gmail.com

Erin D. Crum (Jana's editor)
edcedits@gmail.com

Linda Caroll-Bradd
Lindakcb@yahoo.com

CopyeditingSavesLives.com
http://copyeditingsaveslives.com/wordpress1/

Annie Seaton Editing Services
http://www.annieseatonromance.com/editing-service.html

Karen Lawson - Line Edit and Proofreading Service
http://theproofisinthereading.wordpress.com/

And just for fun, try "Grammarly - The World's Best Grammar Checker"
http://www.grammarly.com/

FORMATTING
(Don't forget to schedule in advance!)

Lucinda Campbell
http://design.lkcampbell.com/

Formatting4U - Judi Fennell
http://formatting4u.com/work-order/

Brett Battles
http://digitalbinder.wordpress.com/

Formatting - Rik Hall
http://rikhall.com/

COVER ARTISTS
(Don't forget to schedule in advance!)

LFD for Authors - My cover artist!
http://mycoverart.wordpress.com/

Hot Damn Designs
http://www.hotdamndesigns.com/

Earthly Charms
http://www.earthlycharms.com/bookcoverdesigns.htm

Wicked Smart Designs
http://www.wickedsmartdesigns.com/

Damonza
http://www.damonza.com

Lewellen Designs
http://www.lyndseylewellen.wordpress.com

Once your book has been released it's time to celebrate! It's also time to think about what you can do to get exposure and promote you and your book. Don't forget to put aside time every day to write your next book.

Feeling overwhelmed?

Take a deep breath and do one thing at a time. Nobody can do it all at once. Don't forget to enjoy life. One of the first things I decided right from the start was to stay positive. This is not a competition or a race. There are so many writers willing to help by sharing information and real data. Nothing is going to sell your book better than word of mouth. That's why your product, your book, needs to be the absolute best it can be.

Believe in yourself. You can do it!

REVIRGINATION

(WHEN TRADITIONAL AUTHORS GO INDIE)

DORIEN KELLY

Some of the Indie Voice authors have been around a while. A long while. Say, like me. I'm a passably smart person. Smart enough to have thrived in this business for a decade and longer. I'm also smart enough to recognize that indie publishing holds value for me. I stepped into indie publishing though my backlist. I was used to being the voices of experience. Newbies came to me for guidance and advice. And now I was the newbie. Damn. A Virgin all over again.

I turned to my voices of experience, who just happen to be Indie Voice members though The Indie Voice didn't exist at that point. My trusted advisors saved me a whole lot of fumbling around in the dark. I'd like to do that for you.

GOT BACKLIST? GET. IT. BACK.

If you have anything ripe for reversion, request your rights back. Now.

1. READ YOUR CONTRACT.

Somewhere in all that boilerplate and egregious bullshit that lawyers love (Yes, I am a recovering attorney but you should construe nothing in this book as legal advice. Go out and hire your own lawyer.), you'll find a clause that will look something like this, which I lifted from one of my ancient Harlequin contracts:

When in the judgment of the Publisher the Work is no longer in public demand or ceases to be salable or profitable, Publisher may give notice to Author of its intention to discontinue further publication (Ed. comment: that would be when Hell freezes over). In the event that any time after the expiry of six (6) years from the last date of exercising any of the rights granted under this Agreement, all of the following are or become applicable in respect of the Work, namely the Work is not in print, not for sale and no other rights are being exercised by the Publisher, its Related or Unrelated Licensees, then Author may make written demand to Publisher to exercise any of the rights granted within this Agreement in respect of said Work within eighteen (18) months from receipt of such demand. ...(Ed. comment: deleting a whole lot of byzantine legal crap)...If none of the rights is exercised with respect to the Work pursuant to said written demand, Author shall have the right to request that the rights revert upon written notice to Publisher.

Write the letter and send it in exactly the manner the contract clause requires. And wait. And wait some more. Let's suppose the Reversion Gods smile upon you and you get your beloved book back. What then?

2. READ YOUR BOOK.

If it was published some time ago, odds are it needs updating. You're a different writer now, and no doubt a better writer than you were back then. If you don't have the work on your computer, use a scanning service to create a new document for you. Scrutinize it not only for scanning errors, but also to correct those editorial changes you accepted against your better judgment. In the case of a contemporary novel, read with an eye to keeping your story fresh. MySpace and pagers aren't what the cool kids are using, right? This is your big chance to make your book be absolutely everything you wanted it to be. Revel in it.

3. READ THERESA'S CHAPTER, "SELF-PUBLISHING TIPS FOR VIRGINS."

The woman is a rock star. And pretty and funny, too. If I didn't love her, I'd be totally jealous. Okay, maybe I have a moment or two of envy anyway.

4. GET AWESOME COVER ART.

I say this with kindness, but don't be a cheap-ass. Yeah, we're used to having the publishers do all the heavy lifting, including coming up with a fabulous cover design. (Let's not get Jane started on some of her less-favorite covers, though.) Now it's all on you. If you're the type who's going to love indie pubbing, this "all on you" thing gives you a thrilling sense of freedom.

Unless you happen to be an amazing graphic artist, hire a cover designer or buy a premade cover. Show the proposed cover to your trusted advisors or author support group (see Jana's chapter, "Author Threesomes and More," about why author support groups are such a boon to indie authors).

Recognize that the cover is there to sell books and pay attention to detail. Bad covers kill sales. Really. Like totally dead. But here's the best news of all about indie publishing: you can change anything anytime you like! If your sales are sucking wind, change your cover. (I suggest with all due deference that maybe Harlequin should break the freaking bank and do that with some of the backlist they've been publishing. I have a cover that makes my eyeballs bleed. The sales on that book suck, too.)

5. TITLE: TO CHANGE OR NOT TO CHANGE?

Authors usually publish their backlist under the same titles they had when traditionally published. There are the exceptions. Say, perhaps, you had a title imposed on your work that's both longer than a sentence by Dickens and nonsensical. If that's the case, you need to ask yourself one thing: Are you prepared to lose all of the reviews (glowing and otherwise) that the book currently has at Amazon and Barnes and Noble? Change the title and poof, they're gone forever. There is no way to have the online retailer link them to your newly titled edition.

Why do you care? Because reviews help power the engine of visibility. Reviews not only bump you up in the algorithm but they are also one of the criteria used by newsletters such as BookBub and The Indie Voice when they decide to give you advertising space for a book you want to put on sale. Most advertisers have a threshold before they'll even look at you. But sometimes the original title was just so bad that you'll go the extra mile and do the extra work.

6. SERIES ARE GOLDEN.

Let's suppose you got the rights back to a trilogy. Traditional publishing wisdom holds that series should be published in close proximity; say, three books in three months. Should you follow that publishing schedule again now that you're releasing the books? Hell, no! Get them all up there at the same time. Readers LOVE series. They love them so much that they go back and buy the next books in the series the second they've read the first one. Do not make them wait. (A word of comfort to those who for whatever reason cannot get an entire series up at once: you are not doomed. You'll just have to work harder to bring those readers back.)

7. THE NUTS AND BOLTS OF E-BOOKS

I'm guessing that you're going to first think about e-books only and save making print versions of your book available for when you're feeling a little less overwhelmed about this brave new world you've entered. The good news is that there are multiple platforms and vendors available to you. Yes, Amazon is the Big Kahuna, but there's more. And of course all of them have their own quirks and requirements.

I formatted my first three e-books myself. I spent long days in August, 2012 staring at my computer and sounding like I'd developed Tourette's syndrome as I learned how to make each of the platforms happy. I thought I'd done it right. Everything checked out and looked right in all of the previewers. And then the quality notices from Amazon began to arrive. "WTF?!? I set the font on automatic! What do you mean the book isn't legible on a sepia screen? There's nothing in the coding that should make that happen! (Insert other random obscenities here.)" After all that work, it seems I learned just enough to be a danger to myself. I now use professional formatters and spend my freed-up time writing more books. Was it a mistake to learn to format? No. Because now I can change the material at the back of my professionally formatted books at will. I understand the formatting process and in a pinch would do it again myself. But not unless I have to. Your own formatting mileage may vary.

8. MINGLE!

It could be that you were traditionally published back in the Golden Years, when the publisher had no expectation that you would have a public presence. If that's the case, be prepared to spend some time creating one. You will be thankful you did. Read Colleen's chapter on marketing. The woman has it down.

If you already have a website and an established presence in social media, get busy. But... Don't be a cheap, street-corner hooker spewing your ads and absolutely nothing else of interest on Twitter. Don't go post on other authors' Facebook pages about your new release. We've all seen it. We've all felt a little squidgy inside at the sight. Don't be that author.

Do interact with your new readers, and you will have them. They might not arrive in a grand stampede the hour you hit the publish button on your book, but they will come. Let them get to know you. You don't have to disclose your deep, dark secrets (unless you want to.) (psstt... Jane's cat runs her household.)

9. CLONE!

Read Tina's chapter (Multiple Positions) about all the different ways your backlist can make money for you. Capture every income stream you can afford to. Which reminds me... When you're over at Amazon setting up your author account, also remember to set up an associate account to use with links in your newsletter. Those clicks and buys add up. You're sending out a newsletter, right?

10. GET MORE BOOKS UP THERE!

If you have a book or series that a traditional publisher abandoned—as traditional publishers have been known to do—getting that backlist up isn't necessarily the end of the road. Keep track of your sales numbers. You'll know if there's a market out there for more. I am thrilled to be writing my Irish contemporaries again. It was too much of a niche market to make a big publisher happy, but my bank account is very, very pleased.

But what about my traditional publisher, you ask? Am I supposed to turn my back on them? That's completely up to you.

There are no rules.

None.

Scared?

Don't be. For the first time in our lives, authors have a financially viable alternative to working with a publisher. You can go full-out indie. You can stay traditional for your frontlist. Or you can be a hybrid. What you craft is all up to you.

FRONTLIST (A/K/A "THE WORLD'S YOUR OYSTER NOW, BABY.")

Smart publishers, and there are many, are seeking ways to work with their authors to both parties' benefit. There have been gains in some contracts (rights to worlds and characters not automatically grabbed by the publisher) and losses in some (non-compete clauses that choke off an author's capability to make a living). But one thing holds true in all cases: this is a business. You should be able to have a businesslike conversation with your editor about your self-publishing goals and how they fit into your overall business plan.

Maybe you'd like to write a lead-in novella for a new series you're traditionally publishing.

Maybe you'd like to contract with a certain publisher but only under contract terms that make sense to you.

Maybe you'd like to write a full indie series while writing another series for your publisher.

The Indie Voice is not here to tell you you're bad or rash or a financial idiot for whatever course you choose. But we are going to remind you that 25% of net royalties on e-books is awful. And that basket accounting is the devil's work. And that non-compete clauses are becoming too damn common. But we all make choices, and sometimes we swallow something horrible to gain a bit of good. Just be sure that it's really, really good.

A couple of our TIV authors have opted for hybrid careers, with very specific reasons for doing so.

Jana DeLeon revirginated to ebooks in late 2010, but still had one foot in traditional publishing, writing for Harlequin Intrigue. Because the Intrigue line is a blend of mystery and romance, like her indie books, she hoped to gain cross-over readership, but was a little apprehensive. The Intrigue line doesn't "do" humor and so her Harlequin books had a contemporary gothic-lite feel, versus her indie books which were full-blown single title and laugh-out-loud humor. Her apprehension was wasted energy. Two weeks after her first Intrigue released, sales of her indie books increased by 40 percent and have remained up. Now, that being said, a traditional contract will not guarantee you crossover readers. Every publisher does not have distribution akin to Harlequin's distribution network. And some readers won't make a leap that's even marginally different in style or tone. But if you chose well with traditional publishing, it is possible to utilize them as a paid marketing plan for your indie books.

Debra Holland started out as a self-published author and then became a hybrid author when Montlake (Amazon's romance imprint) acquired the first two books in her bestselling Montana Sky series. Her idea with Montlake was that they would publish her "big" Montana Sky Series books-

-80,000 plus words. She would self-publish novellas and short stories in the same series, and she discussed that plan with her editor before she signed the contract. Therefore, she specifically structured the option clauses and the non-compete clause to reflect that plan. She also wanted to self-publish any big books that Montlake either didn't acquire or rejected.. She was originally going to limit the word length to 50,000, but then changed it to 60,000. She couldn't imagine that she'd write a novella that long, but Mail-Order Brides of the West: Trudy came to about 55,000 words, so it turned out to be a good call.

Debra thought that Amazon would drive the sales of the first two books, Wild Montana Sky and Starry Montana Sky, and readers would then go to the self-published stories in the series. She also thought the reverse would happen, with readers starting the series with a self-published book. For example, during the holiday season, people might buy Montana Sky Christmas: A Sweetwater Springs Short Story Collection, either for themselves or as a gift. Or readers looking for bargain books might first pick up her novella, Painted Montana Sky, because it's priced lower at $1.99. This turned out to be the case, and she's been very happy as a hybrid author."

Let's suppose you decide to self-publish some frontlist. Everything we talked about regarding backlist applies, plus:

1. HIRE AN EDITOR.

Hire the best editor you can afford. If you think you're solid without a developmental editor, make sure your trusted readers agree. And then after that, still hire a copy editor. An unedited book reads like...well, an unedited book. Indie readers can be forgiving, but why should they have to be? Our goal is to create a product that's absolutely on a par with a traditionally published book. Or better, right?

2. BREATHE.

This "all on you" thing means that you have no one to blame (or praise) but yourself. Try to go with praise for making this leap. If you do, you'll have found new joy in writing and publishing. That's the very best part of revirgination. Now get out there and have some fun!

BREAKING UP IS HARD TO DO

(ARE YOU STILL IN LOVE WITH TRADITIONAL PUBLISHING?)

JANE GRAVES

Superstars have arisen from traditional publishing. Those authors have enormous readerships, get great contracts, demand huge advances, and their publishers handle all the details while they get to do what they do best-- write. Even in today's publishing climate, they're going to survive and thrive, and so are many strong midlist writers. If you're one of those successful traditionally published authors with contract terms you like, a publication schedule that pleases you, you're making all the money you could ever want, and you hate the idea of running your own business, stop now. This chapter isn't for you.

But if you've seen your print runs dwindle in recent years, even more restrictive clauses showing up in your contracts, your advances drying up, your sales starting to slip, or your publisher wants you to do a significant amount of the marketing of your books, then you should consider indie publishing. If you're an author like me who got caught in this midlist hell and would sincerely love to find a way out of it, you shouldn't just consider it. You should get moving and do it.

STOP WISHING FOR THE GOOD OLD DAYS

Have you ever gone to a writers' conference and thought, "Ahh. Life is good. The people at my publishing house know who I am. I'm invited to cocktail parties and dinners. I have an agent. I have made it!" It's a heady feeling, one just about every midlist author who's ever been to a writers' conference has experienced.

Not only were you a star at conferences, unpublished authors who were desperate to cross that threshold to New York publishing looked up to you with stars in their eyes, hoping some of your wisdom and experience would rub off on them. You felt honored. Special. As if you were a member of a club only a few select people were allowed to enter.

Those days are gone.

Okay, maybe not completely gone. But they're in short supply. Now everybody has the opportunity to become an author, and they don't need New York publishing to do it. Many years ago, if somebody said they were self-publishing, it was all too easy to discount their efforts as ignorance and/or desperation. Now suddenly there are self-published authors, one after the other, with bank accounts so big it would shock the hell out of you. How do you tell them they're ignorant and desperate now?

THE MIND GAME

When the Kindle went nuts, readers were looking for content, and suddenly self-pubbed authors were in the driver's seat. A lot of them had been beating their heads against the door of New York publishing for years and nobody answered. So they took those books they'd never been able to sell, self-published them, and found a readership.

So what about those of us with our traditional contracts? Suddenly a lot of self pubbed authors were making more money in a month than we did in the best years we ever had. I know for me, that was a tough pill to swallow. While you and I were watching the decline and fall of our print runs and crying when we opened royalty statements, they were banking.

In the beginning of that revolution, Liliana Hart sat me down and said, "I'm making a lot of money self-publishing." I said, "Hey, that's great!" She was like, "No. A lot of money." Then she proceeded to share some sales figures. When I picked my jaw up off the ground, I realized I wasn't in Kansas anymore.

So there I was, somebody who had never had much trouble staying under contract with New York publishers for thirteen years, and suddenly I realized there were people out there who had been self-publishing for only a few years and already they could buy and sell me a hundred times over. And if there were a whole bunch of authors at that level, how many more had to be out there who were making at least a living wage?

The rumble of my shifting paradigm was picked up on Richter scales three states away.

In a way, I wanted to believe it wasn't true. I wanted to think self-published authors making good money were few and far between, because if the opportunity really didn't exist for the average author, I could sit back, relax, and stay complacent. Then suddenly one person after another was showing me there really was money in self-publishing, sometimes big money. If I wanted what they had, it was time for me to get out of my comfort zone, get off my ass, and get after it.

There was a time when unpublished authors looked up to me as the voice of experience, and suddenly the tables were turned. It's a wakeup call when you realize you don't know the first thing about self-publishing, yet some authors out there are making big bucks. Suddenly I was the newbie, hanging on the words of successful indie authors and hoping some of their wisdom and experience rubbed off on me.

I've found that the hardest thing to overcome as a traditionally published author moving into indie isn't the nuts and bolts of publishing your own books. It's what's going on between your ears. You did things right. You learned everything you needed to know to get published. You got that traditional contract and felt as if you'd finally made the leap. But what happens when you turn around one day and realize that ladder you're climbing just might be against the wrong building?

There's only one thing you can do. Accept the fact that there's a brave new world of publishing out there, one you may need to jump into with both feet.

WHAT REASONS DO YOU HAVE FOR STAYING WITH TRADITIONAL PUBLISHING?

I've seen far too many traditionally-published authors stuck with bad contract terms, terrible advances, and print runs in the toilet who are scared to lose that bird in the hand, even though that bird is weak, anemic, and stopped flying years ago. Here are some of the reasons they stay:

1. I LIKE MY EDITOR.

I've written for five different editors over thirteen years. I've liked every one of them. They've all been wonderful professionals who made my books better, and not once did I have a cross word with any of them. But if the money is somewhere else, I'm not about to stick around just because I love drinking with them at writers' conferences.

Here's the deal. If you cease to make money for that publishing house, they'll dump you in a New York minute and not think twice about it. And they should, too. Why? Because it isn't personal. It's business, baby, and nothing else. So why are you treating it personally when they treat it like a business? Who do you think's going to come out on the winning end of that equation?

2. IF I SELF-PUBLISH, I WON'T SEE MY BOOKS IN A BOOKSTORE ANYMORE.

If this is your primary motivation, you're always going to feel as if something's missing, no matter how successful you are. But digital books are commanding a huge portion of the market and that's growing every day. I'm not saying print is going away altogether. In one way or another, I believe it'll always be with us, and there may come a time when self-pubbed books are routinely distributed to brick and mortar stores. But if you stay with traditional publishing solely because you're dying to see your books on a store shelf, what if you wake up one day and realize there's not much in the way of store shelves left to put them on?

3. I LIKE THE PRESTIGE OF WRITING FOR A BIG NEW YORK PUBLISHER.

Fine. Then keep writing for peanuts. There's bound to be somebody you can impress with those credentials even if you're not impressing your banker. And you will keep doing it. If you're one of those authors who needs the ego gratification of writing for a big New York publisher, you're not going to give that up no matter how poorly you're treated.

4. I'M AFRAID IF I SELF-PUBLISH A BOOK, MY PUBLISHING HOUSE WILL BE UPSET.

Stop feeling as if you'd be rocking the boat. They might not do handsprings over the fact that you want to self-publish, but whether they like it or not, it's a reality they're having to deal with these days. Some publishers even see it as a positive thing--your indie publishing efforts gain more readers for the books of yours they publish.

This is a business. Go where the money is. If your contracts are wonderful and you're making all the money you want, that's fantastic. I wouldn't do anything to jeopardize that, either. Stay where you are and enjoy the ride. Do consider, though, that this industry that was static for decades is now changing so fast it's nearly impossible to keep up. What's good today might be not so good tomorrow.

5. I'M AFRAID I'LL FAIL AT SELF-PUBLISHING, AND THEN WHERE WILL I BE?

I know it can feel as if your big publisher is your only means of selling books, and you're afraid of getting lost out there on the digital bookselling platforms. That's when it's time to read books like this one and learn what you have to do to get your books in front of readers. It's no more difficult than what you had to learn to get your books in front of editors and agents and get them interested enough to buy them. You were willing to do that, weren't you? But the truth is that you have an excellent chance of not failing (more on that in a minute).

6. I THINK SELF-PUBLISHED BOOKS ARE UTTER CRAP, AND I DON'T WANT TO BE ASSOCIATED WITH THEM.

Stop pointing to successful indie authors and declaring that their writing sucks, then blame them for trashing the literary landscape. Here's why. What you think doesn't matter. Editors' opinions don't matter. Or reviewers. Or other authors. The only people who truly matter to indie authors are the ones who click those buttons and buy their books--their readers. They're connecting with readers and selling books. Isn't that what all authors want?

To quote Stephen King, "If you wrote something for which someone sent you a check, if you cashed the check and it didn't bounce, and if you then paid the light bill with the money, I consider you talented."

7. DAMN IT, I WORKED MY ASS OFF TO GET WHERE I AM, AND NOW YOU WANT ME TO GIVE IT UP?

Nope. I just want you to take a good, hard, realistic look at where you are and decide for yourself. It's like getting a divorce. Maybe you've known for a long time that your marriage isn't what you'd like it to be, but lately things have been worse than ever. Sooner or later you have to ask yourself if you're better off with or without your spouse.

Same thing: Are you better off with or without your publisher? The answer to that question determines whether you continue down the same path you're on now or you strike out in a different direction. Only you can answer that question.

WHY YOU'RE LIKELY TO SUCCEED AT SELF-PUBLISHING

If you've written books for a traditional publisher for several years, you have an advantage over other self-publishers who begin from the ground up. You've already proven you can produce books readers want. You have an established reader base. It's just a different delivery method, one over which you have almost complete control.

Your readers don't give a flip where your books come from. They don't care how they got up on Amazon or Barnes & Noble. They just want your books. If you publish them and make 70%, or your publisher puts them out and you make 25% of net, your readers don't know the difference. Even if they do know the difference, they don't care. They just want the damn books. You're probably pricing them for less than your traditional publisher would, so they want them even more.

So really, with a readership already in place, the leap isn't as big as you think. Just learn the basics of self-publishing so you can continue to give your readers the books they love. They'll buy them, only now you can keep most of the profit for yourself.

YOUR AGENT AND SELF-PUBLISHING

Beware. Some agents will suggest you take traditional contracts you really shouldn't be taking, because it's only those deals that make them money. If you self-publish, you're effectively cutting them out of the middle. So be wary when your agent says, "Yeah, I know they're dropping your advance and your print run is going to hell and they want a tight non-compete clause, but that's the state of the market now and it's the best you're likely to get, so I think you should take the contract." Before self-publishing, that might have been a valid argument. What else was a writer to do? But these days your choice isn't between taking a crappy contract or nothing. You can take your books straight to your readers.

Still, your first inclination may be to accept whatever your agent suggests. After all, she has your best interests at heart, doesn't she? The answer is…maybe. If your agent makes no money unless you take that crappy traditional deal, ask yourself if that really is the best direction for you to go. I'm not saying she's deliberately selling you out for her own monetary gain, but I am asking you to look both ways before you cross that street.

Some agents these days are actually setting up publishing arms within their agencies where they'll do the dirty work--covers, editing, formatting, upload, and to a large or small extent, marketing--for their fifteen percent cut (or whatever percentage they choose to charge). Tempting, isn't it? To hand the smell and the mess over to somebody else?

But understand this: in most of these situations, there's very little an agent can do for you that you can't do for yourself. You can personally hire a cover artist, an editor, a formatter, and even somebody to upload your books to the various platforms. Once that's done, then you can collect your money for the remainder of the life of the book without somebody else taking a cut.

So please don't give in to the idea that you're helpless without your agent, or that they always know best. In my opinion, the ideal agent is one who supports your choice to publish your own e-books, and then offers to represent your print and/or subsidiary rights. For the self-published author, that's the best of both worlds.

THE HYBRID AUTHOR

Let's say you're under contract with a traditional publisher. If you have the time, write a book, a novella, or even a short story and self-publish it. That's an excellent way to dip your toe into the waters of self-publishing to see what it's like. As long as you haven't signed a contract with a clause so onerous that it prohibits you from writing something to publish on your own, nothing's stopping you. Of course, if you have backlist books, you need to try to get the rights back (see Dorien's chapter, "Revergination," for the specifics of how to do it). If you already have backlist books that have reverted to you, or books that never sold in the first place, get them up there. They may be worth a bundle, but not while they're sitting on your hard drive. Put them to work!

Here's the irony. If you successfully self-publish along with writing your traditionally published books, your publisher might be even more inclined to give you what you want in a traditional contract. Why? Because you're connecting with readers and making money, and they would love to have a piece of that action. Behave in a professional manner, work out a publication schedule you're both happy with, and you'll probably be able to do both. For many of us, that's a smart thing to do.

THE NEW SLUSH PILE

Authors wanting to get published have routinely sent proposals to New York, which end up in publisher slush piles. Then they wait for a yay or nay from an editor. Now, more and more, editors are trolling the net, looking for successful self-published authors to scoop up. New deals are being made every day. And it makes sense, doesn't it? If you were one of those editors, what would you do? Take a chance on an unknown author who's never been published, or sign a self-pubbed author who has already proven she can sell books?

The day may soon come when the majority of authors that publishers sign for print deals come from the ranks of successful self-published authors. And if that's true, what happens to the traditional midlist author whose numbers are shaky? Will they get shoved aside in favor of self-pubbed authors who already have a strong following? Yet another good reason to make something happen for your career outside of your current traditional contracts.

CONTROL IS THE ULTIMATE APHRODISIAC

Self-publishing offers a number of built-in advantages, giving you the kind of control authors don't have with traditional publishing. Here are a few of them:

1. YOU ALWAYS KNOW EXACTLY HOW YOUR BOOKS ARE DOING.

The first time you log into Kindle Direct Publishing and see one sale, then another, then another, right there in front of you in almost real time, you'll be hooked. Compare that to all those years you spent opening royalty statements every six months before you could see how your book was doing.

To be fair, some publishers these days are providing various means by which authors can get some idea of how their books are faring, whether it's through author "portals" or merely a weekly report to agent and author. These things are all greatly appreciated, but they didn't create those systems out of the goodness of their hearts. They did it because authors are demanding it. And by "demanding it," I mean that self-published authors can see their numbers on a daily basis, and publishers know they have to compete with that.

2. YOU CAN FINALLY HAVE THE BEAUTIFUL COVERS YOU'VE ALWAYS WANTED.

Ever have a crappy cover? I'm the reigning queen of crappy covers. Most were just average, but others were horrific. I once had one so bad--from a major New York publisher--that Publishers Weekly referred to it as "an eyesore." They loved the book and hated the cover. But since it's the cover that gets people to pick up the book, a lot of readers never got around to enjoying the story because they couldn't get past the horrible cover to buy it.

Nothing on earth feels worse than your editor sending you a cover you hate, because there's usually not a blessed thing you can do about it. Unless your contract states you have control over your covers, they might ask you what you think, but they're under no obligation to take your advice. But as an indie publisher, you can finally have the cover of your dreams. You can hire a cover artist and control every aspect of cover design. There's nothing like looking at your book for sale and seeing your vision of your story instead of somebody else's. And if for some reason you think you chose wrong, no problem. Just redesign the cover and upload the new one. Then watch your sales to see how the book does with the new cover.

Let's talk for a moment about creating your own covers. This is where all too many indie publishers delude themselves. If you have no eye for cover design, please hire somebody to do it for you. Many of you think you have that gift, but trust me--you probably don't. If you're not totally sure you're in that top few percent of people who have both the eye for cover design and a working knowledge of Photoshop, please save the rest of us from experiencing the eyesore you're sure to create and hire somebody to do it for you.

3. NOW YOU CAN PUBLISH THAT QUIRKY BOOK YOUR TRADITIONAL PUBLISHER TURNED DOWN.

How many of you have gotten a proposal past an editor and watched it move up the food chain, only to have it come to a screeching halt in that department that really determines what a publishing house buys--Sales and Marketing? The explanation to you for why they were turning it down may have been one of these:

- We don't know how to market it.
- (Insert your genre here) is dead.
- Readers don't want books with a character who (insert his profession).
- Readers won't buy books that take place in (insert your setting).

I could go on. When major publishers put out a print edition, they're very wary of releasing something that's not tried and true because they have a lot of money in the process already. As a self-publisher, you can spend a nominal amount of money, learn the basics of online marketing, publish a book, and it has a good chance of finding an audience. Now that book you love that you were afraid would never see the light of day has a shot at success because the pool of potential readers is so huge.

4. YOU'LL EARN A HIGHER PERCENTAGE FOR EACH BOOK SOLD.

Which would you rather have? Twenty five percent of net (which usually ends up being about 17%) or 70%? Of course you're familiar with that argument in favor of self publishing. And I'm likewise sure you've heard the counter argument, which is, "But in order to earn that 70%, you have to do all the work yourself." Okay, fine. But exactly what does your traditional publisher do to sell your e-books that's worth you giving up 53% of your profit? I know it's a mind bender for the author who's always worked under the assumption that for all that money their publisher keeps, they must be doing something wonderful. But look at your royalty statements. Are they?

Okay, so what about print books? They distribute those to the various retailers, which is something a self-published author can't do. But if you're like most midlist authors, you're getting only 6% to 8% of the cover price, and print runs are going down, down, down. Borders is already dead, other retailers are cutting back on shelf space for books, and Barnes & Noble seems determined to shoot itself in the foot. Those print books you're depending on today may not even have a place to go tomorrow.

5. YOU CAN PUBLISH YOUR WORK AT WILL AND PRICE IT ANY WAY YOU WANT TO.

The publication of a traditional book generally takes longer than it does to have a baby, and it's just about as painful. When you self-publish, you can put your books up whenever you want to without being at the mercy of a publication schedule you had nothing to do with. And you can price your books any way you want to in order to maximize your profit.

BE TRUE TO YOURSELF ABOUT RUNNING YOUR OWN BUSINESS

For as much as I'd like to encourage you to take advantage of the amazing opportunity self-publishing allows, I know there are some of you who wouldn't enjoy running your own mini publishing empire. It's one hell of a lot of work. The learning curve is steep. And in spite of the sales a lot of authors are making, there's absolutely no guarantee of success.

How do you feel about taking over the functions your publisher is currently performing? Covers, cover copy, formatting, editing, and to some extent, marketing? It's not rocket science, but it is time consuming, and you'll have to spend some money if you want to create a quality product. If you're not in a position to spend that time and money, you're uptight about managing all the aspects of your publishing business, or you don't think the risk-to-reward ratio is worth it, then stay where you are. Just understand that more and more, "where you are" can shift like sand beneath your feet.

TAKE ACTION!

Is the opportunity still there to make money, even big money in self-publishing? Absolutely. But the longer you wait, the more technology will get away from you and the more out of the loop you'll feel. Let that distance become too great, and pretty soon you may feel as if it's too steep a hill to climb. Stop wishing for times gone past, get your brain around what's happening in the here and now, and get on board.

If you're willing to listen, learn, and work your tail off, the rewards of self-publishing are there. You're already a published author with an established readership, so you have a leg up. If you shift gears, take the reins yourself, and go straight to your reader, you'll find success. I'm sure of it.

Now go do it!

CONQUERING THE BOTTOM BEFORE YOU CAN BE ON TOP

(WRITING A BUSINESS PLAN)

DENISE GROVER SWANK

Most authors are creative people. Our goal is to write stories and hopefully send them out into the world so that people will read them and lavish our babies with praise. And money. Don't forget the money. ;)

But the reality is that it's tougher than ever to get published in the traditional world, and many authors are self-publishing. The beauty of self-publishing is that there's potentially more money to be made, but it's harder for those authors to get attention. What they really need to do is come up with a plan. Marketing is a topic for another workshop, so for now, we'll focus on laying the foundation of your business.

I published my first four books in the latter half of 2011—and was shocked that I actually sold copies of them. And not just a few. By the end of 2011, I'd sold over 26,000 books, 95% of which were e-books. When I tallied my sales towards the end of December, a light bulb went off in my head.

I could actually make money doing what I love.

But to be successful, I had to separate the writing from the business.

My brother had recently started his own wholesale floral small business and had completed a business plan to get a loan. I decided that I needed a plan like his. A road map of future projects, and projected earnings and expenses. I had personally subsidized my book-publishing venture in 2011—four books that needed covers, copy editing, proofreading, formatting, and blog tours. But I wanted my business to be completely self-sufficient, which meant that I needed to put every line item on paper and plan accordingly.

When I created my first business plan, I couldn't find much information to tailor a plan for authors. (There's much more available now that can be found with an internet search.) I ended up using a blend of business plans I found on the internet, including ones from the Small Business Administration (sba.gov) and inc.com. But before you know what type of plan to use, it's important to figure out what you're wanting from your plan.

For me, I was setting up my business. Even though I'd published my first book six months earlier, I hadn't given much thought to the fact that I became a business the moment I hit publish. First, I had to determine whether I was a sole proprietorship, or if I needed to form an LLC. I consulted with an accountant to decide which was the best path for me at the time. No matter which business type I chose, I needed to come up with a business name. I also needed to register my business with my city and state, as well as set up a business checking account. I also had to submit a DBA form with my state.

The name I created for my business is Bramagioia Enterprises. My first business plan is written for a sole proprietorship. Bramagioia is a combination of Italian words that means "yearning for joy" and while it has deep, personal meaning to me, NO ONE knows how to pronounce it (Bram-a-joy-a). It's not necessarily a big deal, but I am considering changing the name in the next few months, probably to DGS Enterprises. I mention my business name because you will see its name throughout examples of my business plan below.

What do you want your business plan to do? I wasn't really sure what I needed or wanted when I created mine, so I followed business plan templates fairly close. Here's the table of contents for my original twenty-three-page plan:

TABLE OF CONTENTS

A lot of these concepts were foreign to me, and I had no idea how to fill them out. I studied several examples on the internet and then adapted them to what I thought I wanted. Some were simple concepts, like the description of the business and ownership, but they really made me dig a bit deeper than I might have otherwise.

Descriptions are my updated business plan for 2013 unless otherwise noted.

1. DESCRIPTION OF BRAMAGIOIA ENTERPRISES

Use this section to take a good look at what you want your business to do. What kind of salary do you plan to take? What's really important to note is that all funds coming into the business, belong to the business. Any money allocated for personal use is considered a salary.

The purpose of Bramagioia Enterprises is to spearhead publishing and merchandising the written creations of Denise Grover Swank. Most creations are novels, although some will include novellas, short stories, flash fiction and a memoir. Genres at this time include urban fantasy, humorous Southern mystery, Young Adult paranormal/science fiction romance, a new adult contemporary romance series, and a short memoir. All creations will be available to the public for sale via e-books and print for novels. Audiobooks will be created when deemed financially beneficial.

As of January 1st, 2013, Bramagioia Enterprises will provide Denise Grover Swank with minimum income of $XXXX per month, which will be raised as needed, when finances are available. All remaining funds will be left in a bank account until further action is deemed necessary. Denise Grover Swank may only take funds that are not allocated for future expenses for the year.

2. OWNERSHIP OF BRAMAGIOIA ENTERPRISES AND LOCATION OF BUSINESS

My current business plan lists my business as a sole proprietorship, although I'm considering forming an LLC. It's important to remember that a business plan is organic. It adapts to the changes you make along your publishing journey. Don't be afraid to make changes.

This current section is similar to my original plan, but has been changed to add my agent and my part-time employees.

Bramagioia Enterprises is a sole proprietorship operated and managed by Denise Grover Swank. Bramagioia Enterprises currently has one part-time employee, a personal assistant to Denise and two consultants—a virtual assistant and a graphic designer. Consultants such as accountants and attorneys may be hired to offer professional expertise and services. Other professionals will be used to aid the preparation of the creative works of Denise Grover Swank to be made available for sale through various outlets. Such professionals may include but are not limited to: cover designers, developmental editors, copy editors, proofreaders, and book formatters.

Denise Grover Swank is represented by Jim McCarthy of Dystel & Goderich for foreign rights deals, and movie and television options on self-published works and works released through a publisher. Bramagioia Enterprises may need to contract additional professionals or agents outside of the realm of Denise's expertise.

Bramagioia Enterprises will be run and operated in a designated office on the residential premises of Denise Grover Swank. Bramagioia Enterprises will provide Denise Grover Swank with a desk and desktop computer, a printer, and a laptop for mobility. Additional software and equipment will be provided if finances are sufficient and a need has been demonstrated.

3. PRODUCTS

Products include my books, obviously. But they have also come to include audiobooks, as well as a few items I have for sale through Zazzle, and a few products related to my books.

PRODUCTS OFFERED BY BRAMAGIOIA ENTERPRISES

Here is where I list all the books I have available for sale, and the month and year of their release. I list them by the following categories:

Currently available from Bramagioia Enterprises in print and e-book
Currently available in e-book only
Currently available as Audiobook

THE NAKED TRUTH ABOUT SELF-PUBLISHING

When I look at my current products, including e-book box sets, I currently have seventeen products available. This is also where I list my future projects.

PLANNED FOR 2013:

- *The Curse Keepers* (The Curse Keepers #1) published by 47North, due March 2013, release Fall 2013
- *The Death of Me*—a short memoir, February 2013
- *After Math* (Off the Subject #1—a new adult contemporary romance, March 2013
- *Redesigned* (Off the Subject #2)—a new adult contemporary romance, June 2013
- The Curse Keepers short story (1.5), due July 2013
- *Thirty and a Half Excuses* (Rose Gardner Mystery #3) July 2013
- *The Curse Breakers* (The Curse Keepers #2) 47North, due September 2013
- *Business as Usual* (Off the Subject #3)—Fall 2013
- The Curse Keepers short story (2.5) due November 2013

This list is subject to change. Notice that I have a VERY full schedule for 2013. I am usually adding and shifting things around, but it's good to have a general plan. I also have a schedule for each project on giant whiteboards on my office wall with the dates that my projects are due to editors, proofreaders, and when to start cover design, as well as the production schedule in a later section of my business plan.

I have future projects listed I know about for 2014. There are currently three projects already on the list.

I go more in depth with this in the financial plan below.

4. PRICING STRATEGY

Pricing is not only tricky, but polarizing.

When I started out two years ago, the 99-cent pricing strategy was strong, made popular by John Locke and Amanda Hocking. There's no doubt that the lower price was responsible for their success. While other books were priced higher, I knew I was a nobody in the publishing world. My initial goals were to:

1. Sell 1,000 copies of my first book in the first six months of its release.
2. Get readers to recognize my name.

To me, it made sense to price my first book 99 cents. A lot of other books were priced that low, and I wanted readers to buy my book. Buying a book with few reviews from someone they had never heard of was an impulse purchase. By pricing the book at 99 cents, I helped encourage it.

You'll notice that "make money" wasn't in my list of goals, and it really wasn't. Remember goal No. 1 was to sell 1,000 copies in the first six months. Obviously, I hadn't planned on making money if I hoped to earn $350 in the first six months. (35-cent royalty x 1,000 = $350)

I was told to think of self-publishing as a long-tail strategy. While a traditionally published book has a relatively short shelf life, a self-published one can sell forever. You might sell 10,000 copies, but it might take 10 years to do it.

But I was okay with that, because of goal No. 2: get readers to recognize my name, which I learned later is name branding. I wasn't a one-trick pony. When I published my first book, I already had two other books completed in two other series. Publishing was a long-term venture for me. I could be patient.

So when I priced my second book, the first book of an urban fantasy series, I used my original pricing strategy, but also did a bit more market research. I studied the top 100 list in contemporary fantasy and found that around half were first books in a series, priced at 99 cents. All of those were self-published. The other half was a mix of higher-priced self-published books and significantly higher priced, traditionally published books.

When I released the second book of the series two months later, I altered my strategy from Locke and Hocking. They had priced all of their books at 99 cents, but I priced my second book at $2.99. I was now beginning to think about money. I was selling more books than I anticipated, and I realized I could really make a living publishing my own books.

But pricing was key.

By the beginning of 2012, e-book pricing had begun to collectively rise, so I had no qualms raising the prices of my first two books to $2.99. And lo and behold, they still sold.

My pricing strategy has varied in two years. I've used free pricing on three of my books. The strategy worked well when Amazon's Select program was launched in December 2011, but the algorithms changed to limit the bounce-back sales. In my opinion, at this time, the only way to use free effectively is to make a book permafree. And that's only if it's the first book in a series with at least two or three more books already published in the series.

Remember when I mentioned that pricing could be polarizing? Many authors not only refuse to make a book free or price it at 99 cents, but become frustrated with authors who do. They claim authors are weakening the market with lower prices, and in turn, are hurting everyone's ability to sell books. I'll talk more about this down below.

Pricing will change over the course of a year. You cannot set up your business plan and then ignore the market. Market will always dictate price. So when setting up the Pricing Strategy section of your business plan, do so with the realization that this is not set in stone. (Along with the rest of your plan.)

MY CURRENT BUSINESS PLAN FOR 2013:

Digital prices of current products:

"Twenty-Eight and a Half Wishes": $3.99
"Twenty-Nine and a Half Reasons": $4.99
"Chosen": $2.99
"Hunted": $4.99
"Sacrifice": $4.99
"Redemption": $4.99
"Here": $3.99
There": $4.99
Short stories: $0.99

Box sets:

The Chosen $7.99
Rose Gardner mysteries: $6.99

BOOKS PLANNED FOR 2013:

"After Math": $3.99

"Redesigned": $3.99
"Thirty and a Half Excuses": $4.99
"The Curse Keepers": Published by 47North and out of my control

Turbulence in the rapidly changing e-book world should also be taken into consideration. Pricing may be subject to change based on sales, current pricing trends and need to create upward movement in Amazon rankings. Books may be discounted or offered for free if it fits with marketing strategy and promotion.

PRINT:

All print books will be created through CreateSpace unless it is determined another source is better. Pricing of print books is largely based on the number of pages in the book. Pricing is also dependent on making print books available for a wider distribution than just Amazon. Since expanded distribution is used, books must be priced so that the other outlets will be offered wholesale pricing. A book between 360 and 380 pages is $14.99. A book between 340 and 360 pages is $13.99. However, pricing the book for expanded distribution with an effort to keep the price as low as possible often means the royalty on a print book is less than a dollar per book, often close to 20 to 30 cents per book. Since the percentage of print books sold is relatively low (approximately less than 1 percent), Bramagioia Enterprises finds this acceptable.

This plan has already changed. I've lowered the price of "Chosen" to 99 cents as a loss leader to get new readers after declining sales. I've also begun to use BookBub for advertising, which requires posting a sales price.

A word of warning about sales: Some markets, especially new adult, have conditioned readers that books will go on sale at some point. They only have to be patient and wait. Readers mark the book on their Amazon Wish List, and Amazon notifies them when the price is lowered. I marked "After Math" to 99 cents several days before a BookBub ad and quadrupled my sales in six hours of the new price going live, putting the book around the No. 300 ranking on Amazon before the ad even ran.

Does this mean the authors decrying lower prices and free books are right? The performance of one book is not a good indicator of the market. But there is no doubt that overall sales of regularly priced books in the new adult genre are not as strong as they were before June 2013. Is it because the market is saturated or because readers are waiting for the magic 99-cent price point? Time will tell. But this is why it's important to not only study the performance of your own books, but other books in your genre.

5. FINANCIAL PLAN

From all the business plans I studied, this was where the business looked into the future. Expected income. Expected expenses.

This is the longest section in my business plan. This was also the hardest to write.

In both my original 2012 and my updated 2013 business plans, I've listed the previous year's sales in both total books sold and money earned.

But for me, the most important part of this section is the expected expenses. For each project I plan to release, I list the expected expenses including all editing, cover design, any expected promotion and marketing as well as listing price of the book. I can then estimate how many books I need to sell to break even.

With books in a series, I can often guesstimate how many books I expect to sell. But this is truly a guesstimate. You just can't predict when your sales will take off for a book or series or when they will plummet. You don't know how effective your promos will be. When I estimate my expected sales, I always estimate low.

After I've listed all expected expenses—including office supplies, business travel, any equipment (such as computers) I expect to purchase, and now my employee's salary as well as contract labor—I subtract the total from expected gross income, then find my net income. Again, I think it's better to expect a lower number than too high and fall short with expenses.

Don't forget to remember that you'll need to pay quarterly taxes. The more you make, the higher percentage of your income you'll be paying. I don't currently have this in my business plan, but it might be beneficial to note the importance of putting enough money aside to pay your quarterly taxes.

While this section is one of the most important sections, it's also the one expected to be the most inaccurate. As long as you know this going in, you'll be fine.

6. PRODUCTION SCHEDULE AND WRITING PLANS

I mentioned in my Products section that I have dates set for most of my projects with deadlines and dates to turn manuscripts into my editors. (I also have these on a giant whiteboard.) I have projects scheduled with my developmental editor into 2014. The schedules of good editors fill up fast. If you don't want to delay your projects, figure out a schedule, confirm it with your professionals, and stick to your deadlines as closely as possible.

In my business plan, I list every book I plan to write, and the schedule I plan to follow.

Production Schedule
Thirty and a Half Excuses:
Development edit: July 8
DE 2nd read and line edits: July 29
Copy editor: August 5
Proofreaders: August 16
Send to e-book formatter: August 23
Cover needed by: August 1
Expected Release: August 27

7. TARGETED AUDIENCE

When I wrote my first business plan, I realized I hadn't given much thought to this topic. Honestly, I still haven't done much more than I originally did. However, I've added a new genre to my list: new adult. I decided to try a different marketing technique with this by utilizing Goodreads. When writing this section, I list each SERIES and the target audience. My example below is for my new adult book that has March 2013 release.

AFTER MATH

The first book in a new adult contemporary romance. The story is told in first person present from the POV of the twenty-year-old female protagonist. The story is emotionally heavy and contains medium-sexual-heat content. The story is set at a fictitious university in Tennessee.
Rating: R
Number of books planned in the series: Minimum of three
Target Audience: Mature YA readers, romance readers
Best way to reach readers: Review blogs, Goodreads, current newsletter subscribers, give away free e-books to bloggers at Boston Author Event in March 2013.

If you have a good idea who your target reading audience is, you can try to specifically reach them instead of just shooting in the dark.

8. PLANNED MARKETING AND PROMOTION IN 2013

When I wrote my original business plan, I had enrolled in Amazon's KDP Select program. I couldn't predict the effectiveness of running a free promo when I created the plan, nor could I anticipate the ultimate demise of the program. (Note: many people are still enrolled and still run free promos, but there is no arguing that the days of 30,000 to 50,000 free downloads in a two or three day promotion are over.)

So what is effective?

I believe putting books on sale is the most effective sales-boosting tool at the moment. You can still get an ad through Pixels of Ink, but they are rarely available. Multiple sites offer ads, but be sure to ask around to see how many sales other authors have generated from promos. I've found some sites are much more effective than others.

Use a group of authors who cross-promote one another like The Indie Voice. We all send out newsletters promoting our books. This was wildly effective for my Young Adult novel HERE last November, especially on the B&N site. The success of HERE pulled CHOSEN up into the B&N Top 100 for over a month and a half, alone with the rest of the books in The Chosen series. I sold over 11,000 copies of each book on B&N alone in December.

No matter how well a book is selling, just remember that no book will sell well forever. But it doesn't mean the book needs to fade into obscurity. You can boost it with promo and make it visible again.

In my old business plan, I listed each book and what I planned to do for promotions, which also included book blog tours. Over the last six months, I've found most blog tours to be ineffective and have greatly cut back on using them to promote books. My newsletter is much more effective, especially with subsequent books in a series. My newsletter subscribers have read the first books in a series and are much more likely to buy a new book than someone who's never heard of the books.

In my new business plan, I list my proposed promotions by month. I'm usually promoting more than one book within a short period of time.

There's something else to consider when writing this section. It's important to brand and promote your author name. I do this by answering interviews for websites and review blogs who make requests. I also plan to participate in multiple author events, giving me a chance to interact with readers in person. My 2013 branding schedule includes five author events, three book signings, and the RT Booklovers Convention in May.

9. WEB PLAN AND SOCIAL MEDIA

A website is important. A good website is essential—a website that is clear and easy to maneuver. I'm currently working on providing changing content for my website. My own market research shows that dedicated readers visit my website several times a month, looking for news about my books.

Social Media wasn't part of this section in my 2012 business plan, although I'm not sure why it didn't occur to me to include it. Facebook pages are very effective as long as they are regularly updated. Some authors are finding success with Pinterest and Tumblr. If you enjoy those sites, by all means, make a plan to use them to give you visibility and help you sell books. I DO NOT mean posting "buy my book" updates. That is not only ineffective, but annoying. It's one thing to announce a new or upcoming release. It's another to outright ask, beg, cajole or berate potential readers to buy your book. Don't do it. It will backfire.

I focus more on Facebook than Twitter because most of my readers are on Facebook. The majority of my Facebook posts are personal status updates about my family or my writing life. They are usually humorous. I interact with my readers in the comments. This is all listed in this section of my business plan.

The following is my website plan.

Bramagioia Enterprises maintains a website titled Denise Grover Swank: www.denisegroverswank.com. The website is hosted through WordPress. The site currently has links to each series with blurbs, future release dates, and buy links to each available book. The site also has a review page listing some reviews of all books, frequently asked questions, about the author page, and a blog.

Bramagioia Enterprises plans to build a website for The Curse Keepers series before the late Fall 2013 release of the first book of the series. The website will have a .com domain and will be linked to and from www.denisegroverswank.com. The series website will have photos of characters, deleted scenes, "extras" not in books, maps, and anything else Bramagioia Enterprises deems necessary.

10. LONG-TERM GOALS

I find it hard to think about long-term goals and this is my most fluid section. I've added things to my current 2013 production schedule that I would never anticipated in 2012. It's important to make a plan, but be flexible enough to adapt to a changing market or reader response.

In the new version of my business plan, I try to be general with my plans. I've listed a couple below.

Bramagioia Enterprises plans a minimum of three self-published releases in 2014.

Bramagioia Enterprises plans to release one Rose Gardner Mystery per year into 2015, when the series will be re-evaluated.

11. SUMMARY

Just like an essay, this is where I condense everything into a paragraph of information.

Bramagioia Enterprises will see continued growth through 2013 and will release three new self-published novels, as well as smaller works with The Indie Voice. Bramagioia Enterprises will have a minimum of twenty-two books and audiobooks for sale by the end of 2013 as well as one novel available from 47North. Bramagioia Enterprises will continue to strive to produce high-quality, high-content books and stories. Bramagioia Enterprises will push to promote and brand Denise Grover Swank. Name recognition equals sales or futures sales.

While creating a business plan may seem like an intimidating project, just take it slow and give it some thought. You'll have much more insight into the business side of your writing and will hopefully help increase sales. All because you have a plan.

PIMPING YOURSELF OUT

(UNDERSTANDING MARKETING AND PUBLICITY)

COLLEEN GLEASON

When you sell your book to a traditional publisher, your biggest task is to write the book. The publisher then handles all aspects of marketing and brand management. Most of the time, you, the author, are merely along for the ride when it comes to decisions such as format, cover/packaging, genre, price and distribution. (That's not to say the publisher doesn't expect you to support its efforts — whatever they might be — by doing your own promotion, but by the time the book is released, most of the big marketing decisions have already been made — and usually without input from the author.)

It's a completely different story when it comes to indie publishing. In this case, of course, you're not only responsible for the work itself, but also for all elements of marketing the product. For the first time, you make all decisions regarding the four P's: **product (packaging), price, placement** and **promotion**. As well, the indie author must decide how to handle overall branding and brand management—which, of course, is *you* and your work.

It's absolutely vital to have a consistent, professional marketing and branding message regardless of what type of book you write.

So let's take a look at each element of marketing and brand management, and see how it applies to indie publishing in comparison with that of traditional publishing.

(Please note: Everything in this chapter applies to nonfiction equally as well as fiction, but for simplicity, I will use the word "story" interchangeably with "book" or "novel.")

PRODUCT

When marketing anything, the first thing you have to do is create or build the product. Obviously, in publishing, the product is the book itself. However, there are many facets to creating a marketable product as a whole besides just the words that make up the book. (And I say "just" with a gleam in my eye, because at the end of the day, there is no "just." The book has to be great in order to succeed, otherwise everything else is moot.)

So, regarding the product: There is the book. And not only does the book have to be a fantastic story with great characters and a solid plot, it also has to be put together professionally. That means edited, line edited, copy edited and proofread. Oh, and then formatted for the various e-book devices. Yes, there are several steps to preparing the guts of a book for market, and an indie author who wants to be taken seriously has to go through each one of these steps — just as a traditional publisher would.

But another crucial part of "product" is really a fifth P: **packaging**.

What kind of story is it? You have to define and express the answer to this question in order to attract the right readers.

If it's mystery or science fiction, the cover, the marketing, the branding, etc., will all be different than if the book is romance or young adult. This may seem obvious, but I've seen books that are marketed incorrectly — or at least, not as well as they could be.

The cover is the packaging and the very first impression your book will make on a potential reader. That's why the cover is the second-most-important element of your publication (and the first one is...all together now...*the story itself!*), and why you cannot skimp on it.

Read that again: *You cannot skimp on the cover.*

Contrary to popular belief, the cover doesn't have to accurately reflect the characters or an event in the book. It doesn't have to look like a snapshot from something that occurs during the story. So if your main character is portrayed on the cover wearing high-heeled leopard-print boots, but doesn't actually own a pair in the book, you don't have to go back and write that in — or even change the cover. What's more important is whether the *feel* of the cover portrays what type of book it is. If the story is sassy and sexy, and the character is sassy and sexy (or learns how to be), then leave the stiletto leopard-print boots alone!

Readers are trained to look for certain visual cues in book covers to tell what type of story it is, and whether it's something they like to read. Take a look at the Avon Historical Romance book covers, or any historical romance cover for that matter. They all look very similar. Although you will see trends in genre covers — we are currently in a trend where the heads of the heroine or hero or both are strategically cut off; in previous trends we've seen an array of heroines from the back, or non-peopled book covers with flowers or other icons on the front. And then there was the "clinch." The point isn't so much whether the blond heroine ever wears a purple gown in the story while walking in the garden — the point is that historical romance readers know what to look for in a cover.

(*Side note:* One thing that is important to reflect as accurately as possible when it comes to your cover is historical dress. Many readers of historical novels read only certain time periods, and use the image on the front cover as a signal for whether it's "their" time period.)

Thus, there are certain "genre cues" that indicate whether the book is a romance or a women's fiction or a thriller. The best way to identify those "cues" is to look at covers of other books that are like yours — particularly best-sellers. Make sure you pay attention to those cues when you're finalizing your cover.

So once you decide what genre of book you're promoting, you need to come up with a concept — or hire a designer who will come up with a concept and execute the design. Again, you're trying to get the feel of the type of book across — and I'm not just talking about genre (i.e., historical romance versus action adventure versus fantasy).

If your thriller book is funny, don't have a cover with dark colors. If it's a sexy mystery, let us know it by the title and/or the half-dressed couple on the front. And so on.

By the way, the title is just as important a cue for the reader as the cover design. Your title might be the clue for "funny" on a cover that otherwise depicts "suspenseful." So use your title as an element of the packaging as well.

A note about typography: One of the biggest mistakes I see on indie book covers is amateur typography. It's a dead giveaway. Pay as much attention to the type — the font, the placement, the size — of the title and author name as the actual image/design of the cover. I can tell you that a cover done with fonts such as Curlz, Papyrus or any script font like Snell Roundhand that comes standard with Word is going to scream "amateur."

If you're not sure what good typography looks like, take a look at books from traditional publishers. In particular, Signet, Berkley and NAL have excellent typography on their books — both front and back.

Speaking of back and back copy ... that's the next part of **product** and **packaging**. You attract the reader's interest with your cover — which has all of the genre cues you need, plus gives them an idea of what sort of "feel" the book is. Now you have to hook them further by writing excellent back copy.

Back copy is what traditionally appeared on the back cover of a book, but now is also what we use as the book's description on the e-tailer's product page. (And when you do a print version of it — which you will — you will put it on the back cover as well.)

- Make sure your back copy (or blurb) does the following:
- Gives the reader an idea of the *feel* of the book.
- Is short and clean.
- Does *not* give too many specifics.
- Does *not* detail the plot.
- Clearly leaves the reader with a sense of what the conflict is.
- If you have endorsement or review quotes, this is the place to include them.

If you're having trouble with your blurb, you're not alone. There are people who write back copy for a living, and it's not something everyone can do well. So get help if you need it. Look at other back copy — particularly on books similar to yours, and also on books that you picked up and were attracted to because of the blurb. Dissect it and see what the formula is — because there usually is a sort of formula, by genre, for back copy.

And one more important thing to remember … *you can always change it.* The cover. The back copy. The packaging. Nothing is forever. So if one cover doesn't seem to be working, *change it.* Rebrand it. Big companies do it all the time. So can you.

Once you've got your book formatted, a cover and back copy, you're ready to publish and start promoting, right? Eventually … but before we get to promotion, we have to talk a little about two other Ps: **price** and **placement**.

(By the way, in relation to uploading and making your book available on the various e-tailer sites: I'm not going to spend time talking about metadata and keywords — Liliana covers that in her chapter "Taking It in the Back Door." But suffice to say, those elements are obviously important — or we wouldn't have a whole chapter on them!)

PRICE

There are many pricing strategies to consider when you're publishing your books. Traditional publishers have generally stuck with specific price points that are determined by format, and format only. Right now, mass market paperbacks (mmpbs) are usually priced at $7.99. Trade-sized paperbacks are in the range of $12.95 to $15.95, young adult hardcovers in the upper teens ($17.95-$19.95), and adult hardcovers from $21.95 and up.

And as far as traditional publishers go, their pricing for e-books follows the pricing for whatever format the book is published in in print, within a dollar or so. The exception is that some publishers — particularly ones that focus on genre fiction — are experimenting with e-books, dropping the prices on the e-versions to as low as $3.99, even when the print version is $7.99.

For the indie author, pricing can be a lot of experimental fun — and confusing at the same time. How much do you price a short story? What about a novella? How long is a novella, anyway? What constitutes a short story? Should I price a 100,000-word novel the same as I price a 90,000-word one?

The simplest answer to this question brings us to a common tenet in marketing: The correct price is the point at which the (unit sales) x (profit) = highest revenue. Or, basically: Price it at what your readers will pay.

Here are a few strategies you might consider:

Pricing by length or word count only. Set a scale for yourself; there are several well-known indie authors such as Dean Wesley Smith and Joe Konrath who have blogged a suggested scale of pricing, taking into account the length of the work. Using this strategy, you might create a scale that looks like this: a short story (less than 10,000 words) for 99 cents, a novella (30,000-40,000 words) for $2.99, a short novel for $3.99, and a full-length book (over 90,000 words) for $4.99.

Pricing by date of release. Many writers I know price their new releases higher than their backlist. This strategy works particularly well if you have a series readers are dying to get a new book for. You might price the rest of the series at $3.99, then when a new book comes out price it $2 higher for six months or so — or until the next installment comes — and then drop the price. If you are a traditionally published author whose backlist has reverted, consider pricing those books lower than your new ones, for obvious reasons.

Loss leader, aka permafree. This really works best if you have at least three books in a series. Set the first one to "free" at iTunes, Kobo and wherever else you're "allowed" to give away a book, and then at a very low price (99 cents) at Amazon. Amazon may or may not match the free price, but either way, you will have the opportunity to lure in new readers who want to try something on sale. This strategy has catapulted many an indie author to the top of the charts. But beware: Amazon's price-matching policy is not only subject to change, it can also cause you and your books to be flagged by the company and could cause problems if you are pricing your book(s) lower at other places than Amazon.

Another thing to consider regarding pricing is the belief that "you get what you pay for." There are a number of readers who believe that books listed as free or very low (a relative term, but in my discussions with readers, the price point of "bargain basement" seems to be around $2.99) are priced that way because they aren't any good. *They couldn't be good if they are that cheap* is what this group of readers thinks. Of course that's not true, but there is a segment of the market that believes that — and if that's your target market, then you might rethink a low-price strategy.

Genre also plays a role in pricing. Romance readers are particularly voracious, and seem less sensitive to what some call the "cheap factor" of a lower-priced book. However, readers of literary fiction and women's fiction, as well as nonfiction books, often seem to have no qualms about paying higher prices.

The bottom line is: Price your work at where you make the most money. This means you'll have to experiment — and the nice thing about indie publishing is that you *can*. You can change a price at a moment's notice. You can put a different book on sale each week. You can put them all on sale for a month. You can adjust your prices whenever and however you want — so keep track of how they do and develop a strategy that works for you.

PLACEMENT

Placement is another term for distribution; in other words, how and where can the product be found?

Your goal as an indie author is to get as much placement, or distribution, of your product as possible. You want to increase your sales and revenue through market penetration. In general terms, market penetration includes three different tactics:

Product development — creating new products (e.g., a new book in a series)

Market development — finding new markets, or places to *sell* the product (i.e., distributors)

Diversification — finding new markets and creating new products (e.g., a CD of original music or T-shirts or other salable items related to your books/series)

I'm not going to talk about diversification here, but I will talk about the first two items as relates to indie publishing.

PRODUCT DEVELOPMENT

This is obvious. The more books or works available you have, the more products you have. So if you're writing a series, find ways to expand that series. Write short stories, novellas and long novels in that world.

Take that world and tweak it, bringing it into another genre. I've done that with my Gardella Vampire Chronicles series — I've taken elements of that world and brought them to my steampunk young adult Stoker & Holmes books. It's just enough of a wink-wink to my readers and they love to find what we call "Easter eggs" — hidden or subtle references to other books a favorite author has written.

Combine your books into a boxed set — either from the same series, or, if you're like me and write in a lot of different genres, consider a "sampler" set.

MARKET DEVELOPMENT

This is just as important as product development. You want to make your product available to as many people as possible.

This means expand your distribution as far and wide as you can. Make your books available through every e-tailer you can find, not just the (current) giant, Amazon. Even if you're given a "sweet deal" by offering exclusivity, in the long run, this is only hurting you — and your potential readers. The wider the net, the more fish you're gonna catch.

So list your books at Amazon, iTunes, Barnes & Noble, Kobo and Overdrive, and use Smashwords to get to places such as Sony and Diesel. There are new vendors and distributors popping up all over the place — for example, Bookwire.de is a new up-and-coming distributor of e-books mainly in Europe. Check them out, and any others that you hear about. Keep your ear to the ground and keep abreast of news in the digital world

THE NAKED TRUTH ABOUT SELF-PUBLISHING

especially — for the market is always changing. You need to keep on top of it and take advantage of any new opportunities as soon as you can.

Expand your market even further by creating print versions of your books. There are still readers who will not read e-books. You're missing out on a huge potential audience if you don't have a print book available. (Tina talks more about this in "Multiple Positions")

If you have electronic and print versions, why not an audio version? There are readers who prefer audiobooks. This is yet another way to expand your market.

And don't forget translations. Again, Tina talks about this in her chapter, but I wanted to put in a word here about the fact that there's a big world out there, and investing in foreign (to you) translations of your books can really pay off in the long run.

A word to the wise about translations: Just because someone is bilingual doesn't mean he or she can translate your book. It is so not that easy. A good literary translation is like actually writing the book, so make sure if you hire a translator, you have some people you trust — who are native speakers of the language it's being translated into — read a sample translation. Good literary translators are very expensive because literary translation is an art form, just as writing a novel is. In fact, a good literary translator is often a writer him- or herself. If you're going to invest in foreign markets, make sure you get a good translator, because in my experience, there are wayyy too many people who think they can translate a book ... and simply cannot.

And if you have your book(s) translated, make sure you hire someone *else* to proofread it. Yes, it can be an expensive proposition — but once the translation is done, it's yours. Forever. And I'm here to tell you that my foreign translations sell almost as much as my domestic books.

PROMOTION

Whew. Finally! This is what you were waiting for in a chapter about marketing, isn't it? But in order to have effective promotion, you first have to have a solid product and wide distribution, along with a solid pricing strategy.

Before I dive into some promotional tactics, I want to address branding and brand management, because it goes hand in hand with marketing.

Very simply, your brand is you. Your name becomes your brand, particularly if you write in a variety of genres. Your brand isn't your series or your books, but it's you — and the type of entertainment experience you and your books provide.

Above all, you must protect your brand.

Everything you do, everything you put "out there," under your writing name (which, remember, is your brand) represents and reflects on your products. Which, in turn, means you must always be professional in everything you do.

This means neatness and professionalism in your work, your materials, your online presence, your public presence, **ALWAYS**. If you have political or incendiary opinions, feel free to have them — but it's not usually in your best interest to share them publicly. (Paula Deen, anyone?) And remember: Everything you do digitally — on your phone, on your computer, via email, text, blog, IM, etc. — is there forever. Just ask the kids of Steubenville how that worked out for them.

So, keeping that in mind — that above all, you must *protect your brand* — here are some of the best promotional tips I know:

Have a **website** and keep it updated all the time. It's not that readers flock to author websites (they really don't), but you still have to have one. So don't spend a lot of money on one — you don't need flash or other animation, and you sure as hell don't need music! — but you need to have a clean, professional site that's kept up to date *with a place for people to sign up for your newsletter.*

Newsletter. This is the single *most important* thing you can do for promotion. A robust newsletter list helps you control the timing and content of any message you want to send to your readers — people who already love your work. But please: Don't add people to your newsletter list just because you have their email address. This is not only illegal, but it will really piss them off.

Case in point: I have three different author names under which I write. I do not sign up for anything, *ever*, with two of them. In the last month, I have received newsletters from *three different writers* whom I've never heard of at *all three of my email addresses.* Plink, plink, plink — that's how they landed in my email boxes.

The only way these people could have gotten these email addresses is by trolling Facebook or some other social media or online place and stealing them. I am really pissed off. I will never buy their books — which I'm sure is the opposite effect those authors were going for. In fact, I'm really tempted to publish their names *right here* ... but I won't.

Very bad decision. Bottom line: **Don't spam people.**

Be Consistent. Whatever you do, wherever you have visuals that represent you and your brand, do your best to make it look and feel the same. Consistency among your website, your newsletter banner, your name the way it appears on your books, all your swag and promotional items — the more you tie the look and feel together, the more recognizable your brand will be. Do the same with "sound bites" — descriptions of your book and your brand. Use the same phrases over and over, like a politician, to share your message. Even if you write in different genres, try to use the same sort of phrase to describe your work, your inspiration, your brand. No matter what genre I'm writing in, I talk about the kernel or core of my stories: They are all about strong women who find a life partner who accepts them for their strengths as well as their weaknesses.

Paid Advertising. It can work. There are many websites that offer paid ads, or newsletters such as "BookBub" (the current darling of the e-book/indie world), but their effectiveness will eventually wane. It's the nature of the beast, so it's best to use them while you can but don't rely on these sorts of promotions for your bread and butter. For a while it was "Kindle Nation Daily" that would spark huge increases in sales, then it was Pixel of Ink or "eReader News Daily," or whatever. Again, keep your ear to the ground, pay attention to what's happening and spend your money accordingly. This is one instance in which you sometimes can actually measure the effectiveness of advertising — quite an unusual situation.

Social Media. Liliana does an entire chapter on social media. Read it, and put into practice what works for you. Social media can be effective means of developing *relationships* with your readers. This can translate into sales, and, more importantly, it can translate into die-hard fans who will auto-buy anything and everything you write. These mega-fans are priceless. Keep them close and nurture those relationships.

However ... *a word to the wise about social media*: There is a fine line between building a relationship with fans and going overboard with information that's best kept private. Most fans don't really want to know when you've had a fight with your husband or what your political affiliations are, or where you just had a mole removed. Keep it light and fun and relevant, but not too personal. Not only for your safety — and that of your family — but for the safety and well-being of your fans.

Blog Tours/Interviews. These can boost your sales and visibility, but spending a lot of energy doing blog posts and interviews might not be a good use of time when you could be writing your next book. The more product you have out there, the more chances you have to be found by your next mega-fan. Writing anything can drain your creativity and keep you from working on your next book.

Advance Review Copies (ARCs). This is an excellent way to get visibility as well as garner reviews for online sites. Many indie authors offer ARCs to stalwart fans in exchange for honest reviews on or near the release date of a new release. It does help to have reviews up fast and early, but you cannot guarantee what readers will think of your book — so it's a risk.

Speaking of reviews… You're going to get them. Good ones, great ones, mediocre ones and ones that will just about kill you. My rule of thumb: Don't read reviews. Be the opposite of Nike: Just don't do it. Trust me, you'll be much happier if you don't.

Book Signings. Almost every writer I know dreams of book signings with a line of people crowding around, waiting to buy their books. It's definitely more on the dream end of the spectrum than on the reality end, especially now that we're experiencing the e-book revolution and there are a lot fewer people buying printed books. In short, book signings are an inefficient way to greet and interact with a relatively minuscule slice of your readership — and an even less efficient way to attract new readers. Still, it can be fun and rewarding if you have a good turnout … like in your hometown. If you do decide to do a book signing, try to schedule it with other authors so each of you will draw your core readership. Use a website such as eventbrite.com or togather.com to organize and collect RSVPs so you know whether it will be worth your while.

Conferences and Conventions/Public Appearances. This is a fun way to get your name out. If you like to give workshops or have techniques to share, doing lectures or classes at local or national conventions or conferences is a good way to connect with other writers or readers. It can be an expensive proposition, but remember: It's a tax write-off! And you get the opportunity to meet other writers and readers. There are also opportunities to speak at your local library and/or book clubs. Post your willingness to do any of these public appearances on your website, and mention it whenever you have the opportunity.

PUBLICITY (THE BONUS P)

Many people get publicity and marketing confused. The simplest way to differentiate between the two is this: *Marketing* is something you pay for (advertising, printing, website, swag, etc.) and *publicity* (or PR) is free. Publicity is something that happens with or without your cooperation: an article in the paper (with or without your interview), an unsolicited review, a mention by a celebrity, etc.

There's a well-known saying that "there's no bad publicity." I think the jury's still out on that, but in general, it's really not a bad thing to have your name/face/book being mentioned in any sort of media. (Which is another reason I'm not publishing the names of the three authors who spammed me!)

Because publicity happens with or without your cooperation, it's nearly impossible to generate it, especially when and how you want the attention.

However, here are some things you can do to improve your chances of attracting publicity:

- Make yourself and your information as widely available as possible — including via your website, articles, interviews, keywords and tags (yet another reason to be consistent with your message).
- Send out press releases regularly. If you don't know how to write a press release, hire someone or do some research.
- Start local. It's more likely that your local paper will pick you up before the *Los Angeles Times*. Then work your way up and beyond.

One thing you may not want to do is make rash, scathing or incendiary comments on blogs, reviews or other articles under your brand name. These instances have a way of being picked up and distributed. People tend to be more interested in sharing negative news than positive news.

IN SUMMARY

This chapter by no means covers all elements of marketing, brand management and publicity, but it's a good start. It gives you some of the basics and, hopefully, a few things to think about. If you want more information about marketing, there are numerous resources available in this book and elsewhere.

If you have a great marketing or promotional idea, let me know! I love to hear about new and unique things and I will share some of the best ideas with others on The Indie Voice Facebook page and in our newsletter. The best way to reach me is through www.colleengleason.com or my Facebook page.

THE ART OF SEDUCTION: LURE THEM IN AND LEAVE THEM GASPING FOR MORE

(SOCIAL MEDIA AND MARKETING STRATEGIES)

LILIANA HART

Social media can be an author's greatest friend. It can also be her greatest enemy. (I'm almost positive that's a quote from someone really important. Probably Theresa Ragan. She says a lot of important things.)

Everyone has an example of an author on social media who drives you crazy — those who go on political rants or who bash other authors or other people in general. And then there are those who spam you to death with their *one* book for two solid years while they could have been writing 140 characters a day on their next book instead. Hopefully, you're not one of those authors. If you are ... well ... maybe keep reading.

The purpose of social media is to interact with people and form lasting relationships.

I can't tell you how many workshops I've given where an author raises her hand in the audience and says, "But I just don't do social media. I don't like it."

The honest truth is, if an author doesn't use social media she's going to burn in a fiery hell for all eternity. Not really, but it's not going to help your career any. It's hard to sell books when no one knows who you are and you never leave your house, or put on real clothes, or take your hair out of a ponytail.... You get the point. If you want readers you need to *find* them. Not expect them to fall into your lap like an extra from "Magic Mike." All authors need social media. I don't care how technology-unsavvy you are or how much of a Luddite.

If you build your social media audience steadily, you can use it to reach a different core audience of readers every time you post. Your Facebook followers are not going to be the same group of people as your Twitter followers. Your Wattpad followers aren't going to be the same as the people you meet on Goodreads. They're all valuable in their own way and they're all necessary. And it doesn't have to take hours on end.

"Maximize your results for minimal efforts."

FACEBOOK

Facebook is probably the most well known of the social media platforms. I have both a personal friend page, as well as a fan page. My suggestion is that you use both. I'll tell you why when I get to the section on street teams.

Your fan page is your wall to tell the world whatever it is they want to know. Don't be shy about posting book releases or talking about your books in general. If a reader follows your fan page, it's because they're "fans" and they want to know about you. But at the same time, it has to be a good balance of pimping your book and being entertaining. The more likes, comments and shares you get on your page, the more visible you become on Facebook in general.

I like to experiment with different games that will draw people in, while at the same time slipping my book covers in their line of sight. Selling books is all about visibility (after writing a good book, of course).

My book "Kill Shot" came out in May and I knew I needed to do something different to garner interest because it's not like any book I've ever written before. It's a dark romantic thriller with my twisted sense of humor and an emotional plot that doesn't let the reader rest for very long. Because the book is about spies and every character in the book has their own call sign, I decided it would be fun to let my readers have call signs too. So I came up with "What Is Your Spy Name?" (See image 1a.)

[Image 1a]

It received hundreds of comments, over a hundred shares, and more than a thousand likes. My readers *loved* doing this and it was great advertising at the same time. The title is at the top, my name is in the lower right-hand corner, and the website that is specific for this series is in the lower left-hand corner.

Another way to draw your readers in and make them feel that they're involved in your books is to let them make decisions. Give them two cover choices so they can vote on the one they like best. (See images 1b and 1c.)

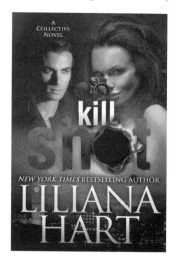

[Image 1b & 1c]

Put up pictures of characters and let them decide who should play the part if your book were turned into a movie. Both of these are a great way to open discussions. The more people who comment on your post, the more people who will see what you have to say. That's how Facebook's algorithms work.

The most important thing is to post something every day. Your readers will come to expect it. Even when I went on vacation for three weeks, I made up my posts ahead of time and scheduled them to appear while I was gone. And when I had a free moment I'd check in to respond to any comments.

You're probably thinking, "Great, Liliana. But how do I *get* the followers?" Your social media links should be on everything you send out. I'll repeat: EVERYTHING you send out. Including bookmarks and other swag, your website, and your email signature line, and in the back of every e-book you have. Make it easy for people to one-click you. The more you engage, the more people you'll have who will want to follow you. And above all else, make sure you respond if someone messages you or makes a comment.

TWITTER

Twitter is a different animal from Facebook. Hardly any of the people who follow me on Twitter follow my fan page on Facebook. That's why it's important to use both consistently. I've also found that my Twitter followers are more likely to use Apple or Kobo devices to read, and my Facebook followers have a tendency to be Kindle users. It's important to know whom you're advertising to.

Most writers I talk to don't really understand Twitter. They don't understand how to use it, what it's for, how to find followers or how to be seen. They'll get an account and then they'll let it sit there without ever having used it for anything. Or if they do use it frequently, they'll do something like spam their book at you every five seconds until you want to stab them with a fork or unfollow them (whichever comes first).

First rule of Twitter Fight Club: *Don't be an asshat or a douchenozzle.*

And I mean that with the best of intentions. Spamming your readers doesn't make you look good. Don't do it.

Second rule of Twitter Fight Club: *For God's sake, pick a Twitter handle where people can recognize you.*

My readers can easily find me @Liliana_Hart. But it'll be a lot harder to find me @crazywriterlady or @sworddancerninjawarrior. I see this all the time with writers. They pick a fun, outlandish Twitter handle thinking they're being hip and cool when what they're really being is unprofessional. Writing is your business. And you're in the business of finding readers. Let them find you and save the fun Twitter handles for your personal Twitter page where only your close friends or family can contact you.

Third rule of Twitter Fight Club: *Don't just find followers. Keep them. And be nice to them, too.*

The same rule applies for Twitter as it does for Facebook. Put a link to your Twitter handle everywhere. This might seem like common sense, but I promise a lot of authors don't think about including their social media links on their promotional materials.

How do I find followers?

Finding Twitter followers takes time and patience, but it's well worth it. First of all, you need to decide whom you want to target. The answer to that is readers. But what kind of readers? Romance readers? Mystery readers? Sci-fi/fantasy readers? Okay, but that's still pretty broad. What about paranormal romance readers or mysteries that have women sleuths? Target your followers for what you write.

I use a program called Tweepi. I've also used Twitter Karma, but it doesn't let you narrow your followers down as much. The first question I ask myself is what other popular authors write books that are similar to mine. For my MacKenzie series, which is hot romantic suspense, it's going to be Maya Banks, Lora Leigh, Cherry Adair and Roxanne St. Claire. Their readers are the ones I want to become my readers. For my mysteries, it's a whole other animal. I'd need to target Janet Evanovich for my Addison Holmes series or Kathy Reichs and Patricia Cornwell for my J.J. Graves series.

Once I know the who, it's easier to get the followers. I just use my Tweepi tool to follow their readers. The awesome thing about readers is they like to read, and if they see that an author has followed them they're more than likely to follow you back.

It's going to take time to build your Twitter following. Maybe six months. Maybe a year. Just be patient. It takes time to build things that last.

"Okay, Liliana. I have the followers, but I never know what to say. I'm not funny. And no one cares what I had for lunch."

Treat Twitter like a blind date. Just be yourself. Though in all honesty, if I were ever on a blind date I'd never be myself. I wouldn't be able to help it. I'd pretend I was a spy or just released from prison, but that's only because my mind is warped and it makes for better book research. But I digress ... be yourself.

You can make something interesting out of almost any situation. And if you're a writer, which I'm assuming all of you are since you spent $4.99 on this book, then you should be able to put a good spin on it. I like to call it tweaking the truth for the greater good.

Here are some examples:

Liliana Hart @Liliana_Hart   21 Jun
Helpful tip: Don't tell people they look tired. It makes them want to
stab you in the face with a fork.
Expand ← Reply 🗑 Delete ★ Favorite ••• More

[Image 1d]

Liliana Hart @Liliana_Hart   19 Jun
Thanks to my #kindle readers for putting me in the top 100
@Amazon! I'm in an @KMFollett & @BradThor sandwich ;-)
amzn.to/19T5seq
Expand ← Reply 🗑 Delete ★ Favorite ••• More

[Image 1e]

Liliana Hart @Liliana_Hart   17 May
Someone at dinner said, "I can't write the serious kind of butt sex,"
and it might have been @janegraves.
Expand ← Reply 🗑 Delete ★ Favorite ••• More

[image 1f]

Or you can pimp other authors that you've read. Readers don't just read
your books, so give them something to do while they're waiting on your
next one. And you get to support other authors at the same time.

#payitforward #we'lltalkabouthashtagsinasecond

Liliana Hart @Liliana_Hart   18 Jun
I got to read an early copy of FALLING INTO US by @JasindaWilder
and I promise you're going to be blown away. It comes out this
Friday!
Expand ← Reply 🗑 Delete ★ Favorite ••• More

[image 1g]

Liliana Hart @Liliana_Hart   19 Jun
Theresa Ragan has a brand new release this week. A DARK MIND
is awesome and chilling. If you haven't started the...
fb.me/241nhSfwL

View summary   Reply   Delete   Favorite   More

[image 1h]

#HASHTAGS AND RTS (RETWEETS FOR THE TWITTER VIRGINS)

Hashtags and RTs are important. Of course, they're also used to express sarcasm or be funny in general, but the main purpose of them, if used correctly, is to gain visibility. Hashtags are a search engine tool, which means every time I use a hashtag like #kindle, it's going to come up whenever people type Kindle into the search bar at the top.

Here's an example of how important hashtags are:

I have around 3,300 Twitter followers at the moment. And who knows how many followers they have, but let's pretend they each have a thousand followers because math is not my forte and I want to make this as simple as possible.

Let's use this example from my friend Jana DeLeon:

Jana DeLeon @JanaDeLeon   11 Jun
The return of Helena Henry....Resurrection in Mudbug is available
now! amzn.to/116vlTl

View summary   Reply   Retweet   Favorite   More

[image 1i]

I'm going to RT Jana's tweet to my 3,300 followers, and let's say that 10 of my followers RT it to their 1,000 followers. Already Jana's new release tweet has been put in front of 13,300 followers. (Tip: It's okay to ask people to RT for you. Pay it forward.)

Now, you notice Jana's tweet doesn't have any hashtags. This is what's going to make a huge difference in visibility. These are the hashtags I would've used for this particular tweet: #Kindle #Amazon #Mystery #Books #amreading. And I would have filled my hashtag space up until I ran out of characters. That takes the 13,300 followers who have already seen her post and opens it up to the potential of thousands more.

Just like Facebook, Twitter is a place to interact with your readers. If you don't know what to say, then just comment on someone else's tweet. Strike up conversations and always reply if anyone tweets you.

*Special note to authors about douchebaggery:
Please don't talk about other authors or their books on Twitter in a negative way. First of all, it looks bad to your readers. Second of all, even if you don't type in the @ with their name so they've been tagged and type in their name of the title of the book instead, all I have to do is enter my name or my book title in the search bar at the top to find it. Twitter is not private by any means. You'd be surprised how many authors bash other people and are surprised they ever found out about it.

AMAZON AUTHOR CENTRAL

Amazon Author Central is one of the most important things you can do on the Amazon website. Every piece of information that you put in about yourself or your books affects the Amazon algorithms. (This fact came directly from Amazon's Dan Slater.) You can put in pictures, add your books, a bio and book trailers, and connect your Twitter feed or blog posts. Do all of it. The more information you have, the better. Take a moment and go to www.authorcentral.com and fill out your page. I'll wait.

Now that you're back, make sure you go to authorcentral.amazon.co.uk and fill out your page on the Amazon UK site. And then go to authorcentral.amazon.de and do the same thing for Amazon Germany and then Amazon France: authorcentral.amazon.fr. You have to do each one separately. It doesn't carry over if you just fill out one. This is going to help give a boost to lagging foreign sales.

GOODREADS

If you don't have a Goodreads account, then go make one at www.goodreads.com. You should be able to sign in using Twitter or Facebook, and this will give you automatic contacts. You can fill out a Goodreads author page, and while you're there you can make sure all your book information is correct. Goodreads is not a passive website. The more active you are, the more readers you'll find. I make sure to always update when I'm reading a new book, or what's in my TBR pile. Readers love to know that stuff. If I enjoyed a book I'll give it five stars.

You can also meet readers by joining the chat rooms. Be careful though — sometimes they don't want author intrusion. But if you join as a reader it's perfectly okay. Just don't spam your books while you're there.

I didn't really notice a pickup in reviews until one of my books was added to Listmania in one of the "Best of ..." lists. If your book happens to appear on one of those lists it's a great way to find new readers.

If you're looking for reviews, a good way to do that is to host a Goodreads giveaway. Patrick Brown from Goodreads gives a lot of helpful tips on how to have a successful giveaway.

- Run your giveaway for at least a month
- Start your giveaway on an odd day. For example, not July 1 to 30, but maybe July 15 to August 16.
- Give away multiple copies. Those who win the giveaways are encouraged to leave reviews.
- Run an ARC giveaway to spur interest in an upcoming book several months in advance.

WATTPAD

www.wattpad.com

Wattpad is another social media site similar to Goodreads, only it has a much different audience. The crowd tends to be younger there, so YA really does well, but my adult novels have done well too. There are different chat rooms, of course, but the best thing about Wattpad is that it's a way for people to sample your work before they buy.

You can create an author page and upload all of your book covers, including keywords and a blurb, but you can also upload sample chapters of each book. I've done this with all of mine, and then at the end of the sample I leave the purchase links.

Another great thing about Wattpad is that people who read your samples have the opportunity to become your fan. All of your fans are joined so if you have a new release or something they'd find of interest then you can blast them an email all at once — like a newsletter.

NEWSLETTERS

Speaking of newsletters, if you don't have one, start one today. Like, right now. Newsletters are an author's No. 1 selling tool in my opinion. Those people *want* to know about you, so if you cultivate a large mailing list, your sell-through rate will increase exponentially. A great way to start building your newsletter is to put the link at the end of all of your e-books. You can also have a direct link from Facebook.

SHELFARI

Shelfari is owned by Amazon, which means any information about your books that appears on Shelfari (like rankings or book information) is going to contribute to your overall Amazon algorithms. Shelfari is a place where readers can go and input details about your books. They can talk about characters and give descriptions, favorite scenes, favorite lines and anything else about your book that can be thought of. The great thing about it is that the information ends up on your book page at Amazon, so the more complete it is, the better.

Here's a sample of "Cade: A MacKenzie Novel" that's been filled out by readers.

[image 1j]

PINTEREST

Pinterest is also a great way to gain visibility. Since book covers rely on pictures instead of words, they are a great way to get your name out there and also make those covers familiar to readers. You can connect Pinterest to both Facebook and Twitter to save time so you only have to post once on Pinterest, and then the same message is flung to both of the other social media sites.

HOW TO DO IT ALL

I try to limit Facebook fan page posts to no more than three per day because of the way Facebook's algorithms work. If you post more than that, then people usually don't see them.

I post on Twitter throughout the day whenever I can. I always have my phone with me, so it's convenient to tweet at any time, and pictures are always great if you can't think of anything to tweet.

Social media are a necessity in this market. The more you do it the easier it will become. I'm very active on all of the social media sites, but the time I spend on them is minimal unless I'm playing "Candy Crush" or in the middle of a fun conversation. I try to have something posted that can be a discussion topic by 8 a.m. every day, and then I only have to check in when I take breaks from my writing to answer. And then I might post a couple of other things throughout the day if something funny or interesting happens.

Your readers want to have a relationship with you. It goes beyond the pages of the book they've just finished and loved. Treat them with respect and kindness and remember always that they're the reason you have success.

STREET WALKERS

(ORGANIZING A STREET TEAM)

LILIANA HART

A street team is made up of a group of super fans who love your books so much that they pimp them to everyone they know. Those fans are out there, in different states and even in different countries, but it's finding them so they can join forces that really makes the difference in sales.

Facebook is the easiest way to find street team members. (See chapter called "The Art of Seduction") The people who have fanned your author page are already ... well, fans. They're there because they like you. The second-easiest way to find members is by putting the call out in your newsletter.

Here's how I do it and the steps I take:

I send out an alert a week or two before I open submissions for my street team. This builds anticipation. I only open my street team up for new members every two to three months (mostly because it takes a while to put welcome packets together and I don't want to overwhelm my assistant), but also because the wait makes them want it more. You want really enthusiastic and excited street team members. Otherwise, what's the point?

The day of open submissions comes and I announce the post on my Facebook page and tell them I'll take the first 50 people to sign up. If they miss the cutoff, they'll have to wait until the next time submissions open. I try to open it at a time that people in both the United States and other parts of the world are awake. Sometimes I will get an email from an Australian reader or something and they'll tell me they missed it because of the time difference and I'll let them in anyway. I usually have 50 new street teamers within 45 minutes to an hour. And then we start a waiting list because, just because they make the first 50, doesn't mean they'll complete the process.

Everyone who makes the first-50 cut gets an email from my assistant telling them what they have to do to complete the process. (We have to do this because otherwise I'd just have a street team of people who wanted free stuff instead of true fans. My street teamers work really hard for me, and they get *a lot* of free stuff and perks so they know how much I appreciate them.) To make the second cut of the street team they need to either post reviews to prove they've actually read my books, or they can do Facebook posts, blog posts, tweets etc. Anything to show that they've read my books and are true fans. They have to do it twice, not just once.

Once they've done this they can send a link or a screen shot to my assistant, and he puts them on the list to receive a welcome packet. Street teamers can receive a new packet at any time if they run out of supplies. Here's a copy of the welcome letter that goes out to all new street teamers. My street team is called Team MacKenzie.

Welcome to Team MacKenzie!

I'm so excited to welcome you to my Street Team. I know, without a doubt, that it's readers like you who help an author have a successful career. I'm honored that you've chosen my books to talk about to all of your friends and family. Belonging to this Street Team comes with a few special perks — such as small thank-you gifts and even free book downloads a couple of times a year. Make sure you join the exclusive Liliana Hart Facebook Group, available only to Street Team members. There you will find a welcoming community and instructions on how to earn even more rewards for helping me promote my books.

Inside your welcome packet you should have:
- Romance Trading Cards
- Bookmarks
- Postcards
- Business Cards
- Pens/Buttons (subject to availability)
- A Small Gift of Appreciation

There are many things you can do with the promo items you've received. You can share them with friends and family, book clubs, libraries, and independent bookstores to name a few. Doctor's offices, hospitals, cruise ships, hotels and grocery stores are a few other ideas current street teamers have thought of. If you choose to promote my books through a blog or a website, I'd be happy to donate signed copies for giveaways.

If you ever run low on promo items, you're always welcome to email me, or my assistant, for more material.

Happy Reading!

Liliana Hart   *Cade MacKenzie*

All of the things listed are also in the packet. Street teams take up a lot of time, so if you don't have an assistant or family member to help you, I'd advise that you wait until you can do so. It's very, very time-consuming and you never want to sacrifice your writing for promotion. The writing has to come first.

New members of Team MacKenzie are also invited to join the private Team MacKenzie group page. It's exclusive only to my street teamers, and it's a place where they can get to know one another, share ideas and just have fun. My assistant moderates the group page, and I'll pop on a couple of times a day to answer questions or join in a conversation.

I'll pick a random street teamer at least once a month whom I've been seeing a lot of pimpage from and I'll send them a signed book or give them a free e-book of their choice. The first time I hit the USA Today best-seller list was for "Dirty Little Secrets," and Team MacKenzie worked really hard that week to promote the book for me. When I hit the list, every one of the street team members got a free copy of Book 2 in the series, "A Dirty Shame." Always take care of the people who have put you where you are.

Any time I'm at a signing or going to make an appearance somewhere I put the word out to my street team. They all know if they come to an event they get something extra I keep behind the table that's just for them. I've got mugs, bumper stickers, T-shirts … you get the idea.

The long and short of it is that a street team increases visibility (there's that word again) and sales. Word of mouth is one of the best sales tools you can have. But like I said, don't sacrifice your writing because of it.

TAKING IT IN THE BACK DOOR

(NAVIGATING ALGORITHMS, CATEGORIES AND KEYWORDS)

LILIANA HART

Figuring out how to become visible in a sea of millions of books is a challenge that gets more difficult every day. Knowing how algorithms work, especially at Amazon where the bulk of most sales are, is important for your business. Because remember, this *is* a business. I look at charts and graphs, read business and financial reports, and try to keep up with what's happening on the technology side of things all the time. I don't care if you're traditionally published, self-published or both. It's crucial to keep up with happenings on the business side of things, whether or not you "just want to write." (How many times have you heard your colleagues say that?)

Anyway, that's a soapbox for another day.

I'll be honest: The more content you have available for sale, the better you're going to do. That doesn't mean toss off as much crap as possible and put it up for sale. It means be patient and wait until you have a certain number of products (yes, they're products, not art you can't part with) to make available. The algorithms "pick up" on authors who have multiple titles, and they're more likely to be featured in the Amazon emails that are sent out daily, on one of the sidebars and on "also boughts" beneath your product description. If you don't have three to five titles to put up when you're ready to self-publish, my advice is to wait until you do. Be patient. It'll pay off in the long run and it'll save you the frustration of making only a handful of sales a month. You'll want to put all the titles up at one time for the algorithms to catch on. Don't stagger the releases out.

Amazon works on a 30-day, 60-day, 90-day release schedule. (See image 1a.) These new releases can be seen on the front of the books page.

New Releases
Last 30 days (96,362)
Last 90 days (308,356)
Coming Soon (55,953)

[image 1a]

Which means once you publish your three to five titles, you have to keep feeding the beast. So you have 90 days from your first uploads of those three to five books before your rankings take a dive and you fall into oblivion. Some people can write fast enough to have a new full-length book out every three months. That's okay. All you need is a new product or title up. It doesn't have to be a full novel. This is the time to think outside the box. Write a couple of short stories or a novella. That counts as a new product to feed the algorithms, and it'll propel you back to the top of the new releases so you'll have better visibility. You can also think about doing a boxed set. We haven't talked about writing a continuing series, but I suggest you do so. It's much easier to sell series than single titles.

My best-selling series is the MacKenzie Family Series. (See image 1b.)

[image 1b]

I released the first four all at one time in August 2011. My sales went from 1,800 the month before to more than 20,000. In one month. Three months later I released "A MacKenzie Christmas" for the holiday season and I made it free for one month. It was downloaded 150,000 times and it had all the links to the rest of the series in the back of the book. (You see why writing a series is good?)

In February, I released "Cade," the next book in the MacKenzie series. (See image 1c.)

[image 1c]

Sales made the book shoot up the charts. The problem was, I didn't have another MacKenzie book scheduled to come out until December 2012. I have six different series going, so I had to put out some other books from those series or my readers would stage a revolt. I also didn't have a release for any book until five months later. I needed to get new content out to satisfy the 30/60/90-day algorithms, so I created a boxed set. (See image 1d.)

[image 1d]

So by combining the five books I already had available, I was able to have what Amazon considered a new release and it increased my rankings even more.

Everything you can think of goes into your Amazon algorithms and helps your overall ranking.

- Tags (yes, you can still do them, so keep reading)
- Author Central (every country)
- Discussion boards (when people comment on reviews or start a discussion about your books)
- Wish List
- Reviews
- Shelfari
- Number of clicks on your pages

The longer people stay on your book pages or author page, the better your ranking will be. Amazon keeps track of all of this information and applies it to algorithms. This also supports the importance of quantity as far as titles are concerned. If you give readers more to look at, the longer they'll stay on your pages.

CATEGORIES

Knowing how to categorize your book isn't as always as simple as it might seem. There's a little bit of strategy involved. When I was first starting out and my sales weren't enough to get me on any of the top 100 lists, I didn't even try to shoot for the big categories. You want to be *visible*. And being ranked 96,000 in the general romance category is not going to bring you visibility. I'm at the point in my career now where I can pick contemporary romance and romantic suspense and show up in both top 100 lists, but if you don't have a chance of showing up in the big-genre top 100 lists, then pick smaller categories where you have a chance of being seen. Be as specific as you can.

Let's take "Catch Me if You Can" and break down the categories. This book sells pretty steadily every month (about 1,000 copies), but it's not a breakaway best-seller like my MacKenzie books are. (See image 1e.)

"Catch Me if You Can" sells about 30 copies a day, which isn't enough to hit any of the major top 100 lists.

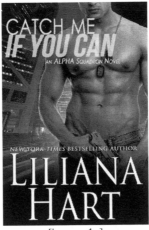

[image 1e]

First and foremost, "Catch Me if You Can" is a romantic suspense. I'm going to go ahead and make that one of my categories because I don't want to be so obscure no one can find me. The hero is also a marine, meaning I can click the military fiction category, which is much smaller than romance and it gives me a better chance to be in a top 100 list. You want to be in as many top 100 lists as possible. It's all about visibility, remember? Selling 30 copies a day is enough to make "Catch Me if You Can" No. 1 in military fiction.

KEYWORDS

I personally think keywords are more important than categories. If you choose your keywords wisely, you're actually opening yourself up to be included in more categories. (See image 1f.)

[image 1f]

Check out my keywords. Sure I picked some of the more obvious keywords such as romantic suspense, thriller, contemporary romance, FBI and Texas. But it's also a military romance. I put it on sale and all of a sudden it's a bargain book. So now it's not only in the top 100 in military fiction, it's also in the top 100 of military romance and bargain books. I just tripled my visibility.

Be creative about your keywords. You never know what list you're going to end up on. Also, keywords are not set in stone. If you start to see a lag in sales, then go in and readjust your keywords to whatever happens to be trending (as long as it fits your book). I change my keywords every few months.

TAGGING

Likes and tags used to be a major part of the Amazon algorithms, but they've removed those functions from the main pages. You can still tag on paperbacks on the main page (another reason to make sure you're using CreateSpace and have your books linked), but the option is gone on the Kindle version. But never fear! Tagging is still an option. I like to call this back-door tagging because … well, I don't need a reason. It just makes me giggle.

Here's how you do it. Say I want to tag "Sins and Scarlet Lace" (the latest book in my MacKenzie series):

Enter www.amazon.com/tag/romanticsuspense. It may show up as amazon.com/tag/romantic%20rsuspense. This takes you to every product that's tagged "romantic suspense."

Go to the bottom of the page. You should see a section that says, "add more products to the tag romantic suspense." I'd type "Liliana Hart" into the search box.

You click "tag this" and it moves your book from the left to the right in the little search box. Just repeat the process until you've tagged all of your books. Feel free to practice on mine. ☺

I can't say the word "visibility" enough. If you combine good social media skills (see chapter titled "The Art of Seduction") with tagging and using keywords and categories to your best advantage, you're going to have a much better chance of being seen.

Other things that will increase your visibility:

- Reviews and review sites
- Writing a series
- Permafree
- Blogging (but only if you do it well and consistently)
- Street team (see chapter titled "Street Walkers")
- Reader conferences

AUTHOR THREESOMES AND MORE

(AUTHOR SUPPORT GROUPS)

JANA DELEON

I'm going to come right out and say it — if you're not part of an author support group, you're probably missing out. Unless you write with a partner, being an author is a solitary profession, and being an indie author is even worse. Why, you ask? Because as an indie author, you are your own business, so you have even more work to do.

Don't get me wrong, we all know that except for a hand-selected few, New York publishers stopped marketing for authors a very long time ago, so that's always been the writer's responsibility no matter her method to publishing. But as an indie author, not only do you have writing and marketing to consider, you have to find an editor and a cover designer, follow the markets, learn SEO, track algorithms, pay quarterly estimated tax payments, and a host of other things that take so much more time than actually writing a book.

Now, if you love working twenty-five hours a day, can't stand your friends and family, and never plan on eating decent food or wearing clean clothes again, then by all means, tackle it all yourself. You will probably die alone, malnourished and stinky, but at least you'll be able to say that you did it all yourself and owe no one. However, if you'd actually like to enjoy your hard work, then having some assistance is the only way to buy yourself that time.

That's where an author support group can help.

An author support group is a pooling of resources, so that every member benefits from the knowledge and work of the others. It means you don't have to do it all yourself. More importantly, it means you have the social reach of every member at your fingertips. Ten authors pushing a book can accomplish much wider reach than one author marketing alone.

That sounds great, right? Then let's talk about how to start one of these groups.

A GREAT AUTHOR GROUP STARTS WITH GREAT MEMBERS AND GOAL-SETTING

Selecting members is the most important aspect of forming an author support group. We've all seen groups or worked in corporate departments where one person has ruined everything good and made life miserable for everyone else. You want to avoid that person like the plague. That person *deserves* to die alone, malnourished and stinky. Leave them to their superior attitude and find people who know something but don't think they know everything.

Clearly, the people you select need to be writers, and to gain the most benefit from the group, they need to write fiction. Beyond that, I don't think rules should apply. Some people prefer to have a group of people who all write in the same genre, and that's fine I guess, but I think it's shortsighted. Heck, I don't even *write* in one genre. Why would I assume most people *read* only one genre? Having a cross-genre mix can be a plus in that you may capture readers who would never have read you before.

Another thing to consider is talent outside of writing alone. If you can select members with various business strengths, you get even more value out of your group. The Indie Voice has an accountant, a lawyer, marketing gurus, multilingual authors, members who can do graphics and build websites, and a host of other talents. The more diverse the talent of the group, the more depth of knowledge you have at your fingertips, and all without having to research it yourself and/or pay for someone else to do the work.

You may already have a couple of people in mind you want to include in the group, or maybe you know some authors from a local writing group or whom you met at a conference or on a writer's loop. When you invite members, then you can ask the new members to recommend other members, until you've reached the number you decided on for your group. The Indie Voice started with four indie authors who met at the NINC conference. Each one of them recommended other authors they could vouch for and thought would be a good fit, and that's how the group started.

Once you've selected some people and you've loosely assembled as a group, you're ready to get to work. But before you start making membership badges and recording minutes, there's one very important thing you need to know:

RULE NO. 1 OF AUTHOR SUPPORT GROUPS: EVERYONE LEAVES HER EGO AT THE DOOR.

Princesses are great for Disney movies but not for author support groups. Everyone in the group needs to agree that every decision made will be for the benefit of the group. Nothing is about one individual. Every choice made by The Indie Voice requires a majority vote of members, except for membership. Selecting members requires 100 percent agreement among the existing members.

Now that all egos are on the front porch and anyone with a crown has been dethroned, you're ready to get to work. And the No. 1 priority is goal-setting. In order for any group to be successful, you must first decide what it is you're trying to accomplish, and every member needs to agree with the main goal(s) of the group and how you're going to achieve them. Until you determine what your group wants to accomplish, members cannot decide if they have the time and money to meet the expectations of the other group members, so it's imperative that these things are spelled out in the beginning. If possible, I recommend your group meet in person, at least for the first meeting, but if that's not possible, then teleconference. Too much is lost in online chatting.

When The Indie Voice first formed, we thought we would cross-promote one another's work, but we weren't sure what else we wanted to accomplish. As not a single member of our group knew every other member personally, we thought meeting in person was a good idea. So eight of our existing 10 members had an author summit in Cancun. (Hey, if it's a tax deduction, it may as well be a good one.) When we started our first meeting, the synergy was incredible. Our smiles were wide. Our excitement was clear. And it was apparent that we had something great in the group we'd assembled. Ideas flowed like water, each one bigger than the next, and all of them far outside the original scope under which we'd formed.

So we took a breath and asked, "Is this what we want out of the group?" The ideas we had required a huge investment of time and money. If someone wasn't on board with what would be required, that was the time to speak up.

Everyone in Cancun voted to go big or go home.

Now, here's where I should mention that the 10 current members of The Indie Voice are not all original. A few members left the group during initial startup for various reasons: personal issues, wanted a genre group and wanted a group with a different agenda. All were perfectly valid reasons, and there should never be hard feelings if an author does not feel she is up to the tasks decided on by the group during the goal-setting meeting. That's exactly the reason you should have your goal-setting meeting before you do anything else.

When we returned from Cancun, we had two members to replace because we'd already determined our magic number was 10. But now, we had a business model and a list of goals. At that point, it was much easier to explain to potential members what the group was about and what would be required because we'd already had our goal-setting meeting. Based on their professional attitude and success with indie publishing and most importantly, based on personalities we felt would mesh with existing members, we selected two new members and invited them to join the group. They were on board with the requirements and the goals, and The Indie Voice was ready to rock 'n' roll.

If you're prudent with membership selection, you'll have a successful group. If you're really lucky, you'll gain partners you respect and friends that will last a lifetime.

So let's review:

- Ask people to join the group.
- Hold a summit to determine goals and member contributions.
- Allow people to walk away with no hard feelings if it's more than they want to tackle.
- Find replacements who are on board with the group plan.

Now that you've got members and goals, you can choose the legal structure and method of accounting that suits you best.

LEGAL AND ACCOUNTING: WHY AREN'T THOSE FOUR-LETTER WORDS?

I know you're saying, "What a minute. I just want to sell more books. How difficult can it be?"

Well, that depends. If your group plans only to promo one another on the Internet and hand out one another's bookmarks at events, then you can give a cheer and completely ignore this section. But if you plan to do joint promotions, how are you going to split the costs? The even bigger question, if your group plans to generate income, how will you account for it?

Consider this scenario: Your group decides to do an anthology. Each group member contributes a short story and the anthology is sold in e-book and print form as a single offering.

Here are some of the issues you'll have to address:

- Who will do the editing and how will you pay for it?
- Who will design the cover and how will you pay for it?
- Who will do the formatting and how will you pay for it?
- Whose publisher account will you use to launch the anthology?
- How will you split the profits and who will prepare the 1099s at year end?
- What happens to the anthology if someone leaves the group?
- What happens to the anthology if someone dies?

Things just got infinitely more complicated.

If someone doesn't mind playing with a calculator or Excel, the first three items are easily enough addressed. One person can coordinate the service and everyone else can send him money to cover the cost. PayPal makes transferring money a breeze, so no need to panic ... yet.

What about the fourth and fifth items? Whoever uses his publisher account to launch the anthology will receive a 1099 that includes all the income for the anthology. That member must claim all income received for the anthology, along with his other income, on his own tax return. Amazon and other retailers are not your accountants. They will not split payments among authors to make it easier on you, and they shouldn't. You're officially your own business, remember? So handle your business.

If the money is to be split, then the person receiving the money will have to calculate the split every month and forward the correct percentage to the other authors in the group. That person will also have to file 1099s at year-end. A copy goes to the IRS and to each group member to account for the share of the profit she received. That means the publishing member must collect a W9 form from each group member, purchase the appropriate forms to prepare the 1099s (you can NOT print them off the Internet), learn how to prepare the forms, and get the forms completed and submitted by the deadline.

Note: The threshold for 1099 royalty payments is not $600 per year as it is for vendor payments. All it takes is a payment of $10 per year and you are required to prepare 1099s for royalty payments.

Okay, it sounds messy, but I could have my accountant do it, or if I don't have one, I can hire one. Absolutely, and as a former accounting geek, I highly recommend hiring a professional unless you're very comfortable with tax forms. The IRS is the very last agency you want to hack off.

So your accounting crisis is over, but we still haven't addressed the last two items on my list. Wait, you say, no one will ever leave *my* group. *My* author group is the best thing since the Mickey Mouse Club. Hey, maybe you're right, but do you want to risk having to pull a moneymaking product from the market because one person wants out, and he owns the copyright to his work? Rest assured, it can happen. I've seen people make moves completely and utterly detrimental to their own careers over ego or some perceived slight. Do you want to stake money and reputation on someone else? Do you really trust anyone that much? Or maybe a better question is, should you?

Perhaps the last issue will come into play. What if one of the members dies? Do you know if every member of your group has left a will stating how he wants his rights distributed after his death? Do you know the family member who gets them? What if that family member doesn't want to deal with the mess and wants out? What if that family member's new hooker wife thinks she can get more jewelry money if the dead member's short story is pulled from the anthology and sold individually?

One solution to the last two items is to draw up a legal document specifying how group works are handled if someone leaves the group or dies. That's the simplest solution, but what if your group voted to "go big or go home"? Then a legal document addressing those two items is not enough. The simplest solution at that point is a separate legal entity.

Here's where, again, I highly recommend talking to a professional — a tax attorney is a good choice — about the different types of legal structures available, the cost of the structure, the annual reporting requirements of the structure and how the structure is taxed. When you decide on a structure, things such as work on an anthology or box set in relation to leaving the group or death can be addressed in the formation documents that every member must sign.

Too many variations in legal entities and state requirements exist for me to cover all possible scenarios in this book, but I will tell you how The Indie Voice is structured, because I think it's a damned good setup.

We formed a 10-member LLC. We picked a state for formation that does not require cumbersome reporting every year and will not require out-of-state members to file state income tax. Two members happen to reside in that state. For tax purposes, an LLC is a "pass-through" entity, which means that the LLC itself does not pay taxes. An informational return is filed for the LLC and all profit/loss is split equally among the 10 members and reported on their individual tax returns.

Our LLC acquired an employer identification number (EIN) from the IRS in order to open publisher accounts with all the book retailers and a bank account to receive income and process payments. Each member contributed an equal amount of equity to fund the LLC. If a member wants to leave the group, the only thing she can take with her is her original equity contribution. She cannot take a percentage of profit. In addition, our formation documents state that any work written for inclusion in a company product cannot be removed due to the retirement or death of a member.

A slightly different twist on this comes into play when authors "lend" an existing book to the company for a short-term box set. In April 2013, The Indie Voice released a box set with full-length novels by eight of the members. Each member agreed to allow the company use of her novel for the term the box set would be available, and all income generated by the box set was designated as company income. The members never pulled their individual books from distribution, and they retained all rights during the box set's available dates. They simply "lent" the usage of the book to the company and allowed the company to keep the income.

I know what you're thinking — won't you all have to pay tax on that income?

Not necessarily. The goal of The Indie Voice is to use all the income we generate to pay for things that further the group and our careers. Members make suggestions on how we should spend available funds and we all vote. Our goal is to spend everything we make. Clearly, some years will have carry-over, but once it's split 10 ways, it's negligible.

Are you starting to get a headache? Me, too. But this is one of those areas where a selective membership process could be a huge boon to your group. One of our group members is an attorney and filed all our corporate documents. I am a former CFO and set up the bank account, got the EIN number, and do all the accounting. Rather than having to hire out for these functions, we are able to keep it in-house, and that's a real plus.

So let's recap:
- Legal documents can be used to protect you rather than restrain you.
- The IRS is bad and you should never, ever piss it off.

Can you now see the huge importance of establishing goals from the onset of group formation? Do you have people in mind you think will share the same vision? Have you chosen people with different skill sets who bring extras to the group aside from their work?

If the answer to all those questions is "yes" then you're ready to get your group started.

THE NAKED TRUTH ABOUT SELF-PUBLISHING

I HAVE A GROUP WITH GOALS AND STRUCTURE. WHAT NOW?

Exchange household tips, give each other pedicures ... oh, wait, that's a different group. Of course, you *can* do those things if you desire, but I don't have much faith in those increasing your book sales. So let's get started on increasing sales.

The first step in becoming a cohesive unit with a single-minded purpose is clear communication. Set up a Yahoo group (or the like) so that you can exchange email among members. Set up a secret group on Facebook. It's easy to start a discussion, then see everyone's comments and add more. That way, all discussion about one topic is in one place instead of scattered among email at all hours of the day.

Once you have your communication channels in place, you can start launching your group plans. Smaller plans may include things such as:

- Every member using social media to blast a group member's new release.
- Every member using social media to blast a group member's book sale.
- Announcing other members' sales and new releases in your own newsletter.
- Collecting and distributing promo items (pens, bookmarks, postcards) for other members.

These things should definitely help every group members' sales. After all, you've now got the social reach of every member instead of just one. Not every fan of an author is willing to try something new, but many will, and they'll recommend it to their friends/family if they liked the book. So you're creating buzz — the grass-roots kind, and ultimately, I believe word of mouth is how books are sold.

But what if you want to be bigger than just pimping on social media and shoving bookmarks at random strangers in the airport? What can you do to increase visibility for all members at the same time instead of just one member at a time? The easy answer is to increase visibility for the group, and here's how you do it.

First, you have to establish a group name and identity. We tossed around a lot of names for our group, but what ultimately narrowed ours down to The Indie Voice was the availability of the domain name. We wanted a .com because that's still the mainstay of domains. It's harder to find a .com domain for basic words, but if you're picking a unique name for your group, you'll probably have an easier time of it.

Once you have your group name, you need to give it physical form, and please, don't set up a blog and call yourself done. Except for the huge bloggers that people still follow, most readers have navigated away from that format in favor of Facebook, which provides instant interaction and a stronger feeling of "knowing" the author, which a lot of readers want.

So set up a Facebook page for your group and have every group member invite their friends to like the page. If the authors have their own author pages (and they should), then have them create a post inviting all their readers to like the new group page. This should get you a fair amount of crossover to start with a good base of readers.

Next up, a website. I firmly believe that a website differentiates the professionals from the amateurs as far as group marketing goes. If you're throwing your group name around like you're a big deal (and you should be), then back it up with a website that provides more information about who you are and what your group is about. You should already have this information because you decided it all during the goal-setting meeting.

You don't have to have a fancy website with a shopping cart and interactive pages. That's cool, but not necessary, which means it doesn't have to be expensive. If you've formed a group with variously skilled members, then you probably have someone in the group who hosts her own website. If a member hosts with someone such as Hostgator or GoDaddy, she can usually host additional websites on her account for no additional funds, so hosting is taken care of.

If you've already tracked down an available domain name, then purchase it. Again, domain names are cheap, and if you don't want to make a big investment in something that may not work, then pay for one year.

WordPress is free and one of your members may already know how to set up a site. WordPress templates are free to moderately priced, and many can be manipulated to set up a professional site. The Indie Voice site is hosted on my Hostgator account, set up in WordPress, and I used a template created by mysitemyway.com that was a mere $39, and allows me to modify all the CSS (that's what controls the appearance of a site) through menus. It makes things simple for those who don't know, or want to know, HTML.

Okay, you say, I have a domain name, I've installed WordPress (or whatever) and I have the basic structure of a site. Now, what do I put on it? That's completely up to you, of course, but I recommend that you have an "About" page, describing your group and your reasons for forming. You should always have a way for readers to contact you, so set up an email account for the group and link a contact page to that email. You should have a page that lists all of your group members with a bio. If you want to make it really count, then include a link at the end of each bio that links to a page listing all of that author's books. If you set up a separate legal entity, then you should apply for an Amazon affiliates account. Make sure you use affiliate links for all the books on your website. If people are going to buy anyway, the group may as well make a little profit on it. No use leaving money on the table.

After those items, the rest is totally up to your group based on your goals.

One of the main purposes of The Indie Voice is to provide indie book recommendations to readers. Let's face it, a billion new indie books hit the Internet every day and not all of them are great. It's getting harder and harder for good indie books to rise to a visible level, and we wanted to help great authors gain a toehold. Now, that being said, we're all authors ourselves and can't sit around reading all day (although we'd probably all like to), so we limited our recommendations to two a week to make it manageable for the members.

A second thing we decided was that we wanted to offer information to aspiring and established writers. We get a lot of questions, individually and as a group, and thought it would be cool to put information on our website, then we'd have a link available to point people to the information they want rather than having to retype the same answers over and over again. Of course, now we took it one step further and have written this book, which we hope is a one-stop shop for everything we've done.

Once you have a website and a Facebook page, the next thing you should do is set up a newsletter for the group. Newsletters are golden. I believe they are the strongest marketing tool that a writer has in her publicity toolbox. Those names are people who took the time to read your book and loved it so much that they visited your site and signed up for information on future works. Those readers are your auto-buys. Having a newsletter for the group is just another way to get your book information out to a cross-readership.

Services such as Constant Contact and Vertical Response are good for building a list of newsletter subscribers and providing the HTML code to drop a sign-up box on your website or Facebook page. Depending on the number of your subscribers and your desired newsletter scheduling, a flat monthly fee may be a better option than paying per subscriber.

IMPORTANT: Never, ever, ever, ever take an individual author's newsletter subscribers and add them to your group newsletter list. The quickest way to piss people off today is to waste their time. Many would rather you run off with their husbands. I have had my email scrubbed from writer's groups and added to author's newsletter lists without my permission, and it has the opposite effect of what they were looking for. I not only unsubscribe, I add that author's name to a list of people I will never buy. And based on conversations on the many author loops I'm on, I am not the only one who feels that way and readers are no different. Readers **HATE** strong-arm marketing as much as forums hate fly-by marketing, and I don't blame them. And other authors are the worst people to force onto your newsletter list, especially if they're doing things ethically and slowly building their list of genuine readers.

So you've established your website and Facebook page, and you're starting to build a solid newsletter list. What now? First, you need to decide what you're going to put in your newsletter and how often you'll send one out. TIV didn't think a newsletter pimping our books all the time was a worthwhile use of our subscribers' time. We wanted our newsletter to have value to readers, so we decided to release weekly and to include two indie book recommendations and sales on indie books. Recommendations are added to our website the week following their feature in the newsletter, so subscribers get the benefit of early review of recommendations and the book sales. We have a place on our website with information on our criteria for listing a sale in our newsletter and a way to submit the sales information for consideration.

In addition to recommendations and sales, we put TIV new releases in a sidebar, we have a link to each member's website and we have a monthly contest. Which leads to the next topic of discussion.

Contests are a great way to get people's attention on your group. TIV has a new contest each month, sponsored by a different member of the group. All of our contest winners are drawn from our list of newsletter subscribers, so there's an incentive to sign up and remain signed up. The contest is advertised on the website and in our newsletter. The sponsoring author is also featured in the newsletter for the entire month they sponsor the contest, giving each member a full month of newsletter exposure. For our launch, we gave the winner a choice of a MacBook Air or $1,000.

Most importantly, don't forget to include social media links in your newsletter. In addition to our website and Facebook page, TIV also has a Twitter account. Include links to all your social media forms in your newsletter.

Okay, so your head is probably spinning, right? I can just hear you thinking "How the hell are we supposed to find the time to do all that, and write, and market our own books, and bathe? Those women must be vampires."

Well, the jury's out on the vampire thing … I have my suspicions.

The reality is that getting a group set up to this level is a shit-ton of work, and it will require members to do a lot of it. But once you've established your website, Facebook, Twitter, newsletter format, etc. you can move on to the wonderful place where you hire a virtual assistant (VA) to maintain it all. We use Melissa Jolly of Author RX to screen sales requests, prepare the newsletter, add our new releases and book recommendations to the website, get Twitter followers, and write and schedule tweets. She's a lifesaver, and the inner accounting, spreadsheet-loving geek in me loves her organization skills.

So let's review:

- If you want to make things easy, exchange social media plugs and get pedicures.
- If you want to go big, establish a group presence.

If you go big:

- Establish clear communication channels.
- Set up a Facebook page.
- Blogs are dying and will soon be chatting with MySpace.
- Set up a website.
- Decide on website content.
- Build a newsletter list.
- Consider having contests.
- When you're ready for a supporting role in "The Walking Dead," hire a VA.

ANTHOLOGIES AND OTHER COLLECTIVE WORKS

I know you read that previous section and thought, "Hiring a VA is a great idea, but you have to actually *pay* them." Yes, that's true. People do expect pay for work, and people who are especially good at their work expect a bit more pay than average, which is only fair. So how does the group pay for things? You have several options for funding, and I suggest using them all.

First, all TIV members capitalized the company with equal equity contributions. So we started with some capital. Then we released the box set, To Die For (covered more in my chapter "Keeping Score"). This box set gained us a No. 7 slot on the New York Times list, and when you have sales high enough to gain a New York Times moniker, the money comes along with it. The box set sold for 99 cents during the sales period, which is when most sales were gained. We raised the price to $9.99 after the sale and still sold a significant number of copies. Enough to net us a little over $30,000 in a matter of weeks.

Instant capitalization.

And all it required was eight authors donating use of a full-length novel for the duration of the sale. I should also note that none of us noticed a decrease in sales of the individual novels on our own accounts, despite inclusion in the box set.

In June 2013, we released the first of what will hopefully be many anthologies. For the anthology, we pulled out all stops. We came up with a fictional island and gave it a legend along with descriptions of island locations, businesses and shared common characters. I created a map of the island, along with many, many new curse words while using Photoshop, then Jane Graves, fabulous graphic artist and picky woman extraordinaire, created a website for the island. (Check out http://seekersisland.com.) Each author wrote a short story in her own voice and style set on the island. We'll add the revenue to our bank account and use it to pay for more of our ideas.

If you're reading this book, then you're well aware that we also collaborated on a nonfiction book on self-publishing. Obviously, I can't tell you anything about sales for this book or the anthology yet, as they are new releases, but I predict they will do quite well.

Mo' money. Mo' marketing.

OTHER FUN THINGS TO CONSIDER

Being a writer shouldn't be only about work and never about having any fun, especially if you've formed a group. Who wants to be in the Stick-in-the-Mud group? So here are a couple of things TIV has done that you may want to consider. First, we believe that it's in the group's best interest for all of us to meet in person at least once a year. This year, we held our opening summit in Cancun. If you're going to talk business 18 hours a day (and bet your ass we did), then you should at least have someone serving you drinks while you do it.

If a group of us happen to be attending the same conference, such as when nine of us were at the 2013 RT Booklovers Convention, we scheduled a business dinner at a nice restaurant and even took a limo. We Skyped in the missing member and made plans for our summer and fall activities.

At the 2013 RT convention, we hosted a black and white party (our group's signature colors) that was invitation-only and specifically targeted our readers. The facility held only about 100 people and trust me, every bit of 100 were there. We paid for the facility, decorations, goody bags, catering and open bar. Everyone had a fabulous time, and we couldn't have been more pleased at our ability to offer such a cool event to our readers.

We are currently planning group book signings and hope to hit several cities by the end of 2013 and even more in 2014.

Now, granted, the ability to have fun at all these events is dependent on you and the other members, so keep all these things in mind when you're forming a group. TIV has a blast whenever we get together, and we wouldn't have it any other way.

Well, what are you waiting for? Go get your author support group started!

KEEPING SCORE
AKA NOTCHES IN YOUR BEDPOST

(BEST-SELLER LISTS)

JANA DELEON

One of the first things authors obsess over when a book releases is lists. Maybe you're saying, "I don't care about all that. It's all vanity." I'm here to tell you, you're wrong. Hitting a list is not all about vanity (although you're allowed that too, at least for a couple of minutes). Hitting a list can make the difference between a nuclear explosion of book sales and a complete fizzle. How, you ask? It's simple.

Advertising, social media and established readership will get you sales, and maybe a good amount of sales, but no matter how good a marketing job you do, you'll never be able to reach all of your potential audience. Lists help capture some of those readers you can't reach through your marketing efforts alone. Millions of readers don't cruise Facebook or Twitter and don't subscribe to any of the book services that advertise sales and get authors in front of new potential customers. But a portion of those millions look at lists to help them select their next book.

Being on a list gives you exposure to a whole new range of readers that you haven't reached before. And hitting a list is a self-sustaining thing, at least for a while. Basically, you hit a list based on current readership, people who have never heard of you see the book because they're reading the list, they buy the book, and that keeps you on the list for longer than you could have managed with only your established readership.

But there are so many lists — which one do I want to hit?

The short answer: all of them.

UNDERSTANDING ALGORITHMS

I can already hear your groan: "That sounds like math. Is it math?"

Yep, it's math. And even worse, it's math that changes whenever the retailer decides it wants to change the rules. So your worst nightmare has come alive — in order to take advantage of lists, you need to have a basic understanding of the math behind them. And once you think you understand, it will all change, and you'll have to do more math.

The simplest of definitions is that algorithms are mathematical equations that retailers use to determine your book's position on a list. The more lists a vendor maintains, the more algorithms the retailer will have in place.

For more in-depth information on algorithms, read Liliana's chapter "Taking It in the Back Door."

AMAZON SALES RANK

Amazon sales rank is determined by the number of sales (and borrows if you're enrolled in KDP Select). Sales rank does not care if you're a best-selling author, if it's your first book or your 100th, or about book price or number and rating of reviews. Clearly, Amazon is not recalculating sales every minute of every day and giving you a ranking according to that minute, so this is where algorithms come into play. The time component of sales ranking works like your credit score — the newest activity counts more than older activity. So while historical sales are taken into consideration, the most recent sales are more heavily weighted in determining sales rank, which is calculated every hour.

The second component of sales rank is the velocity of sales, or how many books you sell in a shorter span of time. For example, if you release a new book and sell 100 books in one hour and then have no sales for the rest of the day, your book will achieve a higher ranking than a book that had 100 sales over the course of 24 hours. But — and there's always a but — if your sales drop off significantly after that initial burst, your trip down will be just as speedy as your trip up. By throttling back the effect of velocity, Amazon limits the benefit of spotlight advertising. You should also be aware that free book downloads do not factor into sales ranking, even once the book is no longer free. However, paid sales of that book count toward ranking immediately upon conversion from free to priced.

The last aspect of sales ranking is how much other books are selling. Sales rank compares your book's performance with the performance of other books. If it's a slow sales week overall, it won't take as many sales to push you up in ranking. But if it's a big release week for major best-sellers, it will take more sales to get you to the same ranking. For this reason, it's impossible to pin down exactly how many sales are required to achieve a certain ranking, but that didn't stop us from trying.

This spring, Indie Voice author Theresa Ragan started collecting data from TIV members and other authors and this is what she compiled for sales versus ranking at that time:

Sales rank 50,000 to 100,000 — Close to one book per day
Sales rank 10,000 to 50,000 — 3 to 15 books per day
Sales rank 5,500 to 10,000 — 15 to 30 books per day
Sales rank 3,000 to 5,500 — 30 to 50 books per day
Sales rank 500 to 3,000 — 50 to 200 books per day
Sales rank 350 to 500 — 200 to 300 books per day
Sales rank 100 to 350 — 300 to 500 books per day
Sales rank 35 to 100 — 500 to 1,000 books per day
Sales rank 10 to 35 — 1,000 to 2,000 books per day
Sales rank 5 to 10 — 2,000 to 4,000 books per day
Sales rank 1 to 5 — 4,000+ books per day

Remember, these numbers are estimates. Depending on the sales of other books for the week, you can have lower or higher ranking based on the sales rates listed here. But this should give you a range of possibilities to consider for sales rank.

AMAZON LISTS

The biggest and best list for indies at Amazon is the Top 100. If your book hits the overall Top 100 best-seller list, start celebrating. This placement alone will gain you more readers. If you can't hit the overall Top 100, do not despair. You can still pick up new readers by hitting a Top 100 genre best-seller list. Genre best-seller lists pull the top 100 books for that genre (or category), which means choosing your category when publishing your book is very important. If your book fits into only one slot, then so be it, but if your book straddles genres, then it might be a good strategic move to select a category with less competition as you'll have more of a chance to appear on a list. And the beautiful thing about categories is that you can change them anytime you want, allowing you to gain the benefit of wide placement in the Amazon store. Amazon maintains separate best-seller lists for paid books and free books.

Three other lists that may garner you additional readers are the Top Rated list, the Hot New Releases list, and the Movers & Shakers list. The Top Rated list is where reviews come into play. This algorithm considers the average review rate and the number of reviews collected to establish a ranking. The Hot New Releases list considers your sales ranking for a 30-day period following release as well as books available for pre-order. The Hot New Releases list is a great place to get visibility for a new book, so the timing of your release becomes more important. If your book releases the same week that ten best-selling authors in your genre release new books, it diminishes your chance of gaining placement on that list. The Movers & Shakers list is based on a 24-hour period of sales and offers incredible exposure, but is also difficult to attain as it is not broken down by genre.

The last Amazon list I'll discuss is popularity lists. Popularity lists are similar to best-seller lists in genre division but do not separate paid versus free books. If you navigate to the Kindle store, choose Kindle Books, and then a category, you will find popularity lists. Many main categories also allow you to drill down to more specific niches within the genre. No one but Amazon employees know for certain what goes into the popularity list algorithm, but if you compare the books in the popularity list and the best-seller list, it's clear that they're based on different factors, even if you eliminate the free books from the popularity list. After watching my books on both lists and comparing ranking to sales, I believe that best-seller lists heavily weight a more recent span of time — maybe 24 to 72 hours — while popularity lists appear to weigh more evenly over a larger span of time, maybe a month or more.

LISTS AT OTHER RETAILERS

No other retailer has as many lists with varying purposes as Amazon, and the vast majority of indie authors I know who are experiencing sales that equate to a livable wage tell me that the bulk of their sales come from Amazon. Because of this, little analysis exists concerning the best-seller lists at other retailers.

Barnes & Noble has a best-seller list that is supposed to be based on sales, but in spring 2013, several best-selling authors who write "hot" books (but not erotica) sporting sexy covers experienced the same problem — their ranking stopped at a certain point at B&N and never dropped lower, regardless of their sales. These authors compared sales with friends who were lower in rank only to discover that the "hot" cover books were outselling the lower-ranked books, often by a wide margin. New York Times best-selling author Hugh Howey did a great blog post covering the issue:

http://www.hughhowey.com/does-bn-manipulate-its-best-seller-list/

Those claims have led to the speculation that B&N is limiting the ranking of "hot" books, and quite frankly, I can't provide any other logical explanation. Now, you might say, "What a crock of crap!" and I agree with you, but if you want to bypass this restriction, then make sure your cover and cover copy don't lend themselves to being labeled "hot." Is it fair — hell, no! But do you want to make money or make the world fair?

iTunes has a best-seller list but given the limited amount of competition, it doesn't take much in sales to make the top 10 list for your genre. Not that making the top 10 is a bad thing, because it's not. I'm just saying don't rush out and put a Ferrari on layaway if you hit it. A top 10 slot on iTunes may equate to only a couple hundred in sales over a period of several days.

USA TODAY AND THE NEW YORK TIMES

Some of you are saying, "Now you're talking!" Some of you are saying, "Who cares?" But you should care and this is why. USA Today and The New York Times are the two lists that carry the most weight with the average reader. People have heard of them. People understand that it means a book on that list has sold a lot, which they equate to its being a good book. And let's talk about the moniker. The absolute best thing about hitting USA Today or The New York Times is that you get the moniker. You can put it on your website, book covers and business cards, tattoo it across your butt, and even have it chiseled into your tombstone. All it takes is a single hit on one of those lists, and that moniker is like a university degree — it's yours forever!

Now, clearly, the goal is to hit the lists more than just once, because that means you're selling books, right? But that first hit can be a boon to your marketing plan. Doors to advertising and public speaking will open up to you that were previously closed. In short, these two monikers come with serious street cred.

So how do I get that forever moniker? Let's start with the USA Today best-seller list.

The USA Today best-seller list comprises the top 150 selling books for the week. The list includes both fiction and nonfiction as well as print and e-books. USA Today does not provide separate lists for genre or format.

One list covers all books for sale in the United States. USA Today collects sales data from various sources such as retailers, bookstores and mass merchandisers.

While it does not make its sources public, the generally accepted theory is that it collects digital sales from Amazon and B&N, probably Kobo, and maybe iTunes. What is apparent is that your book must be available at multiple vendors in order to be considered for the list. So if you're in KDP Select or with an Amazon imprint limiting your distribution to Amazon only, don't expect to hit the USA Today best-seller list, even if you outsell everything on it. Bottom line: USA Today expects your book to be readily available in the marketplace in order to be considered for the list.

The USA Today list counts sales from Monday through Sunday and posts the new list online on Wednesday. It's important to consider this range of time when scheduling launch and advertising. If your intent is to hit the USA Today list, start on Monday in order to get the most push for your advertising dollar.

I can hear you already — "All that's great, but what about sales numbers?"

Well, I hit USA Today in February 2013 at No. 99 with a little over 9,000 in sales for the week. The very cool thing about that (for me) is that it was not a new book that hit. In fact, the book that hit USA Today was my very first print book, originally published by a New York publisher in 2006. So seven years after original release, the book had new life and gave me a coveted best-selling moniker.

How did I do it, you ask? Simple — I picked a week when there were not a lot of new releases by major authors, then I put the book on sale for 99 cents. I had a BookBub ad on Monday, and Ereader News Today and Daily Cheap Reads also picked up the sale. I sent out a newsletter advertising the sale Monday morning. I blasted on Twitter and Facebook, where I also did a paid ad. And, of course, the fabulous ladies of The Indie Voice spread the word, giving me 10 times the social reach I had alone. (Note: If you haven't read the chapter on author support groups, you need to.)

The lowest number of sales that I am aware of that put a book on USA Today is a little over 6,000. That garnered the author the 150 slot. So if you're shooting for a USA Today slot, be aware that 6,000 is likely a good target for the very bottom of the list.

Now, let's talk about The New York Times — the big daddy. The New York Times has many different best-seller lists divided not only by fiction and nonfiction but by format and age division (i.e., children's books versus adult). Indie authors are shooting for placement on the e-book best-seller list.

Where USA Today seems to be straightforward in its method of determining its list, NYT does not. For a long time, indie authors never graced the pages of NYT, even though we are all aware that sales were into the millions per year for some indie authors. When it became apparent that indie books weren't going away, NYT created the e-book best-seller list and things improved, but I still contend that some snob factor remains. The NYT best-seller list calculation is harder to solve than the Da Vinci Code, but this is what seems apparent: While industry professionals insist that sales from Amazon do not count for NYT print lists, they do appear to count for the e-book list. This is great news for indie authors.

As with USA Today, your book needs to be available at multiple vendors. The best guess among industry professionals is that sales from Amazon, B&N and Kobo count toward the NYT list, but that doesn't appear to be the only thing it takes into account. This is where the snob factor comes in. I know traditionally published authors who have hit NYT and the number of books it took for them to hit. I also know indies who have sold 1.5 to 2 times those amounts and never gained an appearance.

The bottom line is that it appears sales alone do not dictate the NYT list. Somewhere in that determination, other things come into play. Maybe they consider historical sales to see if you're an author trending up or simply a flash in the pan. Maybe they look at your bio pic and if they think you're hot, they let you on the list. No one knows except the people choosing the list, and they're not talking. I always have this mental image of a bunch of old, stuffy men wearing tweed jackets and standing in a law library, deciding whether indie authors are good enough to be allowed into their club.

So my suggestion is that if you really want to hit NYT, then don't give them a choice. Come at them with sales so huge, you can't be ignored. In April 2013, eight of the Indie Voice authors each donated a full-length novel to the LLC to create a box set, titled To Die For. All were suspense/mystery novels, and all were existing offerings by the authors, no new releases. Our only goal in creating the box set was to hit the NYT list and gain the NYT best-selling moniker for the eight members who did not have it. And we hit big at No. 7!

Here are the things we did to ensure success:

- We asked Amazon for a pre-order button and got it.
- We priced the box set at a 99 cent sales price with a $9.99 regular price.
- We released the book on Sunday (NYT counts sales Sunday to Saturday).
- We had a BookBub ad on Monday.

- Every TIV member sent out a newsletter on Monday.
- Every TIV member did paid Facebook ads.
- Every TIV member tweeted the box set sale.
- We followed up during the week reminding readers on Facebook and Twitter about the sale.

We sold 38,000 copies of the box set in that one week, gaining us No. 7 on the NYT e-book best-seller list, No. 11 on the combined e-book and print best-seller list, and two weeks' placement on USA Today with the lowest ranking at No. 16.

Now, as far as we were concerned, this plan was a total crapshoot. We didn't know if a multi-author box set would be "allowed" on the NYT list, so we pushed for major sales in that one week so hopefully, we wouldn't be ignored. But total crapshoot plans are what indie authors should be doing. Try everything at least once. You never know what may work.

We've gotten a lot of questions about the pre-order button, so I'll address them now. The "claim" is that indie authors can't get pre-order buttons from Amazon, but we all know that's not true because we see them. Clearly, Amazon is experimenting with giving pre-order buttons to some of the best-selling indies. In our case, three of our group members write for Amazon imprints and the editors were happy to make this happen for us. Gaining a NYT best-selling moniker for their authors is good business for Amazon too, and what did it cost them but a couple minutes of programming? So if you have a contact at Amazon, want to make a push for a major best-seller list and think you have the clout to ask for a pre-order button, then by all means, do it. But make sure you're ready. Unless I was certain I could collect thousands of pre-orders, I would never ask for a pre-order button. Don't make them regret the decision by embarrassing yourself with almost nonexistent pre-orders.

Why do I want a pre-order button and how are pre-order sales reported, you ask? Good questions! Pre-orders collect the weeks/months ahead of release date and all hit your account as sales on release date. We collected 9,000 in pre-orders before our release date. So on the day the book released, we were already 9,000 into our list grab.

Now, for the bad news concerning our stealth NYT grab. First, BookBub no longer accepts ads for multi-author box sets. Yes, we have been accused of breaking BookBub. So sorry, but that avenue for advertising no longer exists for multi-author box sets. They will, however, accept single-author box sets.

More bad news, The New York Times has shortened the list from 35 to 25.

The lowest amount of sales I've heard of someone hitting the NYT e-book list with is a little over 8,000, and that garnered slot 35. Now that 10 slots are gone, it will take more sales to hit the NYT list. We didn't have anything to do with this change. I swear.

So 38,000 to hit slot No. 7 and 8,000 to hit slot No. 35. Somewhere in between that is as good a guess as any as to what it may take in sales for you to hit the NYT e-book best-seller list.

To wrap things up:

- If you want to garner the most sales, watch the algorithms. They change.
- Be strategic with your release/sales dates.
- Be strategic with your marketing dollars.
- Get some help spreading the word. (I recommend an author support group.)

MULTIPLE POSITIONS

(MAXIMIZING PROFIT ON A SINGLE BOOK)

TINA FOLSOM

If you're thinking of self-publishing your masterpiece, most likely your first thought will be e-books. And rightly so. Most self-published authors I've asked sell more in this format than all other formats combined. In most cases, this is also the cheapest version for both the reader and yourself. Production costs of an e-book are extremely low and comprise mostly editing, formatting and cover design. Publishing an e-book also takes the least amount of time.

But should you ignore other formats just because they might not yield the amount of revenue you generate from an e-book?

I'm all for making several different products from one original. Why? Because it's (almost) found money. Would you pass by a hundred-dollar bill that lies on the sidewalk and say, "Oh, well, I'll let somebody else pick that up"? It's the same with other formats you can sell your book in.

Let's look at them in detail.

PRINT ON DEMAND (PAPERBACKS)

Who doesn't want to hold her book in her hands and show it to her family and friends? With an e-book that's rather difficult, but a paperback lets you do that. Apart from showing off to your friends and family, why would you need a paperback?

It's a great marketing tool: Giveaways of autographed paperbacks draw a much larger crowd than e-book giveaways. You can also schedule signings with your paperbacks at conferences or bookstores, if you make sure the book can be ordered by the bookstore.

There are several companies that will process your print-on-demand book. By the way, print on demand means exactly what it sounds like: The book will be printed as soon as somebody orders it. So there's no warehousing, no inventory, yet the book will show as "in stock."

CreateSpace (an Amazon company) and Lightning Source are two large POD companies. The process is simple. You decide what trim size you want for your book, format your book with those specifications—and that's the part that's a little tricky, so you might want to use a professional formatter for this—and then upload a print-ready PDF through their dashboard. Once you know how many pages your book has in this format, you're ready to prepare a cover for it. You can use your e-book cover for the front of your book cover, but you will have to fit it into the template that you can download from CreateSpace or Lightning Source, because you'll also need to design the spine and the back cover of the book. Again, you'll upload a print-ready PDF once you're done.

The rest is simple: You enter your metadata, price and a few other details, and send the files for review. In general it only takes a day or two to receive a notification that your proof is ready to order. Once you've reviewed it and you're happy with it, you'll be able to approve. A few days later, the book will be available at places such as Amazon, and if you've chosen, also at other online bookstores, and may be ordered by physical bookstores.

While the profit margin on a paperback is quite a lot smaller than on an e-book, there's still money to be made. Also, if a paperback version of your e-book exists and is linked to the e-book version on Amazon, it improves your discoverability in searches. In addition, because the paperback will almost always be much more expensive than the e-book, the e-book will suddenly look like a bargain to shoppers. They will instantly see how much they "save" by purchasing the e-book.

AUDIOBOOKS

Another way to generate extra income from your book is to convert it into an audiobook. You might think that producing an audiobook is expensive, and it can be if you want a celebrity narrator; however, there are many good narrators available who will read your book for $200 per finished hour.

Hold it right there, you're saying. What's a finished hour?

According to ACX (an Amazon company that helps you produce your audiobook), 9,300 words will translate into roughly one hour of narration. This means that your book of about 90,000 words will be 9.5 to 10 hours long. If you get a narrator for $200 per finished hour, you will pay about $2,000 outright.

However, there are other ways if you don't want to foot the bill upfront.

ACX.com also allows you to post your narration job, offering a royalty split. This means that you won't have to pay the narrator, but then the narrator will receive 50 percent of whatever royalties you earn on your book. This could be a good solution if you're strapped for cash, but want to get your book into audio format nevertheless.

ACX has a large database of narrators you can choose from. Or you can narrate your book yourself. Only do this if you have a great speaking voice and the right equipment to record the book. Having read a short excerpt of my own book once to provide a little tidbit to my readers, I know how hard it is to get it right. Your time is much better spent otherwise, so have a professional do the narration.

Keep in mind that with only one audiobook available, your income will be relatively low. Yes, many authors make their money back very quickly, and authors such as Bella Andre and Bob Mayer rave about it, but they have multiple books available. The more books you have in audio, the more likely you'll find readers willing to dive into them. Many readers won't pick up an audiobook in a series if only one of them is out. They'll wait until you have more available before they start, so don't be disheartened at low sales at the beginning.

By going through ACX for your audiobook, your book will be available for sale at Amazon, Audible and iTunes, the three major sellers of audiobooks. ACX will set the price for your book, and it's generally set by length.

Here's a guideline of its pricing:

- under 3 hours: under $10
- 3 to 5 hours: $10-$20
- 5 to 10 hours: $15-$25
- 10 to 20 hours: $20-$30
- over 20 hours: $25-35

Producing an audiobook will require a little work by you first: You'll need to listen to auditions and select a narrator. And once the narrator has finished your book and uploaded the files, you should listen to each chapter and make sure he or she hasn't made any mistakes, then have him or her re-record those portions that contain mistakes, missing sentences, wrong pronunciation, etc.

I think an audiobook is well worth the effort. Personally I prefer to pay the narrator, so that I receive the full amount of the royalties. But you may choose a different path, depending on your situation.

TRANSLATIONS

As discussed in the chapter "Hook 'em With a French Kiss," foreign translations should not be ignored and can be a valuable income source from your book.

But how do you go about finding a translator — or should you instead sell your foreign rights to a foreign publisher?

It all depends. If you speak another language fluently and are confident that you can do quality control when it comes to translations, then by all means go for it. I found translators on Elance.com. It's a process that will take some time, since you'll need to weed through lots of proposals and translation samples. Beware that many of the translators claim to be perfect in a language, but aren't. I had many proposals where the translators claimed to be native Germans, but from their samples I could easily tell that they weren't, because they didn't understand the simplest rules of grammar and used expressions that didn't mean anything in German.

Another thing to keep in mind is the law in other countries. For example, in Germany, a translator automatically gets copyright in the translation. If that's an issue for you, you'll have to find a translator who's living in another country. I personally like to own all copyrights to the translations of my books, because it allows me to make whatever changes I desire, without having to ask for permission from the translator.

If you do hire a translator, make sure to have a contract drawn up that states that this is a work for hire and that you will retain all rights to the work. I'm not a lawyer, so please consult a literary lawyer for more information.

There are other things you should consider when deciding whether to take on a translation project yourself. You need a team made up of one translator and at least one or two other native speakers to correct and proofread the translation. Then there's the language itself to consider. Where should your translator be from? If you're choosing to have your book translated into Spanish, this is an important decision. The Spanish spoken in Spain is vastly different from the Spanish you'll hear in Mexico or in Latin American countries.

The same goes for French. The French spoken in France is slightly different from that in Belgium, and quite different from that spoken in Quebec, Canada. Therefore, consider who you're targeting before launching into a translation.

With German, however, you can rest easy. While Germany has many spoken dialects, the written language is virtually always the same. There are a few slight regional differences (and they also include Austria and Switzerland), but these are negligible. Therefore, a translator from Munich (who might speak Bavarian in her day-to-day life) will translate your book into the same correct German as a translator from Berlin or Hamburg. The dialects really only matter in the spoken word.

When pricing your book for the foreign market, take the country's economy and pricing laws into account. In Germany, for example, I price my books about 25 percent higher than in the United States, because Germans are used to higher book prices. However, they also have a very stringent law: *Buchpreisbindungsgesetz*, or fixed book pricing law. It means that if you distribute a German language book via more than one channel, i.e., you sell it through Apple iTunes, Amazon and for example Thalia, you'll have to make 100 percent certain that the price is exactly the same at each retailer. This can make it very difficult to run any kind of price promotions, because you can't sell the same book for different prices at different retailers. And as we all know, trying to get retailers to switch prices simultaneously is virtually impossible.

If all this sounds overwhelming, then approach a foreign rights agent and see if she will consider selling your foreign rights instead. These days, if your books are already selling well, you might get inquiries from literary agents anyway. Turn the tables on them and tell them you're not interested in selling your English-language rights, but if they can do something for you in foreign markets, you're willing to talk. I know several authors who have agents only for their foreign rights and handle their English-language rights themselves.

Having your books available in foreign languages can be a significant source of revenue. In my case, my foreign editions account for about 30 to 35 percent of my income.

ENHANCED E-BOOKS

Enhanced e-books are still in their infancy. Two companies come to mind: Vook and Cine-Books.

Vook.com allows embedding of audio or video content into the e-book. Generally, a reader will need a tablet to play this kind of added content. Not all e-readers support this technology. Since I have not spoken to Vook and since it gives custom quotes for each project, I can't give you any indication of price.

I met representatives of Cine-Books.com at BookExpo America in New York. It is a Ukrainian company of talented programmers and filmmakers. They will use photography and live-action shots with actors to bring your e-book to life. In addition to the visual elements of the book, there will also be professional narration, but the reader can also read along. While the demonstration I was privy to was stunning, the price tag was staggering and had me gasping for air.

According to Cine-Books' representatives, each visual element, i.e., each time a scene changes and you want a different background, will cost approximately $1,000. Considering that a book of 90,000 words, to take one of my own books as an example, with about 40 chapters has possibly 60 to 80 different scenes, this is beyond most self-publishers' budget. Also, since this company is new, they have no sales data available yet. Therefore, any estimate of how many books they think they can sell in this format is a wild guess.

However, I like the concept of this, and short of selling your movie rights, this would be a great alternative. (By the way, your movie rights will not be affected, should you produce enhanced e-books.) I'll be watching this company closely.

IN CLOSING

So, what are you waiting for? Get your ass in gear and clone your books. If I had stopped at e-books and never done POD, audio or foreign translations, I would earn 40 percent less than I do. And between you and me, that's a boatload of money!

HOOK 'EM WITH A FRENCH KISS

(SELLING OUTSIDE THE U.S.)

TINA FOLSOM

If your book doesn't exist only in the English language, but also in one or more foreign languages, first of all: congratulations! You're already a step ahead of the competition. If so far you're only published in English: What the heck are you waiting for?

Many writers these days still can't see beyond the borders of their own country, be that the United States, Canada or the United Kingdom. They think their audience is restricted to their own country. Americans in particular believe that they're writing for the largest market anyway, so why bother looking elsewhere?

It's the wrong attitude. Genghis Khan didn't conquer other countries and people by sitting at home. Do you think Christopher Columbus discovered America by lounging around in his native Europe thinking that where he lived was the be-all and end-all? What these people had in common was a drive to go beyond what they knew.

I know it's scary out there. You don't speak any other languages, you say? You've never been abroad and don't know how other nationalities are different from yours? Don't let that stop you from exploring what other markets your books could thrive in. Get your butt out of that computer chair and follow me!

Let's explore together what countries will give you the most bang for your buck and what you can do to connect with readers in those countries.

UNITED KINGDOM

I lived in London for more than eight years, and I still don't really understand the Brits. I get their humor and their love for a good curry, but beyond that, I don't know what makes them tick. And consequently, I still haven't figured out their book-buying behavior. However, there are a few things that I have learned about the British readers: They are extremely price-sensitive, and they'd rather not buy a book with a racy cover.

How can I use this little information to my advantage in connecting with British readers?

Cater to their taste, both in terms of pricing and in terms of covers for your books. You can upload different covers for the same book by uploading your book to all retailers twice (under different ISBNs) and by selecting the appropriate territory rights for each book. For the cover you want to show to U.K. customers only, select only U.K. rights. For the other version of your book, select all other territory rights.

I generally price my books about 25 percent cheaper in the U.K. than in the U.S. Since I dropped my price to this level, my sales in the U.K. have gone up by much more than I lost on the lower price. It was definitely worth it and has introduced me to many new readers.

Communication with these readers is still less frequent than my communications with American and German readers. However, there's a rather large UK Book Club group on Goodreads where British readers exchange information. It's a place to start connecting with British readers. It's where you can see who added your books to their bookshelves. You can see how they reviewed them. Go through this club and look for British readers who like your books and run blogs, then ask them if they're interested in doing giveaways and reviewing your books in exchange for a free copy.

The London Book Fair, which takes place each year in April, is a huge event. I attended it in 2012, mostly to connect with retailers and other industry professionals, and it paid off for me. It's a great event; however, it's not a reader event, so this will not be the best place to find your readers. However, it's a great place to connect with retailers and other industry people who might be able to connect you with readers. One good connection at the London Book Fair might lead to a hundred connections to new readers. If you can connect with the right journalists in London, they can open doors for you. Don't worry if this sounds a little too advanced for you — just keep it on the back burner and dig it out when you're at that stage in your career. A presence in a foreign country also means getting press in that country. It starts with showing up in another country and showing your peers that you exist.

Contacts I made at the London Book Fair turned into promotional opportunities with retailers and some nice mentions in the foreign press.

Just keep chipping away at it.

GERMANY

Germany is the one market that I personally think has the greatest potential, particularly if you write romance or mystery. Germans are avid readers, and the romance genre in particular is underserved in the German market. It is the largest foreign language market for romance, yet there are few really big German romance authors. The reason? The literary community in Germany looks down on romance authors, so there are few writers who chose this as their field. As a result, the majority of romance novels the German readers consume are translated works from U.S. and other English-language writers.

This will not be the case forever, because once the self-publishing craze spreads among German authors, those closet romance writers who could never get their books published by a German publisher will come out and bring their books to market. In the meantime, there is still time to make a name for yourself with German readers. And once they know you and your writing, they will be just as loyal as American readers.

Consider, though, that tastes in Germany are different. Your Midwest contemporary romance will probably not sell in Germany as well as it does in the U.S. Neither will your NASCAR romance or your contemporary Western. Germans are well-traveled and love exotic locations: You can probably interest them more in a Scottish Highland romance, or a paranormal romance set in New York, New Orleans or San Francisco (where incidentally, my Scanguards Vampires series is set).

To see what kind of genres and sub-genres do well in Germany, peruse the top 100 best-seller lists at retailers such as Amazon.de. Check which American authors are doing well there, and then look at what they're writing. In most cases it's not contemporary romance or cozy mystery. But when it comes to paranormal romance, there are very few German authors in this field, hence authors such as Lara Adrian, Nalini Singh, J.R. Ward and I are doing well there.

As I mentioned already in my chapter about translations, the translation process can be fraught with problems, but once you've conquered those, it's time to make German readers notice you. How do you do that, particularly if you don't speak any German?

The good news is that Germans, particularly the current generation, learn English from an early age. They now start with English classes at age

10. While not everybody will be fluent, at least most of them speak sufficient enough English to communicate with their favorite American authors. This doesn't mean that they want to read your books in English. For those leisure activities, they still prefer their native language.

German readers still prefer to do their reading with actual books. They like paper. But at a recent conference in Berlin, I was able to speak to many readers, and they are — somewhat grudgingly — adapting to e-readers. Many of the ones I met carried their Kindles, Sonys and other reading devices with them. Yet even those readers love an autographed paperback, so make sure that your German-language novel is also available in paperback.

Connecting with readers, in particular those whose language you don't speak, can at first be difficult. Getting reviews (or *Rezensionen*, as they're called in German) can be even more difficult. But it's doable.

In the U.S. we have Goodreads where readers talk about books. Germany has Lovelybooks.de. It's nowhere near as big as Goodreads, but it's a thriving book community where readers exchange recommendations and reviews of books. They also organize reading circles and contests. As an author with books in German, you should set up your author page and post information about your books. It's your first step at trying to communicate with German readers.

Many German book blogs have sprung up in the last few years, some with more regular visitors than others. There's no real comprehensive list that I could find on the Web; however, the German romance magazine LoveLetter Magazin has a nice list of book blogs on its site. You can find it here:

http://www.loveletter-magazin.de/links/

LoveLetter Magazin is the German equivalent of RT Book Reviews and serves the romance industry. It is distributed monthly to about 20,000 romance readers in Germany. LoveLetter Magazin also organizes an annual reader conference in Berlin. During two days, about 500 readers meet with 30 to 40 authors, many of them American or British. It's a wonderful opportunity to meet enthusiastic readers who are eager to discover new authors. Many of the panels and workshops are held in English, and during those that are held in German, translators are at hand. The signings are excellent opportunities to get your book into German readers' hands and get them interested in all your books. If you're writing a series, this is the place to get these readers hooked.

When I went to the first convention in 2012, I was a total unknown to these German readers. After signing 100 copies of the first book in my vampire series, Scanguards Vampires, I gained many new readers. The German presence on my Facebook page went up exponentially, and

German sales of all subsequent books in my series skyrocketed, catapulting each of my books into the top 20 at Amazon's German Kindle store.

Now I receive almost as much German reader mail as American reader mail, and the German release of my books nets me as much revenue as an English-language release. To satisfy my German readers, I produce German language "swag," i.e., bookmarks. It's something your translator can help you with if you're not fluent in German. For conferences such as the LoveLetter Convention (which takes place at the end of May each year), bringing bookmarks with you will endear you to your German readers. If you can sign those bookmarks, even better.

It's also a great place to make contact with blogs. Many bloggers visit this convention and will post reviews, photos and videos on their blog. Make sure to give those bloggers extra swag so that they can raffle it off among their readers. Or offer to do giveaways on their blog. Ask them if they would review your next book in exchange for a free copy.

Which brings me to another thing: Often authors will do giveaways, but limit them to U.S. and Canadian readers, excluding other countries. I understand that postage can be very expensive, especially when you raffle off an autographed paperback, but you can raffle off other items related to your book, which are lighter and where postage won't be as expensive. Readers are very appreciative if you include them in these giveaways.

Try to communicate with your German readers by occasionally posting in German on your Facebook page. Ask a friend who speaks German or your translator to compose a few posts for you, things like "the next book will be out in German soon," or "we're working on the next translation into German, and the book will be out in June." Keep your German readers involved and excited. If you take notice of them, they will stick around.

FRANCE

While I speak French, and was indeed engaged to a Frenchman many years ago (I didn't marry him, but that's another story), my French is nowhere near fluent enough for me to feel entirely comfortable talking to French people in a business setting. That puts me in the same boat as most of you: I feel nervous when I have to talk to somebody who speaks French and assumes I understand everything they say. In other words: My French is just good enough to be dangerous.

The French are still quite far behind the e-book revolution. They still read mostly in paper, and French publishers have been slow at offering books as e-books. This is actually an advantage for us Americans. How so? you may ask. Well, look at it this way: You have a lot fewer e-books to compete with in France. Therefore, even without an existing readership in France, you can be noticed.

A handful of sales on sites such as Amazon, iTunes and Kobo will instantly catapult you into visibility on those retailers' sites. Early on when I started publishing my books in French, I was able to hit the top 10 at Amazon's French Kindle store with only 20 sales. Now, it takes a little more to do that, but it's still easily attainable. Once you have visibility on these channels, word of mouth starts to work for you.

Again, contacting French readers can be difficult. Finding blogs that will review your French edition is cumbersome, particularly if you don't know what French keywords to type into Google. I therefore suggest hiring a French assistant who can handle this for you. All they need to do for you is find a list of French blogs for your genre and write a standard inquiry to them, asking for reviews and offering to do giveaways. For this, you should definitely have your book available in paperback format.

All it takes is a few hours of your French assistant's time and you can get started. Once you start receiving French fan mail, forward those emails to your assistant and have her draft a response, then respond to the reader directly. Your assistant can also draft some Facebook and Twitter messages for you that you can post at various intervals.

Or, if you don't want to spend the money on an assistant, use Google Translate. It's not perfect, and at times it does get stuff wrong, but it will convey the gist of what you want to say. Be open about it to your fans: Tell them you're using Google Translate to respond to them. They'll still appreciate the fact that you take the time and effort to communicate with them.

A way of getting those French readers who're already buying your books in French to correspond with you is to put a note at the end of your French books and ask them for feedback, either on the translation or just in general. You can also encourage blogs that way. For example, say, "If you have a blog in France and would like to host a giveaway, please contact me."

If you're a romance author, you might want to contact Fabiola or Agnes, who run the blog Lesromantiques.com. They produce a monthly webzine in French and do interviews with authors. It's a great place to get your books in front of French readers.

SPAIN, MEXICO AND LATIN AMERICA

The Spanish-language market is highly underdeveloped. There are various reasons for this. In Spain, unemployment, particularly among young people, is close to 25 percent. This means that disposable income in that segment of the population is low.

In the Latin American markets, the standard of living in general is lower, and you'll therefore have to take this into account when pricing your books for those markets. In addition, many of these markets don't have Kindles or other e-readers yet. Until reading devices in these countries are more widespread, your sales will be minuscule in these territories.

What about the Spanish-speaking population in the United States? Won't they buy my Spanish-language books? Yes, they will, but you'll also need to look at the socioeconomic makeup of this segment of the population. For 37 million people in the U.S., Spanish is their primary language. However, when I look at my sales of Spanish language books in the U.S., I don't see a reflection of this figure, even though eight of my books are available in Spanish.

Thinking that my books can't be all bad, considering how well my English-language editions sell, there must be other reasons my Spanish editions don't sell well in the U.S.

I've made assumptions that may or may not be true: Of these 37 million Spanish speakers, many are also fluent in English. Since English-language books are generally released before their Spanish translations, it's entirely possible that those Spanish speakers have already read the books in English. It's also possible that they prefer to read in English, considering that many readers believe that the English original is always better than the translated edition.

Personally I believe that the Spanish-language market still has far to go to come up to a level where it's profitable for an author to invest in translations and time to communicate with readers.

There are forums and blogs in Spanish, both in Spain and in the U.S., and for anybody who speaks Spanish this might be a low-cost way to market their books, but at this point I would not recommend going out and spending a lot of your hard-earned dollars to dive into this market.

CANADA

We share a common language with our neighbors in the north, which would make anybody believe that our books should sell as well in Canada as they do in the U.S. Oddly enough, that's not the case.

I must confess that I've not yet been able to crack the Canadian market and figure out what readers want there. It's only recently gotten its own Kindle store, but sales through this channel are still meager. Kobo is a Canadian e-book retailer, and traditionally, sales of e-books through Kobo are higher for many of my colleagues and me than sales through Amazon or Apple iTunes. It may have to do with the fact that Kobo really markets itself in Canada.

Canadian readers use Goodreads, Facebook and Twitter, just like their American cousins. Since they speak English, communicating with these readers isn't problem. Finding them might be a little harder.

My best suggestion to gain a foothold with Canadian readers is to be active on Kobo. It has the strongest "in" into the market, and it is also very author-friendly. It often offers promo opportunities to self-published authors, and most of these promos are available to Canadian readers. Kobo also operates an active blog and is always looking for authors who're interested in writing a blog post for them. Just contact your Kobo representative and ask.

When you do giveaways or blog tours with contests, make sure to make those available to Canadians too. They like to be included and often get upset when a deal is not available to them. When that happens, and I'm told via Facebook post or an email, I always respond to those readers and explain why — sometimes it's an oversight I can correct, sometimes it's out of my control, such as when Amazon price-matches my book to free on the Amazon U.S. site, but not the Canadian site.

Canada is still in the growing phase when it comes to e-books. I'm watching it closely and hope that within the next year we'll see more growth to make this a viable market.

AUSTRALIA AND NEW ZEALAND

I've had the privilege of meeting several of my Australian readers while they were traveling in the United States. It's given me a bit of an insight into their psyche. Australians (and their New Zealand cousins) are ferocious readers. They love series. And they recommend books to their friends.

Again, you won't have any language problems when communicating with your readers there. However, with a population of only 23 million (and a little over 4 million in New Zealand), Australia is a small market.

Many Australians purchase their paperbacks through the UK Book Depository to save on postage, rather than order their books from Amazon.com. With e-books they generally get charged a surcharge of $2 by Amazon, no matter what the price of the book is. So be aware of that when Australian and New Zealand readers contact you and complain about the price.

ABOUT FOREIGN READERS IN GENERAL

While cultural differences exist between all nationalities, a reader is a reader. And most readers never have any contact with authors. To them we're an oddity, something to look at from afar. Those who approach us are the brave ones. Be kind to them. They've made an effort to find out your email address and pen a few words to express their appreciation for your work. Be gracious to them, and they will repay you for it by becoming loyal followers.

PAYING PEOPLE TO DO IT WITH YOU

(PERSONAL ASSISTANTS)

DENISE GROVER SWANK

Around the spring of 2012, I was becoming busier and busier. I'd released four books, with a soon-to-be-released fifth book, and had begun to sell more books than ever before. I worked from the moment I woke up at eight (checking emails on my phone while still lying in bed) until I went to bed around three in the morning. And I *still* didn't get everything done. I began to consider hiring someone to help with some of the workload, but I wasn't even sure what I'd have them do. At that time, I had no idea virtual assistants even existed.

One of my friends knew I was considering finding someone and she recommended her friend. Her friend had worked in an office and had been in charge of publishing their newsletter. *Perfect!* My newsletter was brand-spanking-new and was a huge time suck since I hadn't even sent one out yet. I was still in the process of setting up a template. I told the woman she could set up my newsletter as an "audition" for the position and I'd pay her a flat amount. A week later, she sent me a huge, jumbled mess.

That was the end of the first assistant.

But I was under a deadline, and I had my new release — the third book in a series — coming out. I realized I'd really screwed up not starting a newsletter six months earlier. The best way to market the sequels to a series was to the readers of the first book(s). But I didn't have time to stop and create one.

I have a house full of kids — six total but only five live at home — and they are forever used to me dragging them into something. I have literally used them *all*. My younger children have been recruited to act out fight scenes for me so I can watch and make sure I'm writing them correctly. (They have begged me to write a scene with swords so they can act that out too, but so far I've stuck with physical violence.) My older children get sucked in from time to time as well, to do bigger things. I tell them this is a family operation. Our livelihood depends on me selling books, which means sometimes their "chores" will include helping me when I need it. Thankfully, they all get that. Occasionally, they even think it's fun.

So in my desperation, a few days after the newsletter mess arrived in my inbox, I pulled my then-14-year-old daughter in my office and sat her next to where I was working and told her to create a newsletter. She asked several questions, but ultimately had one written and formatted within an hour.

I kid you not, I would have hired my daughter on the spot and paid her a monthly fee. In fact I tried to. But she's very active in theater at school and takes advanced academic courses that involve tons of homework. There are days she has absolutely no free time. It would never work.

The search continued.

Several weeks later, I mentioned to my friend Heather that I was considering hiring someone part-time to help me with administrative stuff. My biggest problem was I wasn't sure what I'd even have my assistant do. Heather had just been temporarily laid off from her part-time job and offered to work 10 hours a week for a couple of weeks to help me figure out a job description. I agreed to pay her the hourly wage she was making at the other job.

We decided she'd work three days, the 10 hours split among those three days. The first day she came over to my house I'm sure she wondered what she'd signed up for. My office is set up in my living room and my desk is the dining room table my son and I had moved in. I gave her my desktop computer and my office chair as I sat on the other side of the table sitting on a dining room chair with my laptop. We stared at each other for a few minutes while I tried to figure out what I should have her do first.

The week filled up quickly with us both thinking of things she could do to help me. On the third day, about an hour before she was supposed to leave, she looked up at me and said, "I'd like to quit my other job and work for you 10 hours a week if you're interested in me."

Does a bear shit in the woods?

So began our partnership. Heather's hours soon moved up to 15 hours a week — still three days, but now five hours a day. A lot of Heather's work could be done at home, but she prefers coming to my house to work. We slowly figured out what she could do for me, but the duties have changed and evolved. At this point, Heather is in charge of my street team and all my accounting. She runs my QuickBooks and is the contact person for my accountant. She's also in charge of my giveaways and mailing out books, prizes, etc. (Just ask Heather how much she *loves* our local post office. Ha! She periodically checks my author rankings. She used to track the rankings of similar books. She often creates my newsletters. She's in charge of ordering print books and swag.

The Indie Voice decided to host our first black and white party at the RT Booklovers convention in 2013. RT was in Kansas City and since I live in a suburb, I volunteered to coordinate the party. Heather helped — from finding the venue to coming up with decorations.

Heather is invaluable.

She had to learn pretty quickly that I'll email her at all hours of the day and night, but that didn't mean she had to address it immediately. We worked out that I would text her if it was urgent, otherwise emails could wait. Some days I'll send her 10 to 20 emails of things she needs to help me with or remind me to do. Those emails have lessened as we've developed our weekly work flow.

But months later, I realized that I was still spending time on administrative things that I could pass off to someone else. The links in the back of my e-books needed updating and maintenance. My FAQ on my website is nearly always out of date since I include details about new releases. Heather wasn't interested in increasing her hours, so I decided I needed someone else.

By this time, I'd joined with the awesome women of The Indie Voice. A couple of the women have their husbands helping them with these things. I'm single (technically, a widow, but that word choice makes me feel old), so handing over responsibility over to a husband wasn't an option. Unless I put up a profile on eHarmony.

Professional woman in her 40s seeks:
- Man confident with his Photoshop skills.
- Must know his way around HTML coding.
- Enjoys late-night emergency runs to Wal-Mart for coffee and Diet Coke.

I wasn't so sure that was the best way to find someone.

So I tried the next best thing. My kids.

My second-oldest son goes to community college and still lives with me. He's a huge help around the house and with running my children to all their various activities. I told him I wanted him to start helping with the daily recording of my sales as well as learning how to format e-books.

This did not work out.

I knew from the start that this was not my son's area of interest. He hates numbers. That should have been my clue right there to cease and desist. I've been a supervisor before, so I should have recognized that people working on long-term projects that don't interest them in the slightest won't work for long. For us, it didn't work more than a few weeks. He did it, but he hated it.

Back to Square 1.

I have a friend who had begun working as a virtual assistant. She's also an aspiring writer, so I asked Kristen if she'd be interested in doing some work for me. I wanted someone to set up a Google spreadsheet to list my books and the current links in the back of the e-books, along with any extra content, such as other authors' chapters, or ads for another book or author. (I had my graphic designer create half-page ads for my other series, then embedded links to the appropriate distributor.) I currently have 18 published works. It's easy to lose track of what's in the back of my books. I wanted someone to keep tabs and come to me on a weekly basis, or every other week, with suggestions on what needed to be changed and/or what to change it to. I also wanted the assistant to learn how to format the e-books so I didn't have to constantly send my revised books to my formatter.

I wanted Kristen to check my website at least weekly for outdated information and remove it or update the information. She would work in conjunction with my graphic designer/website developer.

Kristen also keeps track of my daily sales. She records them on a shared Google spreadsheet.

The duties of my assistants change and evolve. I'm very active on my Facebook profile, and have encouraged readers to friend me. But recently I found people searching through my Facebook photos and liking massive amounts of them. People I didn't know. It occurred to me that all those older photos of my kids were available for the world to see. So I had Kristen go in and switch every photo of my kids to private. At this point, I'm the only person allowed to see them.

I often have Heather and Kristen read my books and short stories. I've used Kristen as a proofreader on shorter pieces.

One thing I do not have them do is Tweet for me or post for me on Facebook. Heather will post on my Facebook author page, but she always states that it's her posting. However, she will follow up with winners on any giveaways I post. It's important that it's *me* posting. Part of my early success was the connection readers felt to me via Facebook. To have someone else post as me felt disingenuous. And as for Twitter — it's fairly worthless for me. I have more than 3,000 followers, but when I post links to new releases then track the click-overs, Facebook *far* outnumbers clicks from Twitter. With everything, from blog posts to book product pages. *My* readers are on Facebook. However, what works for me or doesn't work for me isn't necessarily true for everyone. Many VAs tweet regularly for their clients. Do whatever you feel comfortable with. No judgment from me.

Having assistants has helped free up time for me to spend writing, but I must warn you that there is a huge learning curve for everyone involved. I needed to figure out what I wanted my assistants to do, then teach them how to do it. Some things come easily, and others require lots of questions and answers. In the short term, you'll likely ask yourself if the hassle is worth it. And honestly, it's a valid question. With some people, it might not be worth the commitment. If you find yourself hand-holding your new assistant several months in, then you should consider cutting your losses. The whole point of having an assistant is to free up time for you. If you're spending as much or more time telling them what to do, then they're not worth your time or your money. However, keep in mind they won't necessarily get it all the first week or two.

If you hire a virtual assistant used to working with authors, I'm sure you'll find them much easier to break in. But keep in mind that they are also working for several other authors. Even though Kristen has other clients she works with, I'm one of her primary accounts, thus I get primary attention.

Keep in mind that what works for me might not work for you. But hiring an assistant can free you up to focus on what really makes you money: writing more books.

PIRATES AND OTHER FORMS OF PTD'S (PUBLISHING TRANSMITTED DISEASES)

(LEGAL ISSUES FOR INDIE AUTHORS)

DORIEN KELLY

Once upon a time I was a lawyer and hated it, which explains why I write novels. But I still have enough law crammed into the corners of my brain that my fellow TIV authors thought I'd be the ideal person to talk to y'all about some random legal stuff you might run into. But I am not *your* lawyer. In fact it's very likely we have never met. I am *not* giving you legal advice but, rather, giving a general analysis of some nasty situations you might encounter. If you want legal advice or if you have questions regarding your situation, *consult with your own lawyer.* Okay, we're done with that. Now on to the pestilent diseases that are the dark side of the publishing industry. ...

COPYRIGHT INFRINGEMENT

You've finished your novel and you're wondering whether you should copyright it. Good news! Under U.S. law, your work was copyrighted the moment you finished writing it. Cool, eh? Well, sort of. While copyright has attached, there's another step to be taken before you're fully protected. If the occasion arises that you need to file an action for copyright infringement, you'll need to register your copyright with the U.S. Copyright Office if you haven't already. And really, for the $35 an e-filing costs, that's pretty cheap insurance. Plus, then you get the added thrill of being able to look yourself up online, so you might as well do it as soon as the book is done. Cruise on over to http://www.copyright.gov/forms and get yourself started. They also have a really pretty decent FAQ section.

I want to believe that everyone who is reading this book would never infringe upon someone's copyright. We all know that theft is evil and that theft of someone's creative work damns you to a circle of hell so dark and wretched that even Dante couldn't have listed all the horrible agonies you'll suffer, right? And let's not forget the major and well-deserved public shaming. Witness June 2013's exposure of the plagiarism of Tammara Webber's and Jamie McGuire's works by some cloaked-in-mystery person named Jordan Williams aka Jordin B. Williams aka many other aliases. Check out the Dear Author blog at www.dearauthor.com for the details on that one.

Another legal tidbit for you: Though the terms are often used interchangeably, copyright infringement and plagiarism aren't the same thing. Plagiarism (taking someone's work and putting it out there as your own) can give rise to a copyright infringement claim, but even when a work is out of copyright and thus part of the public domain, taking it still gives rise to a plagiarism claim. Do an online search for Cassie Edwards and visit the Smart Bitches' blog at www.smartbitchestrashybooks.com, and you will see how this is so.

But let's talk about what to do should you ever have your copyright infringed or if someone claims (wrongfully, I hope!) that you've infringed their copyright. **Step One: Call a lawyer.** If you belong to Authors Guild, call it. It has lawyers on staff and should at least be able to discuss with you whether your copyright has been infringed or if it just feels that way.

What manner of lawyer-speak is this, you ask?

Well, there's the outright copying (stealing) of your words, which is pretty easy to spot. You'll know it when the hair on your arms stands up. And it will. Trust me on this.

But let's suppose someone has taken elements of your story and not the words themselves: a handsome yet damaged hero and the spirited woman who brings him back from his bad, desolate self, if you happen to be writing a romance novel. Is it copyright infringement if the words themselves are not stolen? I refer you to **Step One: Call a Lawyer.** And while you're waiting for a call back, and to educate yourself a little, do an online search for Rucker v. Harlequin Enterprises. This 2013 Federal District Court decision contains a great analysis of copyright infringement. You'll still need to talk to a lawyer, but you'll have a better handle on what you — and the court — will be looking at.

PIRATED WORKS

Not long after you have published your first indie novel, a pirate is going to steal it. Because pirates, teeming pestilence that they are, do it 24/7. You sleep ... they steal. You write ... they steal. You get one pirated work taken down ... 10 more pop up. I am sure that someone is going to advise you to make sure your books are uploaded with DRM (digital rights management) and that your pirate woes will be gone. In my opinion, that person is living in a fantasy world. All it takes is a few minutes of research and anyone can learn to strip DRM from a work. And DRM stops legitimate buyers from transferring your work among their e-readers, ticking them off. DRM is not going to protect you from this particular Publishing Transmitted Disease. It might make you sleep easier, though, and if that's the case, definitely do it. Just don't think it's going to have any appreciable impact on pirating.

So what can you do?

1. Don't take it personally.

Every writer ends up with his or her work stolen, and while it is disturbing, don't let it take the pleasure out of the business of writing for you. You just need to decide your course of attack (or ignore ... and some people do, though I'm not one of them) and move on.

2. Be vigilant.

Set up a Google Alert for your name as well as multiple separate alerts for each of your books. When I set up one for a book, I'll use the book's title for a search alert, but that net isn't wide enough to catch every time a book is posted; pirates don't always include titles. I'll also create a search based on an unusual phrase from the book, whether it's an odd character name, or, in the case of my Ballymuir books, which are set in Ireland, a curse in the Irish language. In the great sea of language online, nobody much tells people to go to hell in Irish. When they do, I know about it. And if it's one of my characters doing the cursing, I'm ready to take that pirate down ... or at least try to. To set up your alerts, go to http://www.google.com/alerts.

3. Have your takedown letter ready.

In the United States, book theft is addressed under the Digital Millennium Copyright Act. I could give you the whole speech about how the DMCA is supposed to address the concerns of those having their works ripped off versus the constitutional right to free speech, and what each element of a takedown letter is there to address, but life is too damn short. Instead here's a form of a letter:

Dear Sir (yes, you're thinking Asshole but don't give in to the urge to type it),

It has come to my attention that my work(s) titled (INSERT TITLES OF YOUR WORKS) (the "Copyrighted Material") has been posted and/or made available for download either directly or via an index or hyperlink on (INSERT SITE NAME). I located these materials at the following URL(s): (LIST ALL URLS THAT CONSTITUTE VIOLATIONS WITH ENOUGH SPECIFICITY THAT THE ADMINISTRATOR CAN FIND IT)

As owner of the Copyrighted Material, I request that you promptly remove it from the site. Neither I nor any agent of mine gave permission for the copyrighted work to be posted, and I have a good-faith belief that there is no basis for such use. Pursuant to the Digital Millennium Copyright Act, I affirm under penalty of perjury that I, as owner, am authorized to request that the Copyrighted Material be taken down.

Please contact me using the information listed below once the Copyrighted Material has been taken down.

Sincerely,
(INSERT AUTHOR NAME)
(INSERT EMAIL ADDRESS OR PHYSICAL ADDRESS)

4. Send the takedown notice.

When my books pop up on pirate sites, I take an unofficial, straight-to-the-source approach first. I send the takedown notice to the pirate site. That has worked for me with decent frequency and I suggest that you do it first.

But let's suppose that a firmly worded takedown or cease-and-desist straight to the pirate site doesn't work. Then what?

The law provides that you are to send it to the Internet service provider for the site where your pirated works (or a hyperlink or index to your work) appear. The DMCA requires that ISPs provide the agent and address to which takedown notices are to be sent. You can find the list here: http://www.copyright.gov/onlinesp/list/a_agents.html.

Sometimes, though, you're not going to get lucky with the official list. When that's the case, look for the site administrator by searching the site's name at http://www.whois.com. Look for the hosting company and go from there.

So that's the official way to send the notice.

5. What if the takedown notice doesn't work?

It seems as though the bulk of pirate operations are taking place from offshore sites, which leaves Americans very limited recourse at this point. If the pirate is charging for the work, you can always try to choke off the funds flow.

If there's a PayPal button, fill out the form found here:

https://cms.paypal.com/us/cgi-bin/?cmd=_render-content&content_ID=ua/InfringementRpt_full&locale.x=en_US

and submit it to infringementreport@paypal.com.

You can find MasterCard's infringement policy and reporting requirements here:

http://www.mastercard.com/us/wce/PDF/MasterCard_Anti-Piracy_Policy.pdf.

Visa provides the following instructions if your intellectual property rights are infringed at http://www.visa.com:

If you are an IP rights owner and believe a website is accepting Visa as a form of payment for products or services that infringe your IP rights, please provide the following information to us at Inquiries@visa.com:

Description of Violation

1. Please describe the Violation, including a description of the goods that are infringing, and attach all cease and desist letters, DMCA notices, or related correspondence sent by the IP Owner notifying the Merchant of the infringing activity.

IP Owner's Contact Details

2. IP Owner Company Name:
3. IP Owner Contact First & Last Name:
4. IP Owner Contact Title:
5. IP Owner Contact Email:
6. List of IP Owner's Copyright or Trademark rights alleged to be infringed

(include registration numbers and countries, if available):

If a law firm or association is acting on behalf of the IP Owner, please provide

7a. Agent Company Name:
7b. Agent Contact First & Last Name:
7c. Agent Contact Title:
7d. Agent Contact Email:
7e. Power of Attorney or authorization letter signed by IP Owner confirming Agent is authorized to act on behalf of IP Owner

Merchant Suspected of Engaging in Illegal Activity

8. Merchant Name:
9. Merchant Website:
10. Merchant Country (if available)

And if that doesn't work, try the whole takedown thing again. But what's more likely is that one of these approaches will work and you can rest easy … until you turn up the next instance of theft, five minutes later.

I do feel compelled to add that some authors feel that piracy increases their sales. They'll tell you that they had their book pirated into X nation and then their sales in X nation grew. If that makes them feel better, I won't argue to their face. I will, however, think that anecdotal evidence doesn't float my boat. Give me the numbers and show me that there could have been no other contributing cause and I'll buy in.

I'm more tolerant of those who say that pirates are pirates (or thieves are thieves). Someone who steals one work isn't apt to go pay good money for more. I can live with that.

THE AGENCY CONTRACT AND THE PERPETUITY CLAUSE

The author/agent relationship in the indie world is fresh, new territory. You might quickly catapult to the rock star range with your self-published books. Offers for deals foreign and domestic might flood in. After all, we've seen it happen among the TIV authors. So, what to do? Now we're tiptoeing into personal territory. Some folks are happy with a literary attorney to help sort through the proposed terms of a foreign rights deal. Some do it alone. And some retain an agent not only to help with deals that come in, but also to cultivate interest in foreign markets.

If you do want to work with an agent, I have a few words of advice. First, remember that your agent works for you … not the other way around. I have seen too many writers quiver like neurotic poodles when their agent speaks.

"But I'm *lucky* to have him," the writer will say when the agent has done some random, crappy thing and the writer doesn't want discuss it with the agent.

Even though writers like to see their agents and their editors as BFFs, that's not the way it works. It's a business relationship. Treat it as one. Start your relationship as you wish to continue it, with mutual respect, direct communication and transparency — aka no bullshit or pandering from either party.

Suppose the agent who has been courting you presents you with an agency contract? And suppose this contract has language that grants the agent an interest in the works being represented "in perpetuity"? Think very, very carefully before signing it. And talk to your lawyer about the contract. Your lawyer will no doubt tell you that this is a rights grab you might well benefit by avoiding. Ask yourself what this particular agent can do for you that less grabby agents cannot.

It's fair and equitable that the agent remains of record and entitled to his or her agreed-upon percentage for as long as the work is available under the publishing contract the agent negotiated. However, to give that agent a cut of any money you earn off that work for as long as the work exists, *even if* the rights have reverted to you and you're now self-publishing the work — and *even if* you are no longer working with that "perpetual" agent — hardly seems like a deal that would thrill a thinking person. So think. Ask yourself what you're getting in return for giving that agent 15 percent of your proceeds forever and ever and ever. The passion of the moment makes us do a lot of crazy things in life; don't let this be one of them.

PUBLISHING CONTRACTS: 25 PERCENT OF NET

Let's suppose this indie life is wearing you down. You're tired. You want to write, and only write. A publisher offers you a deal for your book. The very first thing you need to do is read Jasinda's "Before You Cheat" chapter. She's in the midst of dealing with all sorts of publisher attention and she has a perspective that is spot-on brilliant.

But let's suppose you want to go ahead and try to negotiate with them. The publisher courting you is whispering all sorts of sweet nothings about what an incredible writer you are and how your story was so touching it made the editorial director weep. Don't get sucked in. Keep an emotional distance and examine what's being offered.

The terms look pretty decent at first glance. You're getting a substantial advance. The base print royalty rate is good and it escalates appropriately the more copies you sell. You've even managed to get some written commitment regarding marketing, and they swear upon their dead grandmother's grave that they're going to get you into Wal-Mart.

But then you look at the royalty rate for e-books: 25 percent of net.

Seriously?

Once upon a time, I bought into the publisher argument that the startup costs in the e-publishing market were massive and that the money had to come from somewhere. But years have passed and e-book royalty rates at most traditional publishers have not been raised now that those costs have been absorbed. I'm way too cynical to be surprised.

As any indie author can tell you, 25 percent of net is a ridiculously low rate compared with what we can earn for ourselves when we self-publish. I'm prepared to say that a little giveback is to be expected since you also don't have to handle formatting/covers/uploading/metadata, etc., but let's not get carried away!

And putting aside that ever-so-critical money issue, you're left to figure out what "net" is. There's a possibility that it has been very tightly defined in your contract so you know down to the item what's going to be subtracted to get you down to that net, but I'm not betting on it.

So what do you do?

Negotiate for a higher percentage. The very worst that can happen is you'll be told no.

Request a clear definition of the elements that make up "net." And even then, try for a floor — an easily understandable figure that "net" may never fall beneath, perhaps X percent of cover price. And make X a hefty one. The whole idea is that royalties on e-books should be higher than those on print, right?

One more thing: All we know for sure is that the publishing world is in a state of flux. Whatever you end up with in your contract, you're also going to want a clause stating that if the publisher begins to offer higher royalties on e-books in its contracts, your royalty rate will be revisited.

PUBLISHING CONTRACTS: JOINT ACCOUNTING (AKA BASKET ACCOUNTING)

Jasinda has described what joint accounting is. I wish I could tell you that there's a compromise position that you could argue, but there's not. Joint accounting is like pregnancy: Either you are or you aren't. Jasinda has explained why this clause is never, ever in the author's favor. Run and run far. And if you decide to embrace joint accounting, don't get all whiny when it chokes off your income stream. (I think somewhere in there was a nice and dirty sexual allusion. This book's title is warping my brain.)

PUBLISHING CONTRACTS: NONCOMPETE CLAUSES

Noncompete clauses are the creeping crud of the publishing world. They started many moons ago in the nonfiction world and worked their way into fiction publishing contracts. I wish like hell we could completely stomp them out. And barring that, all you can do is make sure that the noncompete clause is narrow enough in scope and duration that you can still manage to eke out a living without offending the publishing overlords. If they want it for the length of the contract, you want it to be limited to only the same month as the release date for a work contemplated under the contract. If they want it for all works, you want it only for a work of the same sub-genre, setting and length as your work. (And you also want to own your characters and your worlds. Just thought I'd mention that, too.)

PUBLISHING CONTRACTS: OVERREACHING OPTION CLAUSES

The option clause is the inbred brother to the noncompete. The market being what it is, I straight-up don't understand why someone would be thrilled to sign a contract granting a publisher an option on his or her next work(s). Too much is changing, and too quickly, to be wedded to a contract for any length of time. (Ditto for those writers I know who are suddenly signing multi-multi-book contracts with print publishers after years of being handed one-book contracts. Nervous much, publishers?)

Your first move is to ask for the option clause to be removed. A decent number of publishers will agree to that. But if not, and if you're willing to accept an option clause, negotiate to make it as narrow, specific and short as humanly possible. Those who draft contracts (say, like publishers), draft to their advantage — not to yours. The option clause you'll be presented with will be exactly as broad as the publisher thinks it can get you to sign. It's your job to hang tough.

If you write 60,000-word vampire BDSM novels, make damn sure the option addresses only your next 60,000-word vampire BDSM novel. And do your best to carve down the amount of time the publisher has to respond to the *proposal* you've submitted for the VBDSM novel. Thirty days is a good number. And, yes, make the option submission requirement a proposal and not a completed manuscript.

Finally, make sure that the option clause does not require that the offer you might accept over the publisher's must be on "better terms." That's an incredibly subjective concept. All you really want to do is give the publisher a chance to offer and for you to negotiate with it. You should be able to accept another offer even if it's less than the one your publisher presented. It's entirely possible that you don't think your publisher did such a hot job with the first book and that you don't want to work with it on another one.

Or you just want to go flat-out indie, right? It's your life. Your words. Your choices. Keep control on your side, always.

Whew!

I have managed all the legal talk I can handle without flashbacks to my lawyer days, and that's a dark place I don't miss at all. If you take one thing from this chapter make it … never, ever be a lawyer. Just hire one instead.

BEFORE YOU CHEAT

(THE POTENTIAL COSTS
OF A TRADITIONAL DEAL)

JASINDA WILDER

Hey. 'Sup.

Jasinda here.

So. Let's say you write a book. You edit it yourself, and then you have it professionally copy edited (more later), you get a sexy cover made (by a pro, again, more later) and finally it's ready. You hit that sexy yellow "save and publish" button and your stomach is in your throat. Then suddenly (since you've taken to heart all the tips we've put together for you in this book), you see your title start to climb the charts. It goes up to the top 500, then the top 250, then it breaks that magical barrier, the top 100. You're freaking out, dancing in the streets and screaming incoherently, and then it's No. 20 … No. 13 … No. 1! You've written a book and it's selling like hotcakes and you're watching the sales reports jump from the hundreds sold to the thousands.

That's an intense feeling. Boy oh boy, is it intense.

Then come the agent queries. "Dear So-and-so, I'd like to congratulate you on your recent success with 'My Labradoodle Is A Teenage Vampire Slut.' Are you currently represented by a literary agent? If not, this is a step you may want to take, and soon…" and then you're wondering what's going to happen next. What if a publisher makes an offer? Should you accept?

I found myself in this situation.

WHEN YOU NEED AN AGENT

It started, initially, with "Wounded." I really love that book. It's kinda scary for some people since it seems to be, on the outside, a war book. It's not, it just happens to be set during wartime. Really, it's a love story about overcoming hardship and finding love in unexpected places.

Anyhoo. That book debuted pretty high — I don't remember exactly where, but fairly high for a new release — and it climbed. That baby got legs, like quick. It went up into the top 100, and holy jeez, was I freaking out. I must've hit refresh on my browser a dozen times every hour, waiting for the ranks to shift. "Wounded" got as high as 36, I believe, and that's when I knew I had a real shot at making this writing thing go far. Within 24 hours of "Wounded" hitting No. 36 on the 'Zon, I got an email from a publisher in, of all places, Hungary. They wanted to buy the rights to publish my book in that country. The advance was something like $2,500, I think. Not a huge amount, I remember thinking, but … it's Hungary. How much could Hungary really afford to pay out? I had no clue. Was that a good offer? Bad? Should I accept it? Should I get an agent? A literary attorney? Just say no and flag the email for posterity?

I asked around on writer's boards and a few other writers who I knew had some experience. The answer I got was that foreign literary deals are notoriously tricky and full of loopholes. You're dealing with people for whom English is a second language, for one thing, and they're out to get the best deal for their publishing house, for another. They may not have any scruples about dicking you over with some tricky legal language. I'm not disparaging anyone, there or anywhere else; that's just business all over the world. The bottom line: Have a literary attorney look at the contract, at the very least. Best option is to find an agent to navigate those waters.

But I'd looked at all the agents and none of them really appealed to me, and I'd only gotten one tiny offer so far. I sent a polite email thanking Hungary for its interest but I wasn't interested in selling my foreign rights at that time. They responded very kindly, telling me to reach out if I changed my mind.

I put the experience away as a good memory and went about my life, plotting the next book.

I'd had some success to that point with "Wounded," obviously, but also with "Big Girls Do It," which, I knew, was a bit of a niche series. I'd been perusing the top-selling titles for some time at that point, trying to figure out why they were so hot. Some, after I read them, puzzled me. There were titles full of grammatical errors and typos and homophone mix-ups galore (there/their/they're, then/than, affect/effect, etc.). There were books with weak writing and little character development. But yet these books were selling thousands of copies a day and getting good reviews. The reviews were saying things like, "This book needed to be edited, but so-and-so was so hot and I just couldn't put it down. ..."

People were reading these books, reading past the mechanical sloppiness, and devouring the meat of the book, i.e., the characters. All of the top-selling indie titles were character-driven stories. *All* of them. Most of them were "new adult," which to my mind was a fairly loose categorization. New adult, to me, meant college-age main characters, a coming-of-age sort of plot, lots of angst and heartache, and hot sex.

I knew a few things for a fact: I could write hot sex. Hubba-hubba, could I write hot sex. I'd had some pretty intense experiences myself during my college years, and in my previous career as a music and theater teacher, I'd come across some crazy and tragic stories via my students. One story in particular stood out to me. A student of mine was dating a wonderful guy. They'd been together for a couple years, and everyone saw them getting married some day. The boy's father was a congressman or a senator or something, and they lived in a rural area. One day, while working in a field, my student's boyfriend was struck by a falling tree and killed. It was instantaneous, and utterly heartbreaking.

As I read the top-selling titles, I realized I needed to write a book that would fit into that trend. Something new adult-ish. Something intense and sexy and coming-of-age-ish.

The key phrase there is "ish." See, I'm not a trend follower. I've never ever been part of the generic mold, in any aspect of my life. I knew if I was going to write a book to fit into the new adult mold, it would only loosely fill those genre slots. It would be a book that screamed my unique taste and style. It would be something only Jasinda Wilder could write.

So, I took that experience of my student and put my own spin on it. What if the female character watched that boy die? How would she cope? What if they weren't just boyfriend-girlfriend, what if they'd grown up together? What if his death totally wrecked her? How would she find her way back? The rest grew from there. Then ... Colton walked on to the scene.

Oh my. Colton. *Swoon!*

That was a risk. I knew it was a risk. Nell falling in love with her dead boyfriend's older brother? That could be a make-it or break-it move. I believed in the story, I believed in my ability to make it work, so I did it.

The result was "Falling Into You." I'd meant it to be stand-alone, a single novel. After which I'd do something different. Maybe another Big Girls/Rock Stars spinoff. Something light and fun. Nell and Colt had been through enough, and I just didn't see how anything else featuring them would really work.

I took another huge risk before I published it. I put an entire chapter, a pivotal chapter at that, on my website. People ate it up. They were moved by that chapter. A few influential book bloggers (a writer's best friend) picked it up, and the viral nature of that chapter went even more gaga. So I sent out the manuscript as an ARC (advanced review copy) to those bloggers, and they did kind and wonderful and stunning reviews, which only increased the demand for "FIY."

When I hit "publish," things were in a frenzy. I was a nervous wreck all that night, waiting for it to publish and the initial sales to go through. I watched the numbers on my real-time sales reports jump exponentially, and I just couldn't believe what was happening. I, in other words, lost my shit.

Then the rank popped up, and I just about pooped my pants. I'd debuted at 30 on Amazon. *Thirty.* Of all sales. Holy amazeballs. Was this really happening?

Within days, I was in the top five and I'd gotten a dozen query emails from agents. That made me laugh. When I was first starting out, I couldn't even get an agent to answer my queries. Not even a "not interested, thanks" email.

Now, upon my success, they all wanted a piece of the pie. Ssshh-yeah. Nice try, losers.

A few agents were on my radar, though. I've been online friends with Hugh Howey since he was still writing the original "Wool" sequels, before his crazy success (yay, Hugh!), and his agent was always my first — and really, only — choice. I queried her when "Wounded" hit the top 100 and she turned me down, saying she wasn't sure she would be able to represent it properly. Then, when "FIY" started getting attention, my friend from The Indie Voice, Jana DeLeon, called Kristin (who is also Jana's agent) and told her she was an idiot for sending us away. I got a hysterical email from Kristin later that week asking if I was still interested in having her rep me, and we've been working together since.

Through Kristin's agency, I've sold "Falling Into You" in something like 14 or 15 countries, which I would never have been able to do on my own. Kristin's foreign rights agent, Jenny, is an absolute magician and a fantastic human being. Just sayin'.

So this leads me to say: Agents can be wonderful. But before you sign with an agent, even a great one, ask yourself one question: What is the agent going to do for you that you can't do on your own, for free?

I couldn't have sold my foreign rights as I have been — which is helping me reach a whole new audience — without Kristin and Jenny.

But what about world English and U.S. rights? Could I finagle those deals on my own? Did I even want a trad deal? I wasn't sure. I'd gotten emails from a few big publishers already, but they'd not been willing and/or able to even discuss what I really wanted from a deal: print-only distribution.

Let's back up a bit, and discuss publisher offers and agents in general.

Most offers from publishers come down to a few simple factors, and if your book is selling well enough, the publishers will come to you directly, whether you have an agent or not. An agent is someone who knows how to navigate the shark-infested waters of New York publishing. They're negotiators. Go-betweens. They can see through the bullshit a publisher is going to feed you and get — ideally speaking — the best deal for your book. *For you.* The best deal *for you.* Not just monetary advances, though, because ... that's just numbers, and the agent makes 15 percent of the advance (so make sure your agent is in this with your interest in mind, rather than that 15 percent). Until that number becomes real money in your bank account, actual zeroes and decimal places that you can spend, it's just numbers.

My agent, Kristin, said at the outset, before we ever signed on with her agency, that she would never pressure us to do a deal we weren't 100 percent excited about. All she was going to do was open the discussions with New York. Until we heard a deal that had us squeeing with happiness, we would say no, and ask what else they could offer.

So far, we've gotten a lot of nothing.

We got an offer from one of the biggest publishing houses, and it was ... laughable. They offered me $500,000 for "Falling Into You" and "Falling Into Us." With a DNC (Do Not Compete clause), all rights into perpetuity. Joint accounting.

Pssshhh. *Hell* no.

We literally laughed together on the phone (just Kristin and me), and then Kristin sent the publisher an email saying, in effect, "Are you kidding me?" See, FIY had sold 250,000 copies in the first *two weeks* it had been up on Amazon. At $3.99, with me making 70 percent of the profit. That made the offer on the table look like the crassest kind of insult. The advance alone was a paltry fraction of what I'd made on just "FIY" alone, just this year, never mind the then-unwritten "Falling Into Us" and never mind what I'd make on both titles in my lifetime.

It's just numbers.

And there's a *lot* more to an offer than how much they're paying as an advance. Ask anyone in The Indie Voice and she'll tell you this is true. The dollar figure is often the least important factor.

The dollar amount is just a number.

This is especially true if your book is selling well, meaning if it's staying in the top 100 for weeks or months. You need to weigh how much you *could* make on this book given its current sales velocity against how much New York is offering you, and then you need to look at the terms of the offer. Is there a DNC? That's a crucial factor.

CONTRACT CLAUSES THAT CAN KILL CAREERS

DNC: Do Not Compete clause. It says that, after you sign and are paid, you cannot, under penalty of breach of contract, publish *anything* that would definitely or could possibly compete with the title you sold the publisher. Meaning, you can't publish. At all. Anything. The clauses usually show up in terms of a number of months, e.g., for three months, six months or twelve months.

That binds you up, hogties your capacity to generate income.

A huge benefit to being indie is that you can publish as fast as you can write, edit and polish. You can put out a dozen titles in a year, and each one can make you money, because — counter to New York thinking — there's no such thing as oversaturation of the market. People will read everything you buy if they like it, and they'll be begging for the next title within hours of finishing the last one. A DNC clause stops you from producing, which cuts into your profit margin, and that, friends, is why you're in this biz.

So, I hear you asking a question. Why are the DNCs included in contracts then?

To New York, you're your own competition. Say what? Yeah, you read that right, and it's absolutely true. Ask any indie who was once traditionally published. You write a book, New York buys it, then spends the money editing it, packaging it and marketing it. All this takes months, maybe a year. In the meantime, you've written and self-published another book, and the one they bought doesn't sell as well as it could have if you'd been tied up with a DNC. You've undercut yourself, in their eyes, since they don't own that second book you put out.

Writing? It's an art, yes. You're an artist. But you're also a businessperson, and in business, the profit is the bottom line. Never agree to anything, *ever*, that will cut into your ability to turn a profit with your talent, both short-term and long-term.

THE DEVIL'S ACCOUNTING

Joint accounting. Another big no-no, and something publishing houses like to sneak into deals, just to screw you over with clauses you wouldn't think to ask about. There are two ways of accounting the profits a book makes. Joint accounting means that when you sign for, say, a four-book deal, you can't start earning out on Book 1 until you've earned out on Books 2, 3 and 4. Read on for a discussion of "earning out." For now, just remember that you'll almost *never* earn out. The contracts are written so as to make that impossible. Ask any traditionally published author other than, like, J.K. Rowling, Stephenie Meyer or Stephen King. The other way of doing it, and how you should demand to have your contract set up — should you be considering one — is separate accounting. It means your series is set up so that each book earns out on its own. So if you sign a $50,000 deal for five books, meaning $10,000 per book, each book would have to sell $10,000 before you started seeing royalties. In joint accounting, you'd have to sell $50,000 across the entire series before you saw any royalties. That, my friends, is nearly impossible. Worse, it's intentionally designed to be that way, so you can't earn out. It means *they own your soul.* For that book or series, at least.

HOW IT ALL ADDS UP

Back to the discussion at hand:

It's just numbers.

I'm not a math person, but I can compare basics.

Such as, if I write "Tap That Ass," a sexy new romance that hits No. 1 on the 'Zon and goes on the NYT e-book and combined best-seller lists and USA Today and The Wall Street Journal and it sells 250,000 copies in a few months ... and then Simon & Schuster (just for example ...) comes to me with an offer to buy this book *and* the next *three* books for $1.6 million dollars ...

Initially, that sounds crazy-amazing.

ONE POINT SIX MILLION DOLLARS.

$1,600,000.

That's a lot of dollars. Not many authors are ever offered an advance that big.

Back to the numbers. Get out your calculators, peeps, we're gonna try to do some math up in this bitch.

You sold, before S&S came a-knocking, 250,000 copies at $3.99, netting 70 percent of that. Crunch it: 70 percent of $3.99 is $2.79; so, then, before the offer, you've made $697,000. And that's just in a few months. Plus, that's 70 percent of *gross*, of all sales. The only cut taken is by Amazon.

Ouch, my brain hurts now.

If you sign a traditional deal such as S&S will offer, you're selling your rights to that book *forever*. The deal is worded in such a way that you'll probably never earn out that advance.

Earn out — think about the phrasing we've been using. The money paid upon signing a deal is called what? An "advance." Meaning, you haven't earned that yet. It's what New York thinks your book *might* sell, basically. They're banking on the fact that you've already sold 250,000 copies, so your book will likely sell enough to make them that amount back, *plus* a profit. Because once you sign, you're going from 70 percent of net profits, to … a *lot, lot* less. Your agent gets 15 percent from the top, then the publisher gets most of the rest, like 70 percent or so, leaving you *maybe* 15 to 25 percent of what's left. Twenty-five percent of net is industry standard. Percent of net means *after* cuts have been taken off the top by the publisher and agent and the seller. So you'll go from making $2.79 per sale of a $3.99 title to pennies, like a nickel per sale at 15 percent of net, and yes, 15 percent of net does happen. It's vicious and disgusting, but it does happen.

Now go back up and reread my little discourse on joint versus separate accounting, and apply that to this deal. They'd insist on joint accounting, no doubt about it, or no deal. So you'd have to sell $1.6 million across the four-book deal before you saw even the puny 25 percent royalties.

Let's go back briefly to the fact that I'm *not* a numbers person. It took me a few tries to remember how to multiply the numbers to get a correct percentage. If I can do this math, so can you.

So, that $1.6 million offer for four books, three of which you haven't even written yet? You made, in the first couple months, nearly $700,000. On *one* book. They're offering you $1.6 million for *four*, and the rights are theirs *forever*.

Crunch that shit: Make it $650,000 per book (meaning, that's all you'll ever make on that book, *ever*, which is baloney and bullshit); that would be $2.6 million. That's an entire million dollars away from the minimum number you should have been offered just based on the premise of having sold 250,000 books. Now, remember, they're making this offer before the 30/60/90-day algorithms have kicked in, so you're still hanging around the top 100 or 200 and making a few grand on that book alone per day. So you'll still make a lot of money before it starts dropping. Then, you'll publish the sequel or whatever, and sales of the previous book will kick back up as new readers find you.

Now, multiply this by four books …

… The offer doesn't work.

$1.6 million doesn't sound so appetizing, once you compare it with what you could make.

It's just numbers.

It's easy to walk away from the deal because the offer for a million dollars is just numbers, ones and zeroes out in space. Until you sign and get paid, it's just numbers. It's just a theory, an idea. Don't look at an offer in terms of, "Dear lord, what could I do with a million dollars?" Especially since Uncle Sam takes a neat 40 percent on income that big, so you're only really making $600,000 or so. Think of it as numbers, cold facts. It becomes easier to walk away from what should be insulting offers, because you've been smart and looked at the big picture.

A deal shouldn't *equal* what you have made, it should *surpass* what you've made *and* give you a nice fat profit you couldn't have made on your own. A deal should be something you just simply cannot say no to, because it's *so much flipping money.*

If the deal doesn't have you hyperventilating, don't sign.

This is your life. It's your future. It's college for your kids and a new house and not worrying about bills or retirement. It's not just a million dollars right now, it's what that book could do forever, earning you 70 percent of gross while you sleep, while you eat, while you write the next one. It's your baby, your art, your craft, your business, and you owe it to yourself to make smart decisions. Don't sign away the rights to your book on the promise that they'll get you into Wal-Mart, Barnes & Noble, Books-A-Million and Target, or on the promise of a million dollars. Sign because the offer furthers your career. Because it does something for you that you can't do for yourself.

That phrase right there, that's the mantra of an indie: What can they (anyone offering you anything) do for you that you can't do for yourself?

You *can* make a million dollars on your own. You really, really can. Not everyone will; this isn't a magic formula or a promise of riches and fame. I'm just saying, if that number — one *million* dollars *(mwah-hah-hah!)* — is your goal, then it is possible without signing a trad deal. You have to work hard and long, and you have to have a book that people want to read, and you have to talk to your fans and all the other stuff we're talking about in this book. But if you have everything in place and you keep working and being smart, it is possible on your own. New York can blind you with big numbers and flashy promises, but if you remember that it's just numbers, you can see through it and make a decision that makes sense for you and the future of your career.

And for the love of God, certainly don't sign a deal for the vanity of having the name of a New York publishing house on the front page of your book. It means far more to have done it on your own, through your smarts and talent and hard work.

At least, if you ask me.

That's not numbers, that's just me expounding on the benefits of being indie.

I'm not against hybrids, though. Or trad authors. Don't get that message from this. After all, some of my best friends are hybrid (indie authors who are also traditionally published, in case you're unaware of what the term "hybrid" means). Hugh was one of the first hybrids ever, and I *love* that guy.

If the deal makes sense to you, if you're fine signing everything over to them and going on your merry way, then do it, more power to you. You'll never hear a negative word from me. Just please, *think* about it before you sign. Look at the numbers.

So, let's back up a bit. What if you're not there yet? What if you're just starting out, writing your first book and only able to dream of selling a hundred copies, let alone a hundred thousand?

It's still just numbers. *Everything* for you is just numbers at this point, really.

Don't worry about how many books you'll sell or the price point or BookBub ads or how many Twitter followers you have.

What should you worry about?

WRITE THE BOOK!

Finish it. Quit agonizing over this word or that sentence. Plot point sticking? Keep going. Make a note that the plot is goofy in this spot and keep writing. A character feels flat? Their motivation isn't quite strong enough? Keep writing. Finish the book. Not sure the climax is screamy enough? Keep writing.

You can't fix what doesn't exist, but once you've finished the book, guess what? You're not just an aspiring writer (I hate that term; stop aspiring and write!), you're an author. Twitter followers won't write the book for you. No one on Twitter or Facebook can make you a better writer. All those people having conversations about "craft" who sound so wise and cool and trendy? Guess what they're not doing? They're not writing a book. Tell the story. Finish it. Then walk away for an hour or a day or a week and let it sit, untouched. Give it time to simmer, and then reread it. Find what sucks and make it awesome. Find what works and what moves you, and leave it alone (but remember for later so you can do it again).

The price point doesn't matter if you don't have a book to sell. That's just numbers, and it doesn't matter until you're ready to think about that. Others here will talk about price, so all I'll say is, don't sell short, and don't sell too high. Price according to what you have and to where others in your genre are pricing.

Ads? Don't do it unless you can afford the price of the ad without getting hurt if the sale doesn't earn out. Most of the ads I've done were a wash; I didn't lose money, but it didn't make me enough to have been really worth it. 'Nuff said.

If you're just starting out, just write. Don't talk about writing … *write!*

If you're not sure you're doing it right, then find someone successful and ask for their advice on something specific, and *listen* to what they tell you. I can guarantee you one thing: They won't give you a magic formula to success, or one trick to making millions. This isn't a get-rich-quick scheme;

it's a business you have to learn, a trade you have to work at with terms and theories to understand. It's hard, but it's worth it. And it all comes back to the first point: *Write the book*. Then worry about the rest.

When I was doing "Big Girls," I looked around and decided who I thought was doing it right. I emailed Liliana Hart and asked her for some specific advice regarding the algorithms and such, and I listened to her advice. I took it to heart and used it, and it helped me succeed. Later, when I met Liliana in person and we became friends, she told me that of all the people — and there'd been many — who asked her for advice, I'm one of the only ones who actually listened.

I've gotten it myself. Someone will ask me for my advice, and I'll give it to them, and then I'll watch them do their own thing, the opposite of what I told them, and it won't work and they'll whine about it. Don't be that person. If you're going to ask for advice, then listen and use it. Even if it's hard; most good advice is hard to accept and use.

My final thought: This is a business, so you have to invest in it. Pay for a copy editor. No matter how many times you edit the book yourself, no matter how good an eye you have, you'll miss things. Pay a professional. *Be a professional.* Make it perfect, or as close as you can come (*after* you've finished writing it, remember). Set yourself apart from the wannabes and the hacks. Nothing says "self-pub noob" so much as sentences like, "John loved his sisters, but he just couldn't make it to there open house," or "This is you're life, Billy, so live it!" I'm squirming in my seat just thinking about leaving those sentences alone. I want to fix them. Make them right. That's part of the craft: learning to use the right words and to spell correctly, using commas and periods and semicolons correctly. No one will take your work seriously if you're not taking the trade and the craft seriously.

Some people (*cough* haters! *cough*) will still say, "Oh, it needs editing," but they'll say that to anyone, about any book. Nothing is ever perfect. That's not the point. Get it as clean as possible. If money's tight, I guarantee you there's someone who'll edit a full-length novel for about $200. That's not a huge amount of money. Scrimp and save as you're writing, cut down on the meals out and cook in, dip into your beer money or your new-purse fund. Find the money and pay a copy editor. Being clean, mechanically, sets you apart. It may not sell your book on its own, but I promise it will set you apart from the sloppy, typo-ridden masses.

Also, I'd advise you to pay for professionally designed cover art. Your Canon and Photoshop and some Word Art isn't going to cut it. This goes back to the point I just made in the preceding paragraphs: Be a professional. Professionals know what they can do themselves and what they have to outsource for, and they scrape up the funds to do so.

Overwhelmed yet?

Don't be. If you love writing and you're willing to stick to it until it works, then you'll make it. Work on it one day at a time, one book at a time. Write the book. Don't aspire, just write. There's a lot to learn about this business, but you can do it. Take it one day at a time. Writer's boards are helpful, but you have to find good, honest, successful people to listen to. Advice from unsuccessful writers who aren't selling books doesn't mean diddly. Find those who are doing well, and make friends with them, but don't get caught up in the nonsense and the drama. Learn, live, make mistakes. Take risks. Write the book, publish it and see what happens. If it doesn't do all that well, try again. Write another book, something different. Don't write the same thing over again ("insanity is doing the same thing over and over again and expecting different results"), but rather look at what's selling well right then and write something that fits the trend, yet is your own take on it.

If there's anything like a magic formula, that's it — the ability to identify market trends and marry your talents to that trend will take you places.

That's how "Falling Into You" happened for me, after all.

Be smart, be savvy, be dedicated, and don't be afraid of failing.

Also, cupcakes.

ARE YOU READY TO GO ALL THE WAY?

(HEALTHY OUTLOOK FOR THE INDIE AUTHOR)

DEBRA HOLLAND

Self-publishing requires a different mindset from traditional publishing because you are no longer just an author, you are now a *publisher*, with all that involves. Therefore you will have to handle every aspect of the business yourself, even though you may have other people doing some of the actual work for you. And self-publishing is truly a *business*, into which you'll be investing, time, money and emotion. However, you (not your publisher) will reap all the profits from your work.

As a self-published author, you don't just think of turning in a book to a traditional publisher and washing your hands of it (which you can't do anyway, because you're still expected to do promotion). But you need to strategize for years to come about that book and the rest of your career. I think this mindset may be easier for unpublished authors to grasp than it is for traditionally published authors, who throughout their careers may have felt powerless to influence anything about their books, as well as endured years of conditioning concerning the importance of reaching good sales numbers as soon as a book was launched.

Most traditionally published books (aside from popular, best-selling authors) don't have much time to establish themselves. Woe betide the author whose book doesn't sell well in the first few months (or maybe weeks). She may find her next book has a smaller print run. She may find her series has been canceled. She may have a harder time selling her next book to the publisher, or she may even be dropped from the publisher. If she's dropped, she may have a difficult time finding a new publisher.

Therefore, fear, anxiety and stress surround a book's release, for an author's career may rest on those early days. These negative emotions brand themselves in the psyche and aren't easy to shake.

Unpublished authors who are involved in the writing world through various organizations and conferences have heard enough stories over the years to absorb some of the same fears. Therefore, it may be difficult for a newly self-published author to change her mindset. She must learn to cultivate the necessary patience needed to ride the slow growth wave most authors experience without becoming discouraged — to think in terms of the "long tail" of sales numbers, not a quick explosion.

At the same time, *self-publishing means freedom!* Freedom to throw off the shackles of fear of what will happen to your career if your book doesn't do well. Freedom to choose your own stories (not write what your editor wants you to), design (or have designed) covers that you feel convey the right impression for your book, and time the release of short stories, novellas and books to your schedule, not your publisher's. You have the freedom to make each decision in your self-publishing career. For many authors that is a scary proposition. For others, it's exhilarating. Everyone may need mental retraining to think of success in years rather than weeks and months.

The authors who write good books, who make the effort to prepare their books for e-publishing and who spend time promoting them, can find opportunities (sometimes wonderful ones) in self-publishing, such as a growing readership, positive reviews, fan email, money (perhaps more than they ever earned in traditional publishing or even dreamed of earning), a supportive community of other self-published authors, agents who want to represent you and editors who want to acquire your books for their publishing houses.

SELF-REFLECTION

You need to do some thinking about your reasons for choosing a particular path. It's important that you evaluate *why* you're choosing to self-publish — if doing it yourself is a good fit for your knowledge, personality and time constraints, and if self-publishing is the best choice for your particular book or series.

Take a little time to get naked in front of the mirror. I'm not talking about stripping off your clothes, but about making a thorough examination of your personality, strengths and weaknesses, life circumstances, and support system. The better you know yourself, and the more willing you are to work on your weak areas, the better you and your career will thrive. You need to consider three areas: yourself, your book or books, and your knowledge of the publishing industry.

KNOW YOURSELF

Below is a series of questions to think about before either self-publishing your story or sending a book to an agent or editor.

Do I like having control over my choices, my product and my promotional efforts? Or do I prefer to write my book, turn it over to a publisher and let someone else do that work?

Some people are too fearful, busy, insecure, financially in need of an advance or focused on their dream of traditionally publishing to take the leap into self-publishing. Sometimes they make a well-thought-out decision not to self-publish. Other times authors blindly do what they've always done, without thinking through the ramifications to their career.

Yet self-publishing may involve a leap of faith. Authors won't know the excitement that comes from having complete control of their books (for example, being able to exercise their creativity in designing or working with a designer to make the perfect cover for their book) until they try the experience.

What's my level of fear or anxiety?

Often people make fear-based choices, and that's one of the *worst* ways to decide anything in life, especially something important like your writing career, where an anxiety-based choice can have long-lasting consequences and cost you a lot in lost earnings. What's worse is that many times, people don't recognize that their decisions are made from fear. They'll make justifications to themselves and others. They'll let a fearful fantasy play out in their mind and take control of their decisions.

It's important to ask yourself if your fear is real, or if it has only a small percentage chance of actually happening. It's easy for authors with their creative imaginations to make anxious thoughts become so vivid they play out like a movie on the screen of their mind. The fearful "movie" causes physical reactions such as an increased heart rate and/or shallow, rapid breathing, which in turn can intensify the emotional reaction of fear and anxiety, becoming a vicious cycle.

How deeply ingrained in my mind is my dream of selling to a

traditional publisher and seeing my book on the shelf in a bookstore?

This is one place it's important to know the market as well as understand your own hopes and dreams. Nowadays, authors have fewer opportunities to get their books in brick-and-mortar stores, and with Barnes & Noble teetering on the edge of continuing as a viable company, there may be even fewer opportunities in the future.

You have to weigh the importance of fulfilling your dream against the reality of financial success. You may be willing to sacrifice making money on a book in order to see that book in the store. But be aware that is what you are doing. Don't blithely assume that the *possibility* of store placement means automatic success.

My friend Tracy had been writing her first book for a long time. While she shopped the story around trying to find an agent (she tried for a year and didn't succeed) she wrote Book 2. Both were excellent stories and some savvy agent should have snapped her right up. But as often happens in this industry, no agent took her on. Tracy knew of my success with self-publishing, and at one point asked me some questions. But she made the decision to go with a small but growing publisher that promised to "maybe" get the book into bookstores.

She didn't ask me my opinion beforehand, which is a pity because I have some other friends with that same publisher. I could have told her my friends tend to make a couple hundred dollars a year and the editing of their books has been substandard. Tracy might have still made the same choice, but she would have done so from a more knowledgeable position.

Ask yourself if your dreams have changed. Sometimes you outgrow them without your being aware of it.

What are my expectations for the book if I self-publish?

Most authors in the early self-publishing wave had little to no expectations of selling their first books, especially if they had years of rejections under their belt. I know that feeling was true for me. Although I knew one of my friends was making $3,000 a month self-publishing her books (and I wanted that for myself) all my rejections had conditioned me to feel pessimistic about my stories (although I never stopped saying and writing positive affirmations about my writing career). Thus it was a big surprise when my two books took off.

Now self-publishing has become the latest get-rich-quick scheme, with authors or would-be authors flocking to publish a book or books, believing they will become wealthy in a matter of weeks or months. I'm not saying some of those authors won't eventually become successful, because they might. However, there is usually a great deal of time and effort invested (and many more books written) before that happens. Also, as more books flood the market, selling big right out of the gate becomes more difficult.

Yet new self-published authors often ask established authors how long it will take for them to have good sales. (As if anyone has the crystal ball to even know the answer.)

Figure out your expectations. You can set goals for writing, cover design and promotion, but you can't control the actual sales of your books. And if you have expectations, you may be disappointed, which could in turn lead to making decisions such as dumping money into advertising or going back to traditional publishing that you wouldn't have made if you had a "long tail" mindset.

Am I semi-self-disciplined and organized?

If you want control of your self-publishing career, it helps if you are semi-self-disciplined and semi-organized because you're going to need both skills in this new business. Those who are driven, Type-A personalities (and good writers) will have the greatest chance of success because they're able to produce books so quickly. You don't have to be a driven personality to succeed in self-publishing (I'm certainly not) but it does take some amount of self-discipline to organize the time to write and actually sit yourself down in front of your computer and type away on your book. You also have to manage the rest of your life and all the tasks associated with self-publishing.

You must treat writing as your job, and therefore write whether or not you feel motivated to do so. In the other jobs you've held, you didn't allow yourself to avoid work just because you didn't feel like showing up that day. You did your job even if you didn't want to be there. Writing and self-publishing require the same attitude.

How much pressure do I put on myself?

There's a fine line between self-motivation and unhealthy pressure. You don't want to sacrifice your mental and physical well-being in your drive to succeed. I know a lot of authors who are working *long* hours because they feel they have a window of opportunity, and they want to take advantage of it. I feel the same way, although I don't always put in the long hours most Indie Voice authors do. (This week's an exception.)

Mental pressure, especially critical thoughts, only causes you more stress. You can still work hard and strive to write the best book you can without being self-critical.

How are my computer and technology skills?

The more tech-savvy you are, the more you can do some of the tasks such as formatting, cover design, websites and blogs — a cost savings. You can certainly do more to promote your book or books because you know of Internet opportunities and how to make the most of them. For example, TIV author Jane Graves designed our Seeker's Island website: http://seekersisland.com. The website is so awesome, I want to vacation on Seeker's Island. I could never create a website like that. My brain just doesn't work that way. TIV probably would have had to pay a web designer several thousand dollars for a site like that.

I'm certainly proof that you can be tech-challenged and still be successful. However, I know that I'd be far more successful if I could do some of those technological thingies that make my eyeballs roll back when someone tries to explain what she is doing. I was anxious about uploading my first book, "Wild Montana Sky," on the Kindle Direct Publishing (KDP) site. I was afraid I wouldn't be able to do it, and someone would have to rescue me (what usually happens). But to my great relief, Amazon makes the step-by-step instructions so user-friendly that I could upload the book in about half an hour. (Now it takes me ten minutes.) Barnes & Noble's Nook Plus, Smashwords and Kobo are all similar. If you can do KDP, you can do those as well. I tell anxious tech-challenged people, "If I could do it, you can!"

But that's about as far as I've ventured into technology. I've hired experts for formatting for both electronic and print books, cover design, the construction and maintenance of my website, the construction of my personal and author Facebook pages, and my newsletter. (TIV member Denise Grover Swank had to drag me into actually *using* my personal Facebook page.) It took me about a year of trial and error to put together my "team," but now they are a solid group of people I depend on to transform my manuscript into a book.

✳✳✳

As you can see by my example, for things you can't or won't do … that's what experts are for, and why you pay someone to do the tasks. Or you find someone to help you for free. (A lot of authors have spouses or children who are good at formatting or cover design. My cousin is learning how to be my personal assistant.) The nice thing about self-publishing (at least among romance authors) is that we try to help one another. If you are struggling with some aspect of self-publishing, there will be someone who knows what to do and will be glad to explain it. Or you can barter for services. For example, in January 2012, I swapped with Louella Nelson, my former writing teacher and current developmental editor. She came to my house and watched me upload a book on Amazon and Barnes & Noble. I explained each step, and she took copious notes. In exchange, I received an hour of free editing. (Louella charges by the hour.)

The truth is that Louella could have figured out how to do this on her own. But she was more comfortable with learning from me. I would have done the same thing if there'd been a local self-published author I could have observed before I self-published my first book. But I had to figure it out on my own.

Sandra, one of my multi-published friends, had many of her books out of print. When her publisher sent her a new contract to make her out-of-print backlist books into e-books, she accepted its terms. I cringed when I heard her choice, because the publisher was paying authors a pittance for those rights. But as my friend said, "I *know* I'll never want to learn what I'll need to in order to self-publish." So for her, allowing her publisher to bring out the books was the correct decision.

The big point is: Are you willing to move beyond your comfort zone? In self-publishing, you *will* learn some new skills. However, that's part of this whole writing business. After all, think of all the craft you've had to learn to write a good book. Self-publishing is another extension of that.

Do I have a belief that I'm lucky or blessed? Do I believe that I deserve success?

After a year and a half of interacting with self-published romance authors, I've come to see that luck plays a part in success. For everyone who's successful, they've had some kind of lucky break or breaks — and it's different for everyone. (This supposes in the first place that they have a good book.)

Therefore, at some point you, too, will probably have some kind of lucky break(s) happen to you that cause you to have better sales. I think the luck is more likely to come to you if you *believe* it will happen to you. Also, you can't sit back and wait for it. You have to make the effort to continue writing and promoting, which will make it more likely to happen.

One of my friends, Amy, the most negative person I know (but she has a good heart), has had 15 years of discouraging rejections or other problems in the industry. When she first started to self-publish, she carried the same negative attitude. At some point, she posted on our writers' group (which has several self-published authors) about her lack of sales and her discouragement. She received both a stern talking-to (okay, writing to) and a pep talk from several of us because we love her and want her to be successful. Amy took our words to heart and worked hard to cultivate a more positive attitude. When she did, her sales started increasing. Then they multiplied.

Then Amy's sales started dropping for several months, and she became fearful that they'd continue. But she focused on the fact that she was still making far more money on book sales than she ever had before. Her husband was able to retire. She wrote to us that she paid more in taxes for 2011 than she and her husband had earned in their day jobs for that period. Then, she posted that one of her books was made a RT Book Reviews Top Pick. Her lucky break had arrived.

Do you have a negative or positive attitude?

This question goes alongside your belief in luck and blessings. Plain and simple: *If you're a negative person, you'll tend to repel people and opportunities, and if you're a positive person, you're going to attract them to you.*

People with a negative mindset tend to *focus* on what's bad or difficult in their lives or around them and ignore the good that may be happening to and around them. Other people, especially successful ones, tend to avoid those who will drag them down or drain them with their whining and complaining or other unpleasant behaviors.

Recently one TIV author sat next to a big-name author at a book conference. The other author was so critical and back-stabbing that our member returned home and said, "We *never* want to be involved with this person!" Sure enough, we had an opportunity to work with some other authors on a future project, and she was *not* one we chose, although before the conference, we might have.

In another example, one of our authors posted on the Kindle Boards that TIV has a weekly newsletter, where self-published authors can advertise their sales for *free*. We have a few minimum requirements, such as 20 reviews with an average of four stars. While some people thanked her, a few other people jumped on her with both feet. One man was particularly virulent about the post. He was angry because we required the reviews, railed about the need for reviews and how difficult they were to obtain, and implied that most self-published authors with a lot of positive reviews either must have friends and family write the reviews, or were buying them. Reading the rant made me shake my head. A positive person would make note of the opportunity, and then set it aside as something to do when he'd met the requirements. A positive, *gracious* person would have thanked the Indie Voice member for letting the group know about the opportunity and also taken us up on it when he could.

I'm sure I'm not the only person on Kindle Boards to make a mental note to never read this guy's books. Conversely, I've sometimes bought and read authors whom I've met online or have read about in blogs. Usually there's something about that author and his book that appeals to me. So I'll take a chance and buy the book. (Self-published books are usually very affordable, which makes it easier to take a risk on an unknown author.) I've discovered some wonderful new-to-me authors that way, and then bought the rest of their books.

How much patience do I have?

One of the next things to consider is your level of patience. Are you able to think in terms of the "long tail?" Or will you become discouraged if you've sold only a few books at the end of the month? Are you able to stay open to possibilities of the future? Can you continue to believe that sales and other good things will happen when they happen, and it might not be for months or even years?

I'm a little guilty of impatience. I'd written off Barnes & Noble as a place where I could have many book sales. For example, in March 2012, I sold 340 books on B&N, compared with over 10,000 at Amazon. Yet (the next month) in April I sold 10,935 at B&N, and in May, 10,558. (I don't know the reason for the jump, but I think I "lucked out" and had a Nook internal promotion of some sort.) It took me 11½ months to reach this point on Barnes & Noble. But it just as easily could have taken two years or five years before this happened. This experience has been a pleasant reminder to remain mentally (and positively) open to the possibilities. The sales have since declined to what they were before, mostly because my Montlake e-books (first two in the Montana Sky series) are no longer available on B&N.

Patience (and some perfectionism) also comes into play. You need to have the patience to produce the best book you can. The impatience to get your book up and selling can lead to some poor decisions that can negatively impact your sales. Or you can make mistakes such as uploading the wrong book (which I did once when it was late at night and I was exhausted) or checking the wrong box and screwing up your royalty rate.

My friend Scott is a screenwriter, and I've helped him polish a script. He heard my stories about self-publishing and decided to write a book. He did so in a few months. When he mentioned to me that the book was ready, I told him I'd be able to edit the manuscript the following week. (I assumed he'd want me to.) Then Scott told me he'd already published it. I couldn't believe he'd self-published an unedited book, especially when he had a friend who was willing to help for free.

I downloaded a sample and read the first paragraph, which was great. Relieved, I read on for a few more paragraphs, and saw that the book rapidly went downhill. (Screenwriters don't need to know about point of view, interior thoughts and emotion.) Although I spoke with him about the flaws, he's too busy to do anything to change the book. Needless to say, he's gotten some bad reviews and few sales.

KNOW THE INDUSTRY

Most people who've been around Romance Writers of America (RWA) and other prominent writers organizations such as Novelists Inc. (NINC) have learned about the publishing industry from listening to speakers, communicating among themselves and reading articles about the industry. They know how to write a query letter, how to submit to an agent or editor, how to promote their books, which publisher is doing what, what type of sub-genre is popular right now, and a lot of other details that almost-published and published authors learn (unless they live in a cave). Published authors have studied and continue to study the market. Highly successful authors might not as much because their publisher often does everything for them. But that's not true for most authors.

It behooves both unpublished and traditionally published authors to also study the self-publishing market. It astonishes me how many traditional authors have *no* idea of the benefits of self-publishing. This is changing in RWA and NINC circles, at least as the buzz about self-publishing grows ever stronger. But for many authors who toil in their proverbial cave, they still have the "old" vanity press idea of self-publishing, and it's something they'd never even consider.

Last year, I spoke at a conference in Louisiana and flew there with an author who'd written a book that had been made into a popular Disney movie. (He's written other books too.) He spends a lot of his time traveling to schools speaking to the students. That's how he makes a big chunk of his income. He sadly told me that he does this less and less as school budgets are cut. I pulled out one of the postcards I carry with my book covers on each side, handed it to him and started to talk about self-publishing. I could tell he had *no* clue about it — hadn't even heard about the new self-publishing movement. But he definitely took notice when I told him how much I'd made in one month. By the end of the conversation, I could see the wheels turning in his head. I'd opened a new door to writing income that he hadn't known about.

Even if you don't want to self-publish a new work, I think it behooves traditionally published authors who have the rights to their backlists to self-publish those books. Authors of outdated books can update them to the current times or they can keep them set in the time they were written. Although if you self-publish "classic" books, put the date in from the first chapter, for example, 1998.

There are lots of blogs about self-publishing that are very informative, especially for writers standing at the decision crossroads. The old adage about first finding an agent to represent you no longer makes as much business sense as it did before. And you certainly should research the type of agent you want, including how his or her self-published clients feel about the representation. Taking the time to educate yourself *before* you jump into the self-publishing or traditional publishing waters can save you from making mistakes that can cost you time, money and sales. Plus in knowing the traditional publishing industry *and* the self-publishing industry, you have a chance to make wiser decisions as your career progresses.

KNOW YOUR BOOK

Different books are better candidates for self-publishing. For example: Is your book genre fiction or literary fiction? Self-published genre fiction (for the most part) sells better than literary fiction. This makes sense when you think of how genre fiction has a built-in readership that returns again and again to their favorite types of books. Is your story a young adult (YA) or adult novel? (YA still has a bigger print readership.) Or is your book a nonfiction self-help with a broad readership base, or will it only appeal to a small niche market? (A niche market isn't necessarily a bad thing. You may do very well with a niche book. However, make sure to target your marketing efforts to your potential readership pool.)

Some books just will not fit into traditional published boxes. They aren't the current hot genre or they cross genres. Or maybe the story is completely different from the type of story the author is known for.

In Stephanie Laurens' newsletter, she announced she is putting out a medieval romance she wrote many years ago at the beginning of her career. Although she didn't say she was self-publishing the book, she also didn't mention a publisher. Putting that together with her very pro-self-publishing keynote speech at the RWA National Conference in 2012, it makes me think she's doing the book herself. The New York Times best-selling author is known for her Regency romances. The medieval, she wrote in her newsletter, "just sat, complete and finished, in my bottom drawer."

Often, a brand-new author doesn't know what she doesn't know. She thinks her work is the next best-seller, when it really belongs under the bed. She rushes to self-publish and receives poor reviews and few sales. These are the types of books that give self-publishing a bad name.

The best unpublished candidates for successful self-publishing are those writers who've studied the craft. They have one or more *knowledgeable* critique partners or a critique group with other writers who are savvy about craft, meaning it's not a case of the blind leading the blind. They entered contests and received feedback. They've finaled and/or won contests and have good feedback about the book(s) from agents and editors, even if ultimately they were rejected. These authors have received enough critiquing to help weed out flaws and strengthen their stories.

Therefore, a new author should first learn the craft of writing. Take classes, read writing books, join a critique group or have a critique partner. Submit to some contests and get some feedback. Try querying agents and editors to see their responses. Revise. Revise. Revise. Then pay an editor to developmentally edit the book. After you've finished those edits, find some beta readers to read the manuscript. Finally, pay for a professional copy edit or even two different copy edits.

Once you've written a good book, write another one, preferably in the same genre as the first. Even better is to make your books into a series — a series has a built-in readership because readers go from book to book to book. I'm not saying you shouldn't write in other genres, but (I've learned to my dismay) many readers will not genre hop or sub-genre hop. Only a few readers of my Montana Sky series also read The Gods' Dream Trilogy. So be aware that you might have to build up a readership for each a different type of book, and some will sell better than others.

PUBLISHING YOUR BACKLIST

For traditionally published authors, self-publishing their backlist gives them a chance to fix things that bothered them about the book. Maybe their editor did a hack job. Most certainly, they are better writers now. But the best thing going for traditionally published authors is that they already have a fan base. They start out at a better level than an unknown author.

A traditionally published author might also want to write (or has written) a book that's different from what she usually writes and her publisher isn't interested. Self-publishing gives her a way to do that.

However, as I said above, a traditional author might be better off leaving her book as is, except for polishing it a bit. This is especially true for thrillers or romantic suspense stories, where a plot point hinges on a character not being able to find a pay phone. A current version of the book wouldn't work because of the Internet and cell phones.

Some previously published books are best tossed under the bed (as are some of an author's early manuscripts). One of my friends got her rights back to a previously published book, and thought she could make some revisions and self-publish it. She asked me to edit the manuscript after she'd worked on it. This friend is an excellent writer who *knows* her craft. So I was shocked to read her '90s-era book. Frankly, the book is horrible. It's so bad,

I don't see how it could have gotten published in the first place. It should not see the light of day ever again. There are flaws in the writing, flaws in the plot, flaws in the characters (not the kind they overcome) and flaws in the relationship. I could barely stand to read the book. I couldn't believe the author wasn't aware of the problems. But she had a story in her head that was so strong, she couldn't see what was actually on the page.

The book will probably need three or four rounds of edits to make it salable. In my opinion, the author should start from scratch or scrap the book entirely, and I tactfully told her so. But she doesn't want to, so she's plowing her time into something that will probably take far longer to fix than writing a new book would. I still don't think the final product will be good, and it could negatively impact the rest of her backlist. Readers probably won't jump to her other books if they start with this one.

REAL EXAMPLES

I'm going to end this chapter with two real-life examples of people who may or may not do well with self-publishing.

Poor Candidate

I had a woman write to me that she was crying every day at her lack of book sales. She saw my sales numbers that I'd shared on my blog and that information made her weep more. She believed she deserved success for her books, and although she didn't attack me, there was an accusatory tone to her email, almost as if she blamed me for my success when I didn't have the same type of *literary* background she did. From her email, I could see she didn't know the market, nor realize she needed to promote her book.

When I went on Amazon and read her book description, I saw a convoluted blurb that contained an error. Her cover didn't do a good job of conveying her story. She was definitely guilty of not knowing herself, her market or her book. Because of that, she had worked herself into an emotional black hole, and (in my expert opinion) required psychotherapy and maybe medication (although probably not entirely because of self-publishing).

Good Candidate

After giving a self-publishing workshop at a conference in Louisiana, I had one of the attendees come up to me. She mentioned she'd be attending the next RWA national conference. She hoped to attract an agent with the new manuscript she was trying to finish by then. She told me she'd been a Golden Heart finalist with me in 2001. Like me, she'd had an agent, had come close to selling and had several unsold manuscripts.

I suggested she consider self-publishing her old manuscripts, while finishing her new manuscript to attract traditional publishers. Good sales numbers from her self-published books might also attract an agent. I also warned her to make sure any agent she chose would be supportive of her self-publishing efforts and to carefully read both the agent's and any potential publisher's contract (among other things) to make sure her self-publishing options weren't limited.

Now that you have an idea of what's required of an indie journey, you can decide if you're ready for the challenge.

STAYING SANE AND SEXY
IN AN INDIE WORLD

(MIND AND BODY AND THE INDIE AUTHOR)

DEBRA HOLLAND

Writers are creative people who aren't allowed to just sit at a keyboard and enjoy wrestling with their muse (which in and of itself can be a stressful process). They must also cope in the publishing world, regardless of their affinity for business.

Writing is a profession that requires you to multitask. To be a successful author, you must also be good at sales and publicity, accounting, networking, public speaking, dealing with the public, arguing with your editor with just the right degree of tact, plus many other things. To be a *self-published* author means you add additional tasks onto an already long to-do list.

As a published author, your cherished work is exposed to public scrutiny, not just with a small group of people, but a national and maybe worldwide audience. Not only do you have the internal and external pressure to do your best work, but once it's published, then anyone, no matter how ignorant, can criticize your book. Reviews, gossip, sales figures fly across the Internet and phone lines. And since you can't please everyone all the time, there is always someone who doesn't like your book, and of course you get to hear or read their critique, which can be hurtful and shaming.

For most authors, the writing income is uncertain. You must make financial decisions and budgets when you don't know when the next chunk of money will come, or how much it will be. Worry about money is one of the top causes of stress, and the No. 1 topic couples argue over.

WRITING AND SELF-PUBLISHING

In reading blogs, articles and books about self-publishing, or in talking to self-published authors, you will see and hear over and over again that indie publishing is *a lot of work*, especially with all the promotion you have to do. Up until the last six months or so, I would have disagreed with that comment. Now I believe self-publishing *can* be, and often *is*, a lot of work. How much time and effort you put into your career is going to be an individual decision that will change from week to week.

As you will read elsewhere in this book, promoting your book is a given, whether you are published by a publishing house or you do it yourself. For the most part with traditional publishing, authors are expected to do their own promotion, and even big-name authors usually augment their publisher's marketing efforts. Therefore, you're going to have to make just as much of an effort to promote yourself and your books *regardless* of which publishing path you choose.

My first year and a half of self-publishing (beginning at the end of April 2011) felt fairly effortless because I'd already written (and had professionally edited) "Wild Montana Sky," "Starry Montana Sky," "Sower of Dreams" and "Reaper of Dreams." I farmed out the formatting and cover design to experts. I did almost no promotion except an occasional blog or guest blog post. My Montana Sky series books sold themselves, mostly because I hit two underserved niches — sweet/clean/traditional/classic romance and Western romance, especially *historical* Western romance. Although I had Facebook and Twitter accounts, I didn't really use them. I had a newsletter subscription list, but hadn't sent out a newsletter in several years.

Would my books have sold more if I promoted them? Probably. But I was satisfied with my sales at the time. I sold almost 97,000 my first year and hit the USA Today best-seller list with "Wild Montana Sky."

However, I didn't put the books into print or audio or have them translated. I started my first print book of "Montana Sky Christmas" in December 2012 because I thought it would make a nice Christmas gift. Since then, I have been working on making the rest of the books available through CreateSpace. I am beginning the work of my first audio version of "Sower of Dreams."

The more projects you take on (especially overlapping ones) means more work and often more stress. Just think of all you have to do to prepare a manuscript as an e-book, as well as a print and audio version.

I'll give you an example of my current workload (in no particular order of importance). This list doesn't take into account the rest of my life — working as a psychotherapist and corporate crisis and grief counselor, spending time with family and friends, and (this week) preparing for a trip to Montana in four days where I will speak at a conference and explore and do research.

- Finish writing "Harvest of Dreams" (the end needs work) so I can put the book up for pre-order to coincide with a promotion I'm doing for "Sower of Dreams" on June 30.
- Read through the formatting of the print version of "Sower of Dreams."
- Write my two chapters for this book (due in a week).
- Finish the developmental edits for my next book, "Mail-Order Brides of the West: Trudy."
- Make the changes to a newly edited version of "Lywin's Quest," the first book in my space opera, Twinborne Trilogy (140,000 words), that I need to finish in a week for a promotion scheduled for the month of July.
- I'm self-publishing a Montana Sky series Christmas anthology that I've invited my friends to contribute stories to. My own two short stories need to be written in the next seven weeks. In the meantime, I'm managing the project with 11 other authors.
- I've just finished contract negotiations with Montlake and soon will have an eight-month deadline for "Glorious Montana Sky." While I'm not currently going to work on this book, that fact that I will soon begin (and have a deadline) stays in my awareness.
- Write the monthlong overdue blog post I promised someone, with another one due next week.
- Write and send out a newsletter (I include several articles) announcing the release of "Mail-Order Brides of the West: Trudy."
- Finish reading a friend's book for the endorsement I've promised her.
- Judge three contest entries. Due tomorrow.
- Critique the 16,000-word short story written by my developmental editor. (We're doing a critique swap, which will save me $500.) I told her I'd get it back to her in about three weeks.

Obviously, right now if you ask me if self-publishing is a heavy, stressful workload, I'll say YES! But if you look over my list, at this point in time, all my projects (except for writing these chapters and the contest entries) have self-imposed deadlines. In other words, I'm doing this to myself! Therefore *the choices are all ones I've made.* I have the control.

Why am I doing so much? (Sometimes I ask myself that question.) The answer is because I have tremendous opportunities right now, and I want to take advantage of all of them. I see this as a time in my life where I'm going to work very hard to get my stories out into the world, making the most of my success. (This is a common feeling among self-published authors.) I plan to ease up on the workload in a few years.

However, my workload is a drop in the bucket compared with some of my colleagues. I admire and envy some TIV authors for their ability to write a wonderful book in only a month. At the same time, I know the sacrifices they're making in their personal lives (and in their sleep) to accomplish everything they do.

It definitely helps to have a driven, Type-A personality, as most TIV authors do. I'm a Type B, more reflective and laid-back. I have hypothyroidism Type 2, so I must build self-care into my schedule, and that hasn't changed with self-publishing dropping into my life.

When we did a TIV summit in Cancun in February 2013, all the other authors got up in the morning and wrote. I went to the gym and worked out. When we had a break from our conferencing in the afternoon, we all went to the pool. Then the other authors went back to their rooms to write. I took a nap. This is not only vacation behavior for me. This is my normal life. I work out most mornings — women's fitness boot camp — and almost always take a nap in the afternoon. I know from experience that after I fully wake up from a nap, my head is clearer and I can write better. Just these two activities mean I won't write as much in a day as other authors. Yet that's a sacrifice I'm willing to pay for looking and feeling good mentally and physically.

PRACTICING SELF-CARE

To write for a living exposes authors to the unique stress of the publishing profession.

Writing isn't a job where you show up at 9 a.m., do the work someone assigns to you, and leave to go home at 5 p.m. Nor do you have someone else supervising you and keeping track of your projects.

Writing requires the self-discipline to spend long hours at home on your computer, regardless of what you'd rather be doing. When you write, you cannot leave your job behind at the office. In fact, many authors have a day job, and still have to carve writing time out of the rest of their day. Even when you write full-time, family, friends, household errands and tasks, and other commitments pull at your time and energy.

For most authors, they *always* have writing hanging over their heads, either to meet a current deadline or to come up with new proposals/books. The "I should be writing" guilt is difficult to shake off, thus making it hard to completely relax. Story ideas or characters sometimes don't leave you alone. They may not let you sleep or be completely present when you interact with others.

A frequent question I hear from writers is: "How can I live a healthier life when I'm so busy?" Another common question is: "How can I balance my life?" In our busy society, with so many choices and possibilities that suck up our time, it can be difficult to find ways to take care of ourselves.

I'm going to be frank with you. Some of what I've written in this chapter, such as exercise and eating well, you've read or heard a hundred times before. You might be tempted to skim or skip those sections because you don't want to think about or do them. Do yourself the favor of taking the time to not only read the self-care tips, but seriously consider how you can fit them into your life. Your health and well-being (and thus the well-being of those who love you) may depend on your making some lifestyle changes.

TIME MANAGEMENT

If you've written a book, you've probably learned to squeeze writing time into your schedule. However, writing because you want to write, rather than writing because you have a deadline — either from your editor or a self-publishing one you've chosen — are two different experiences.

One of the best and worst things about self-publishing is the lack of a deadline imposed on you (and written into your contract) by your publisher. A deadline focuses you to write on a regular basis with the goal of finishing by a certain date. With self-publishing, you have no external deadlines. You don't have the pressure of a deadline, but you also don't have that mental whip driving you to work on your book.

When you self-publish your books, you can go at your own pace, no matter how fast or slow without the stress (and incentive) of a deadline. Or you can make a deadline for yourself by scheduling a delivery date with your editor or announcing on your website/blog/social media when your next book will be out, so your readers are expecting you to deliver the story on time.

Information overload places stress on the brain. Sometimes it's difficult to focus when you have conflicting priorities pulling at you. So throughout the day, it's important to *stop* and ask yourself on a regular basis:

- "What's important to me?"
- "What are my priorities?" (Importance and priorities may be different.)
- "What's the best use of my time?"

Then take a look at what you're doing and what you're about to do and see if you should make other choices about your time. Do your best to eliminate clutter in your home and ease out of unnecessary activities.

Realize that what you're doing is "good enough." Not everything needs to be perfect. Decide what is most important in your life. Choose which tasks deserve your best effort, and simplify or relax the others. For example, in my life, I put my perfectionism into my books, being a competent psychotherapist to my clients and being a good teacher to my students. I don't put a lot of effort into keeping a tidy, organized house.

You also need to take a serious look at your budget to see if you can afford to hire out services such as housecleaning and gardening, as well as various stages of your self-publishing projects. I've used a housekeeper for years, who initially came twice a week. Long ago, I figured housework was not the best use of my time. For me, the five hours she spends cleaning my house (which costs me $75) are better utilized elsewhere. For example, I can get a lot of writing done in five hours. Now I can afford for her to come every week, which helps me, but also helps my housekeeper. She's a single mother of five, who ekes out a living. That extra $150 a month makes a big difference to her.

Don't use guilt (either your own or what someone else tries to inflict on you) as a motivator. *Should, ought* and *must* are guilt words. Many times you force yourself to do things because you *should* do them, not because you *want* to. And there are many shoulds in life that are important. There are also many shoulds in life that are imposed on us from someone else's standards. For example, if your mom kept a spic-and-span house, and drilled the importance of tidiness into your brain, you may feel guilty about not keeping your house to her standards.

Therefore, if you're feeling guilted into doing something, step back and try to see the situation with fresh eyes. Then ask if the task is really necessary and if so, can it be changed, postponed, given to someone else to do, or gotten out of the way as soon as possible so it's off your to-do list and out of your mind? It might help to pretend an impartial stranger is looking at your life and making your decisions. How would she answer those questions?

REPLENISH YOUR ENERGY

Keeping your energy tank relatively full is one of the most important things you can do to have a balanced life and accomplish all you have to. Like a car with an empty gas tank, you won't go far without fuel. Therefore you need to pay attention to who and what *gives* you energy and also who and what *drains* your energy.

The first thing to know about yourself is whether you are an introvert (most writers are) or an extrovert. Many people think an extrovert is someone who's outgoing and enjoys social gatherings, and that's usually (but not always) true. They also view an introvert as someone who's very shy or lives in a basement with little human interaction. However, an outgoing personality isn't necessarily a sign of introversion or extroversion — how you *replenish your energy* is the defining factor. If you are an extrovert, you recharge your energy by being around people and with social activities.

If you are an introvert, you can easily be overwhelmed or drained by too much social stimulation. Introverts replenish through *solitude* and *solitary activities*. Introverts often feel (and may also be judged by others) as if something is wrong with them for enjoying their time alone. Extroverts often drag introverts to social gatherings, thinking that getting out will be good for them. And maybe it will — however, it's usually also draining.

You can be an outgoing introvert (like me) who's good with people but still needs solitude to recharge. Or you can enjoy your alone time, but as an extrovert, the best way for you to feel better is to be around people. Therefore, you need to structure your time so you do activities that will replenish you.

One of the best things you can do is accept whichever personality type you are and then arrange for activities in your life that give you energy. Once I learned about introversion and extroversion (and that I'm an introvert, not an extrovert as I'd assumed) I started scheduling solitude into my busy life. Naps and reading novels are my best ways to recharge. For example, when I'm at a conference, I love spending time with my friends and meeting new authors. However, at times I retreat to my room for some quiet time to read and sleep, relax and recharge, before venturing out into the social scene again.

DEEP BREATHING

Deep, centered breathing is the quickest and easiest way to trigger the body's relaxation response. Throughout the day, you should stop, check your breathing and take deep inhalations. This is especially important when you're stressed, because the body tends to tighten up and the stomach clenches at the very times you need oxygen the most.

After a stressful or difficult situation is over, take some cleansing breaths to release any negativity you might have had to deal with or still are holding on to.

When you breathe, you need to inhale, making sure the air goes deeply into your lungs and your stomach expands. Exhale and pull in your belly. For additional peacefulness, relax your shoulders and change what you are thinking about to a calming scene. A walk on the beach or through a forest is a peaceful image.

Meditation and yoga are good ways to relax and help you manage stress. Both practices involve centering yourself in your body and taking calming breaths. Studies show that yoga and meditation can ease anxiety, help you sleep better and enhance emotional stability. If you don't have time to take a class or indulge in long meditations, learn a few yoga poses and do them in the morning or when you need a break. Meditate for a few minutes by sitting comfortably, closing your eyes and taking deep breaths. Imagine yourself *breathing* in peace and calm, and *exhaling* stress.

Even if you don't do yoga or meditation, it's good to remind yourself to take deep breaths, which will help your body relax.

STRETCH TIME

I teach my clients to do a time stretching exercise, based on one developed by Deepak Chopra. This technique helps in those busy moments when you feel too stressed and overwhelmed, or you have a lot of things going wrong and slowing you down.

- Stop and say (out loud), "I'm going to stretch time."
- Take a deep breath, and tell yourself (again aloud), "I have all the time I need to _____."
- Take a few more deep breaths.
- Repeat Step 2.
- Get into motion by doing a stretch or another quick body movement.
- Shift your thinking. Sing a song, put on some music, dance around the room, play with your pet, call a friend, read something inspirational for a few minutes, or say a positive quote or affirmation out loud.

TAKE TIMEOUTS THROUGHOUT THE DAY

Sometimes all you need to to de-stress is to quiet your mind or switch your thoughts for a few minutes. For example, just covering your eyes with the palms of your hands for a minute — giving them a lack of visual stimulation — can be soothing. Here are some possible timeouts:

- Take a short walk.
- Do a small household chore.
- Take a bath or a shower.
- Write a poem, even if it's silly or bad.
- Listen to your favorite music.
- Play with your pet.

JOURNAL

Writing in a journal is one of the best ways to process your feelings. Research shows that journaling may also keep you physically healthier. Writing about your emotions can give you insight by helping you understand and process your feelings. Journaling also does the following:

- Helps you sort out your thoughts.
- Gives you insight and perspective.
- Gets your surface thoughts out of the way so you can focus on what you really want to write.
- Reveals your feelings.
- Defuses intense emotions.
- Changes how you see things.
- Helps you figure out what you want and don't want.
- Leads to problem-solving.
- Gives you a reference point to come back to later and see changes or patterns.
- Helps you work things out with someone (living or dead).

FIND YOUR PEACEFUL PLACE

Have a spot in your home that brings you calm, makes you feel good and enhances your creativity. Retreat to that place when you need to de-stress. Or go there with your laptop or a notebook and pen when you need need some peacefulness to help you with your writing.

My peaceful place is the balcony off my bedroom. For several years, the wood had deteriorated from dry rot until the decking wasn't safe to step on. With funds earned from self-publishing, I had the balcony rebuilt, bought two comfortable chairs and a small round table, and added some flowerpots. Now I love sitting there in the morning, having breakfast and reading the manuscript pages I'd written the day before. I'll write outside (wrapped in a blanket during cooler weather) long into the evening, when it's too dark to see anything but my computer screen.

If you don't have someplace in your home that feels like your calming oasis, seek one out. Perhaps a bench at a local park, the library, or a beautiful hotel lobby will work for you. If you like the stimulation of people around you, you might write at a coffeehouse or other busy location.

FOLLOW YOUR INTUITION

Your intuition is your connection to your higher self and the divine. This intuitive part of you communicates in various ways — a "gut" feeling, goose bumps, a small voice, a sense that something doesn't feel right or that something's wrong. But much of the time you might not pay attention to the messages you may be receiving — that is, until something happens, and you think, "I knew I should have ____!" or "I knew I shouldn't have____!"

Intuition is often different from logic, different from emotion and different from what other people will tell you to do. You can logically list why a decision might be right, or feel afraid about a decision and thus make a choice based on emotion. Or you might decide something based on a combination of logic and emotion. However, intuition will often defy logic, or be the opposite of what you emotionally feel or want. That's why it's so hard to "hear" it, much less follow where your intuition leads. If your intuition is giving you a message, you need to listen, not discount your instincts.

Too many times, I've heard authors say, "I *knew* I shouldn't have signed that contract, but ..." Each author has his own buts — he wanted the sale, or the money, or his agent or someone else told him to, or he was afraid he couldn't get a better deal, or he'd be dropped by his publisher. ...

I owe my self-publishing success to my following my intuition. Often along the 10-year journey of attempting to sell one of my books, I had a sense that it wasn't yet my time. That feeling often comforted me during the disappointing and frustrating rejection process.

I had a couple opportunities over the years to sell "Wild Montana Sky" and also to submit the book to some small publishers that probably would have taken it. But at each decision point, something didn't feel right, so I said no. If I'd accepted those offers, tried to twist my book to fit what those publishers wanted, I wouldn't have had the series available to self-publish in April 2011. I would have missed the opportunity that came from my books' being available at that very time. Since then I've continued to listen to my intuition. For example: My being part of TIV felt "right" from the very beginning.

CELEBRATE YOUR SUCCESSES, NO MATTER HOW SMALL

Research has shown that people who reach 100 are usually optimistic and handle stress extremely well. Positive people embrace the wonders of life. They take pride and satisfaction in their accomplishments and strengths, and in doing the things they love.

There are special moments along the self-publishing path, many of which have nothing to do with sales and income. I was moved to tears the first time I received a fan email letter raving about my Montana Sky series. Sometimes reading a five-star review of one of my books can give me goose bumps. The complete shock of making the USA Today list with "Wild Montana Sky" made me cry and shake from excitement. Then I went out to dinner with a friend to celebrate.

On the Indie Romance Ink Yahoo group for self-published authors (see the chapter on "Tips for Virgins" to find the link) we have a 10,000 celebratory "cake." When an author reaches an important sales goal she announces that it's time for her "cake" and the other members congratulate her.

When Darcie Chan, self-published author of the best-selling "The Mill River Recluse" (over 650,000 books sold to date), sold 100 books in her first month, she danced with her husband in their kitchen.

Along with celebrating your successes, it's important to celebrate the successes of other self-published authors. A success celebrated means hope and joy for you as well. Congratulate others and wish them well. Being upbeat and supportive makes you feel good. Positive comments, saying thank you, smiling, listening and praying for others are all ways to spread good energy.

BELIEVE YOU DESERVE GOOD FORTUNE

When you write for a living, you have to cope with fear. Fear that you can't come up with a new story idea, write it well, meet your deadline, sell, make enough to live on. ... The list goes on and on.

It's hard not to get caught up in other people's fear or negativity, especially when your livelihood is at stake. Negative rumors sweep through the publishing industry: "The midlist is shrinking" and "Everyone's having a hard time selling" are examples of some common rumors. If you're considering self-publishing you'll hear or read some common criticisms, such as:

- Self-published books are "crap."
- Most authors don't sell 100 books in a year.
- The market is oversaturated.

TIV authors all prove these pessimistic comments wrong. Even if there's some truth in the negative rumors, they don't have to apply to you. Opportunities exist in self-publishing, and (provided you write good books) you can still do well. *Positive/optimistic thinking PLUS hard work equals success.*

To help yourself stay optimistic, take time to picture what success would look like to you. Write down affirmations and post them where you'll see them. Draw a picture or make a collage from photos torn out of magazines and hang it where you'll see the images every day.

About nine years ago, I created two posters (drawing stick figures and other symbols with colored pencils) and hung them on the walls of my bedroom, where I could see them from my bed. I drew one poster for my writing dreams, and on the other I outlined my goals for the other areas of my life. The posters have been there for so long that the paper yellowed and the colors faded. I practically forgot they were there.

Then a couple of weeks ago, I focused on those pictures. I walked over to study the writing poster, and goose bumps broke out on my skin. Across the top of the paper, I'd printed in big letters, "New York Times Best-Selling Author." I had symbols and titles of books I planned to write, which are now written. I had a picture of me doing book signings with people lined up to talk to me. I had the advance money I wanted to earn per book when I sold. Nine years ago, those images seemed like an *impossible dream*. I couldn't even sell a book to a publisher! Now I'm a New York Times best-selling author. I've made the amount I'd wanted for an advance in the space of *one* of my best self-publishing months. And my latest contract for Montlake paid me *more* for "Glorious Montana Sky" than I had printed on the poster. WOW!

Visualizations, affirmations and positive thoughts are all good, but those in and of themselves are not enough. If you don't act (write), you won't succeed. It's the *action* that gives you the results. If your dream is to be a successful author, then you need to *write*.

ESTABLISH A POSITIVE SUPPORT SYSTEM

I owe my publishing career to my support system. I had help, from my very first writing instructor (who is now my developmental editor) to my friends in Romance Writers of America, to the group of friends who began to self-publish just before me and coached me along the way, to the members of Indie Romance Ink, and other authors I've met along the way. TIV has been an amazing experience as we all strive to reach new sales levels through mutual promotion.

Authors have provided networking, education, commiseration, critiquing, cross-promotion, industry tips, life support and just plain fun. I couldn't have done it without them. My family and friends have also been supportive and instrumental in my success.

I've also put together an awesome team of editors, cover artists and formatters who enable me to make my books a success.

CULTIVATE AN ATTITUDE OF GRATITUDE

It's hard to stay stressed or continue with a poor attitude when you count your blessings.

Research on gratitude, including SPECT scans of the brain, shows how thankfulness and appreciation impacts the brain in positive ways. People who practice gratitude:

- Are healthier.
- Have lower levels of stress hormones in their blood.
- Tend to have more energy and alertness.
- Sleep better and wake up feeling more refreshed.
- Exercise more.
- Are more optimistic.
- Experience less anxiety and depression.
- Are kinder toward others, including romantic partners.
- Possess higher long-term satisfaction with life.

- Tend to have more energy and alertness.
- Have enhanced empathy and fewer aggressive thoughts and behavior.
- Are better able to let go of bad memories.
- Create more joy in their lives.
- Tend to have more energy and alertness. (Are you getting the point?)

It's sometimes hard to feel gratitude when you're stressed and overwhelmed. During difficult times, you may dwell on your weaknesses (or someone else's) or what you haven't done or should be doing.

It's easier to have a positive attitude when you take the time to appreciate what's going right or the blessings you *do* have. So stopping during the day to feel and express gratitude helps to calm and center you, reminding you of what's important. Another way to practice gratitude is to write down five things you're grateful for daily. If you do this exercise in the morning and before you go to bed, you'll begin and end your day on a positive note.

The writing profession is very competitive, yet the writers aren't necessary the ones doing the competing. It's the publishing professionals who are making the choices, and the consumers who are buying your books. There are even lists to shout to the world where you stand. And even if you are not competitive by nature, it's hard not to compare your writing output with someone who might be able to write more books a year than you, or feel a twinge of envy when you hear of someone else receiving a hefty advance or making the New York Times list, or having great self-publishing sales, especially if you know your writing is just as good or better. Every time you read a good book, it's difficult not to compare your work with another's and have self-doubts.

Comparing yourself can lead to discontent and dissatisfaction, which can be deadly to your sense of well-being. Everyone is on his or her life path. When you start to compare, remind yourself that there will always be people who are better off than you and far more people who are *worse* off. Give thanks for your blessings and focus on your own life, not someone else's.

When faced with the to-do list I mentioned at the beginning of this chapter, I say to myself things like, "It's all good challenges," or "I'm choosing to take advantage of opportunities," or "I'm grateful to be living my dream." Then I prioritize what needs to be done and get to it.

Other ways I express gratitude are by mentally thanking the readers who leave reviews of my books. (Some are harder to feel grateful for than others.) I also like to look at my sales figures and think of the people behind the numbers. I thank them for buying and reading my books.

EAT WELL

It's always important to eat nourishing food to sustain your body and health, but especially so when you're stressed. Stress and anxiety, as well as emotions such as fear or anger, can produce temporary changes in the brain, which cause cravings for food that contain high calories and few nutrients (even when you're not hungry). When you're super busy, you may not have the inclination or energy to cook. You may subsist on fast food or junk food because it's easier and the high salt and sugar content satisfies cravings. It's also very addicting and a good way to pile on the weight. Letting yourself go physically can contribute to low self-esteem and make you feel bad about yourself at a time when you need all your mental and emotional resources.

Do your best to prepare food that's nourishing for yourself and your family. If you go out to eat, choose healthy restaurants or at least ones that will have healthy choices. If you don't want to cook, stock up on frozen meals (either store-bought ones or ones that someone else cooks for you) that you put in the oven or microwave. Keep on hand what I call "grabbables," healthy foods that are ready to eat, so when you go to the refrigerator looking for the solution to the blank page of your work in progress, your hand emerges with something healthy in it.

When you're at work or on the go, take healthy snacks with you to munch on throughout the day. This will help prevent blood sugar drops and keep your energy even.

I always have a cooler with me that contains grabbables such as: cut-up apple slices, nuts, yogurt (especially plain Greek yogurt, which has twice the amount of protein), baby carrots, cut-up red and green peppers, small containers of hummus, olives, containers of blueberries or raspberries, slices of chicken or turkey, hard-boiled eggs, string cheese, cottage cheese, protein shakes, and protein bars.

Of course, you first have to take the time to grocery shop and prepare the food. But if you look at my list, the prep work is minimal.

In addition to healthy snacking:

- Consume plenty of fresh vegetables, fruits and fish.
- Eat breakfast. Make sure your meal is low in sugars and high in protein.
- Drink plenty of water. Dealing with difficult situations depletes the body of water, leading to drowsiness, listlessness and more stress.
- Limit consumption of alcohol, caffeine, tobacco and sugar. These

cause the body's stress response to become heightened.

• Take your vitamins, minerals and other healthy supplements. Stress causes the body to burn more vitamins and minerals, specifically vitamin B complex, magnesium and zinc, which are needed for blood sugar balance. When their levels drop, stress levels increase. Also, the adrenal glands require more vitamin C and pantothenic acid (part of the vitamin B complex) during stressful times. Vitamin D3 helps keep your immune system strong. Fish oil (in capsules or liquid) is good for your brain.

EXERCISE

Working out is one of the best things you can do for your physical and mental health. Yet exercise is one of the hardest tasks to make a regular part of your day because it is physical work and often hard to do. Exercise can be one of the self-care habits that you drop when you're too busy attending to all the tasks of self-publishing and life. Yet (among other benefits) exercise:

• Increases your energy level.

• Slows down the aging process

• Reduces the release of stress hormones.

• Increases mood-boosting endorphins in the brain, which reduces the sensation of pain and increases your sense of well-being. Exercise also helps fight anxiety and depression.

• Helps keep your weight down and build strong bones.

• Helps keep you mobile and flexible, and increases your strength and stamina.

• Lowers your blood pressure.

• Gives you an adrenaline rush, which can make you feel happier and more energized.

• Improves your brain power, boosting IQ and improving cognitive function and helping you stay more positive, focused and alert.

• Focuses your mind on your body, enabling you to let go of the story in your head, as well as anything else that might be on your mind.

• Improves your immunity against common colds, the flu and other illnesses.

• Reduces your risk of cancer.

- Encourages a better night's sleep, helping you fall asleep faster and sleep more deeply, and often cures insomnia.

Effective workouts don't have to take a lot of time. You can do aerobic interval training, which burns more calories in less time — usually about 15 to 20 minutes. In interval training, you alternate bursts of intense activity with slower-paced movement. For example, when doing intervals, you push yourself for 30 seconds and go slower for 90 seconds. Then repeat until you reach your 15 or 20 minutes. Cool down for two minutes and stretch. If you're a beginning exerciser, you might have to go longer than 90 seconds at first. But you can work up to a shorter "rest" time.

You may also feel you can't muster up the energy to make yourself work out. When you do start exercising, you are going to be tired for the first couple of weeks. But DON'T GIVE UP! Your body will adjust, and after a workout, you'll soon have energy and feel good about yourself.

If you haven't exercised before or can't bring yourself to do much, it's good to take walks. Aside from receiving the benefits of exercising, walking gives you time to yourself. You might use the time to think of your work in progress and figure out what will happen in the next scene you intend to write. Or you might use the time as a way to get away from your story and clear your head.

Studies show that we enjoy almost every activity more (even those we dislike) when we're with people we like. If you're having trouble motivating yourself to exercise, include a friend or relative to keep you (or both of you) on track.

MOVE YOUR BODY

If you aren't willing to exercise, at least move your body. Research conducted on astronauts shows that your body declines rapidly when sitting for long periods. Turns out, our bodies aren't designed for sitting (or standing) for prolonged stretches of time. Sitting for hours is an *independent risk factor* for poor health and premature death.

You don't have to interrupt the flow of your writing. Keep thinking about your story, stand, stretch, and sit down and continue typing. Twenty minutes to a half hour later, do it again, or stand and do a couple of squats or knee raises and sit. *Repeat* throughout your day. This activity is *not* about exercising. It's about changing your body's posture. I've found that even during the most intense writing, I can stand and sit right back down with barely a pause of my fingers.

GET PLENTY OF REST

Research shows the importance of sleep for staying healthy and maintaining a normal weight. Sleep-deprived people have higher stress levels. Sleep deprivation affects blood sugar levels, increases cortisol (the stress hormone) and reduces the production of leptin (a hormone that signals that you are full).

It's hard to juggle family time, writing and other self-publishing duties, exercise, eating well, all the various errands and activities on your to-do lists, and trying to get enough sleep. Sleeping also may be difficult when you're busy and stressed.

Create a routine for getting enough sleep. If possible, try to follow your body's natural inclination to be a morning or evening person. A regular sleep schedule dramatically reduces stress.

Try a cup of warm milk before bedtime. Milk contains the enzyme tryptophan, a natural sedative. Also, the body absorbs calcium better at night. A warm bath might also be helpful.

Turn off the part of your thinking mind that's worrying or planning for tomorrow. Use that writer's imagination of yours to visualize taking a walk in a beautiful scene from nature. Play in a fantasy world, but make sure it's not one from a future book. (Then it's work.) Keep a notepad by your bedside to jot down anything that pops into your mind that you need to remember and that might keep you awake.

Take naps. A nap will help you shut down your mind for a while. Then when you wake (fully) up, you're refreshed and clearheaded. You can take long naps, or if you don't have time, set an alarm for ten minutes. Even with a short nap, once you're fully awake you'll have a pop of energy.

DEVELOP COMFORTING RITUALS

Research shows that those who have a strong faith or spiritual practice and pray often also score high in happiness and purpose in life. Taking time to meditate, pray, worship and study about your beliefs helps you de-stress.

The word "ritual" has a spiritual connotation and is often used as a way to connect you with God. However, a ritual can also connect you with yourself, and may or may not be spiritual. The familiarity of doing the ritual on a frequent basis, perhaps every day, can calm you, especially when so much of your life may be filled with work and stress. Performing the ritual may soothe your mind and emotions.

Anything that's repetitive or calming can help. I've already discussed walking, journaling, yoga and meditating. However, other activities can soothe you. Some possibilities are:

- Reading a self-help, inspirational or motivational book for a few minutes in the morning or evening (or both).
- Quilting, knitting, sewing or crocheting.
- Fishing.
- Working on a puzzle or playing solitaire.
- Baking or cooking.
- Woodworking.
- Gardening.
- Singing.

SHORT-TERM INDULGENCES

There's nothing wrong with *occasionally* using some of your favorite short-term indulgences if you need a break from stress or as a way to comfort yourself.

When I'm overwhelmed or upset, or need some comforting, I allow myself *one* temporary fix — Mexican food and my favorite Lindt dark chocolate for dessert, which I eat while reading a novel. Then I take a nap. Giving myself a little emotional distance frees me to process my feelings or deal with what's stressing me *after* I'm more centered. However, I'm careful to indulge *knowingly*, instead of unconsciously acting out. I stay in control, I limit my indulgence to one, and I'm careful to do this only on the rare times when I really need to.

The problem comes when you indulge in activities you can't afford, such as shopping, using mind-altering substances such as drugs or alcohol as a way to *cope*, or going on a spree, whether it's shopping or eating or anything else that takes over your self-discipline. I'm not saying you can't enjoy shopping or drinking or eating (TIV authors happen to love all three), just make sure you control your indulgences rather than let them control you.

ENJOY THE JOURNEY

For artistic people, exercising their creativity is a fundamental way of life and gives them a sense of purpose and accomplishment. Therefore enjoy your writing journey.

When you're stressed about being an author and all you have to do, take a few moments to remember the positive effects of the writing life. Remember your beginnings and think about how you've grown. List what you've accomplished. Appreciate the good friends you've made. Keep a journal/scrapbook to remember the good times.

No matter how stressful, if you're a writer, you're living a dream — your dream. You might not have the success you want yet, but allow yourself to savor the journey. Never become so stressed or complacent that you forget to appreciate your blessings.

A WILD RIDE

(WHEN YOU HIT IT BIG)

JASINDA WILDER

Let's set aside tactics and techniques, craft and contracts, price points and social media for a few moments. There's one important thing to keep in mind as you embark on this crazy journey of being an indie author: This is your life.

It's so easy to get caught up in the wild frenzy of activity, the pricing game and the gritty trenches of the indie publishing revolution. The whole process becomes a whirlwind and you can easily get swept away by it all.

Don't let that happen.

The more dangerous riptide happens if/when you start becoming really successful. Don't get me wrong, when you find yourself selling books and being able to not just pay off an energy bill or a car note, but see that decimal place in your bank account shift to the right by several digits, it's thrilling. It's beyond thrilling, really. It's life-changing. Getting to the place where you can pay off university loans and entire mortgages is, honestly, mind-blowing. And here's the thing: That's possible. You *can* get there.

This book is dedicated to helping you find that kind of success. The caveat, however, is that not everyone will. There is no magical formula. There is no one thing I or anyone else can tell you or sell you that will make you instantly successful. So, as an aside, if someone is selling you a magic formula for success (in writing or anything else in life) then don't buy; they're scamming you.

DON'T FORGET TO HAVE A LIFE

Back to my first point: When that kind of success zips into your life and starts taking over, time becomes a scarce commodity. Suddenly, it's 1 in the morning and you haven't left your desk since dinner. Your butt is numb, your hand is cramping from typing, your neck is stiff and your eyes are sore from screen glare. Your kids, your husband/wife/significant other, your bunnies and those pet pygmy elephants … they're all wondering if you're ever coming out of your cave. You haven't seen an episode of your favorite TV show in weeks. You might possibly have carpal tunnel.

My advice? Put it all aside, every once in a while.

The latest report from Amazon.com can wait until tomorrow. Those 256 fan emails can wait. Twitter can wait. Facebook notifications can wait. Now, yes, that stuff will pile up. I know that. *Believe me*, I know that. But at some point, you have to step away from the computer and live a little. I don't mean put it off all the time. I just mean, before you get to the point of overwhelmed burnout, take some *me*-time.

Because in the end, all that is just a series of numbers coded to mean something. It's not you, it doesn't define who you are. The two most important things in publishing: No. 1, *finish the book*; No. 2, *live your life*. You can't spend your existence in the writer's cave. It's not healthy.

STAY TRUE TO YOURSELF

Secondly, don't let the industry change you. If you're an active person, running and swimming and snowboarding and doing Bikram yoga and chasing chickens in your backyard, keep doing that. It makes you who you are. You don't have to give that up to make time to write. Lessen how much TV you watch if you're tight on time. Stay in on a Friday night and finish the chapter. Forgo your weekly mani-pedi and do your nails yourself. Give up your poker-night spot for a week or two. Write the book.

Most people have plenty of extra time in their lives, taken up by random things. That 15 minutes you just spent leafing through Better Homes and Gardens? That's a good couple of paragraphs you could've written. Not that there's anything wrong with magazines. If it's important to you, make time for it. See the above point. That's my main thrust, here: If something is important to you, you'll make time for it. Prioritize. If you really, *truly* want to be an author, then you'll make time for it — along with everything else that's important to you. Which had better include your family. Again, see above. Writing takes long hours alone in front of a computer, so make sure you set aside time to play with your kids or go to dinner with your love interest, or whatever your situation is.

DON'T BUY AN ISLAND

Third: money management. If you become successful, meaning money starts pouring in, don't go crazy. Bank it. Pay off your debts. Invest it. Hire an accountant and a financial manager and make sure you don't ignore the change in your tax bracket, 'cause that'll sneak up on you like quick. If you suddenly sell half a million books and everything is going haywire in your life, take time out to be you. Close the laptop, silence the phone, leave the emails, and do some yoga, or tinker with your car, or throw the ball for the pup. Scratch your kitty. No, not like *that* — or do, if that's what you like. Ignore the fact that you've got more income pouring in than you literally know what to do with and just be you. But be smart and wise with that increased income.

Meaning, don't pull an MC Hammer.

When things started happening for me with "Falling Into You," my husband and I had a list of things we wanted/needed. It ranged from little things such as new laptops and a storm door for the front door, to big things like a bigger family car and new carpet and appliances. We prioritized our list in two ways: from smallest purchases to largest, and in order of importance. We replaced our dying laptops one month. We caught up on our energy bills the next (priorities, right?). We replaced our 10-year-old kitchen appliances the month after. We updated our sad wardrobes a bit. I bought a Coach purse I'd been wanting for two years.

What didn't we do? We didn't rush out and buy a Maserati. We didn't move into a 10,000-square-foot mansion. We didn't start eating caviar and sushi for every meal. We didn't alter the basic fabric of our lives. We have kids, and the one thing kids need more than anything else in life is stability and consistency. It doesn't matter to your kids if you're rich or poor, not at the heart of things. Even if all you have is a two-bedroom shack in the ghetto, if you love them and provide a safe home for them where they're loved and sheltered, they'll be happy. They may not have the best toys and newest game systems, but they'll make do with what they have.

For a long time, we had very little. The rags-to-riches nature of my story is coming to public light bit by bit, but what I'll tell you now is this: For several years, I worked 80-plus hours a week, six and sometimes seven days a week to provide for my family while my husband finished his degree. We often had to rotate which bill we were going to pay each month since we couldn't afford all the bills every month. We almost lost our home the month before "Big Girls" really started to earn enough money to pay bills. Literally, we were on the verge of being homeless. That month, I published "Big Girls Do It Better," which sold 600 copies the first day and earned enough that month to *just barely* pay rent. Like, the house note was $1,265, and we earned $1,280. Our kids played outside. They had a Wii we'd bought for Christmas two years before, and that was it. A splurge to spoil them was buying a Lego set for the boys, or a Barbie doll for my daughter.

My point is, I know what I'm talking about. Kids are resilient. Love them, make sure they're fed, clothed, bathed and sheltered. Be there for them. Keep things consistent, and they'll be fine. They'll never know, or ever need to know, how much you struggle to keep it that way.

So then, when our books really started to sell, building up from earning a thousand dollars per month to tens of thousands, we didn't change our lifestyle. We still live in the same house. We don't buy our kids whatever they want whenever they want it. Our lives are pretty much the same, to be honest; my husband and I are just less stressed about bills. We pay the bills as soon as they come in. We pay double on our cars and are rebuilding our trashed credit. We're starting to ramp up the payoff on our mortgage so we can get that out of the way. We're looking into trusts for our kids and life insurance and retirement funds and investments. The only material thing we've really changed is we take vacations. We take a weekend trip somewhere (when we're not at signings, that is) and buy our kids souvenirs, where before we wouldn't have been able to go at all, much less buy any knickknacks for our kids.

This is what we did. Do what's right for you, just be smart, responsible and wise about it.

If you start publishing and you find success, enjoy it. But be smart about how you enjoy it. Pay off your debts, pay off your car. Pay off the house. If you move, don't be ridiculous. Just because the bank approves you for a $5.5 million mansion on a hill with a five-car garage doesn't mean you need to buy it and fill the garage with luxury vehicles. The feeling of just having money in the bank, having your income outweigh your debts, is priceless. Really and truly, that's worth more than any luxury car or mansion or Rolex. If you've been where we've been, poor and desperate, then simply not having to worry is absolutely incredible.

THINK BEFORE YOU LEAP

It's been a wild ride for us. "Falling Into You" took off so suddenly, catapulting us into a whole new stratosphere of success, that we're just trying to hold on right now. Even as I write this article, I think about the last year and I can't believe how things have changed. Just last summer I was digging in couch cushions and the pockets of my winter coats for change to buy a $5 pizza so my family could eat. This summer we can pick up and take a trip to Chicago at the last second and not have to worry about affording it. It's dizzying.

The temptation to go crazy is overwhelming. You watch your monthly financial reports from Amazon make wild jumps in decimal places, and then you get that first six-figure deposit and you want to go out and do something outrageous.

You want to. You can. So why not?

To resist this temptation, my husband and I made a decision: Since so much is already changing this year, we aren't going to make any major life-altering decisions this year. We aren't going to buy a bigger house. We have nice, new cars that fit us all (and no more room in the garage or driveway), so we aren't going to buy any new cars. No major purchases, no major moves or changes. We made this decision for our kids primarily, but also for ourselves.

Again, this is what works for us; that doesn't have to be your decision.

We're adjusting to the drastic shift in income, to the burgeoning media attention, to the demand from the fans and the expectations for each book. When a book sees such huge success, the pressure to follow up with something not just as good, but better, is huge. That by itself is enough to overwhelm you. You have to manage the pressure. You have to keep the insanity contained. Trying to deal with the pressure of success is a full-time job. I don't mean that to sound like a complaint; it's not. I love my life. I wouldn't change a thing. But it's a fact. Ask anyone who's found sudden and drastic success: It's a massive series of huge changes that can be overwhelming.

THE MOST IMPORTANT THING IS STILL THE STORY

Another aspect of the wild ride to success is, with success comes more extraneous work. Suddenly, I'm not just sitting in my office writing or answering a few hundred emails a day, I'm doing interviews, talking with my agent almost weekly and signing foreign rights contracts, and I'm answering *thousands* of emails a day. I finally hired my sister to help with some of the emails that don't need my direct, personal attention. I still answer every fan email myself, respond to every Tweet and Facebook post myself. I will never assign that to a virtual assistant, because I feel that the connection between my readers and me is a vital element of my success. They know me, they feel connected to me. There's a sense of ownership and community, I think, and that's due directly to social media, and that's not something I can shop out.

But all that is time away from writing. You still have to balance all that *plus* find time to write. Because, in the end, you still have to put out new material. If you're not publishing new books, then the social media and interviews won't mean anything, because attention will shift to someone else who *is* producing.

The point I'm trying to hammer home here is that you have to continue, no matter how wild things get, to write, edit, polish, publish and repeat. Create new characters, new stories. Find fresh perspectives and bold new plots. I *love* writing. I love creating. I'm one of the fortunate few who get paid to do the one thing I love more than anything else in life. But I make sure I carve out lots of regular time to actually write.

You have to be prolific. Personally, I feel one of the key components to success as an indie author is prolificacy. You have to write, write, write, and then publish, publish, publish. If one book doesn't sell super hot, then do something different and try again. And again, and again. Even if one title is only selling $500 a month, if you have six titles all selling at that pace, then you're earning $3,000 a month. That's a damn good income, especially if you're still doing this as a supplement alongside your day job. And if you're doing it right, you can write and publish six full-length titles in a year, which still gives you two full months.

I hear some of you fainting out there. "Two months to write, edit, revise and proofread an entire book? Are you crazy?" Well, yes, I am, but that's irrelevant. The industry is changing. For one thing, full-length for a novel is now more like 60,000 to 80,000 words, whereas it used to be that a novel was 100,000 words. That was a pretty hard line that you couldn't go over or under. That difference, that 20,000-40,000 words, makes it possible to do in a month or two.

Here's the thing, though. I think part of what else is changing in the publishing world — now that indies are taking over the world and e-books are burgeoning into the lion's share of the reading market — is that the sense of polished perfection is fading. For a long time, books were smooth, slick, polished, perfect things. Factory-made, store-bought. All the edges were sanded off. Imperfections were boiled away. Anything unneeded was cut out.

Now, indies like you and me are doing things our own way. I write the book I want to write, the book I'd want to read, and I don't answer to anyone but the readers. This scene here may not be strictly necessary to the plot, and a fancy-schmancy New York editor may tell me to cut it, but damn it I *like* this scene, so by God I'm going to leave it in. And you know what? I can. My books may not fit into a neat pigeonholed category in the way New York likes to do things, and that's intentional. I don't want to be pigeonholed.

There's a sense of roughness to indie storytelling. It's not as polished, and I think that's a good thing. I think that's making storytelling a more honest art. You have to tell a good story, above and beyond anything else. As indies, we don't have a team of editors finagling around and massaging false life into a weak story. We only have ourselves. Good storytelling will sell, bad storytelling won't. The market is its own gatekeeper of talent. We don't need New York telling us what to read or who's the next hot ticket; the market tells us that. The Amazon top 100 tells us that.

It's part of how my own success happened. I was already selling thousands of books before "Falling Into You" hit big. I had 24 titles out before I published "FIY." Some of those were short stories, novellas or novelettes, but they were published titles earning dollars, gaining me a readership base, and finding a market. "FIY" capitalized on that, and went further than I could ever have imagined, but the basis was there. I was publishing at a frantic pace, and I've only slowed down a tiny bit.

That's not to say you have to write at the pace I have been. Do what works for you, at the pace that works for you. Push yourself, but not into burnout. Work hard, but save time for your family. Have I said that enough times yet?

I work hard, and I take time for my family. I enjoy the benefits of success, but I keep things consistent. I have to keep my head on my shoulders and think about my decisions before I make them. I consider the impact on my children of everything I do, and if it will negatively affect them, I don't do it, or I find a way to mitigate it so it's acceptable. I keep things consistent. Above all, I write stories I want to read, and I take time out for my life.

It's a wild ride, but it's one I wouldn't give up for anything.

GETTING PAID TO DO IT

(LET'S TALK MONEY)

THERESA RAGAN

When I first started writing, I had no idea what publishers were paying and therefore no idea of my potential earnings. The only thing I knew with certainty was not to give up my day job and that I would be lucky to get a $5,000 advance on a book that took me five years to write. The only site that I knew of to find out what publishers were paying was Brenda Hiatt's Show Me the Money.

Brenda is now collecting data for Indie Earnings, but she needs as many authors as possible — whether you are traditionally published and self-publishing or solely an indie author, she needs data!

Personally, I like knowing what's possible. For the past two decades, like many writers, I didn't make one dime, but I kept on writing because it's what I love to do. But I also realize this is a business and as a business, I do need to earn money if I want to be able to stay home and write full time.

Stephen King is estimated to be worth $400 million.
Stephenie Meyer is said to be worth $125 million.
J.K. Rowling is said to be worth $1 billion.

We all know that King, Rowling, Meyers and, of course, E.L. James are rolling in the dough. But what about everyone else? I believe we are going to see more and more indie authors hitting the million-dollar mark. Many already have. It used to be that once or twice a month I would read about another author making a sale to a traditional publisher. Now I'm reading about authors quitting their day jobs. How cool is that? Of course, it's all relative — if you have zero kids and a husband with a full-time job, you're probably going to be able to quit before the single writer with kids to feed.

Some indie authors, whether they are both self-published and traditionally published, or not, are making $20,000 a month and some are making $500 a month. And some have yet to make a total sum of $500. Not everyone who self-publishes is going to make a ton of money.

I read an article the other day where the blogger stated that too many indie authors are telling other writers that there's money to be made so hurry up and release everything you have and see what sticks. I like to think that writers are smarter than that. Of course, there are always going to be people who are going to try to take shortcuts just for the sake of earning a quick buck. But why waste time worrying about those people? This is not a competition. It's also not a good idea to compare yourself with other authors. Better books than mine will earn less money and vice versa. That's never going to change. There are too many variables for it to be any other way (genre, story, pricing, timing, cover, blurb, luck).

Let the possibilities of big money motivate you to finish your book, but don't let these same possibilities put unnecessary pressures on you, and certainly don't let *expectations* ruin all the fun if you don't earn $20,000 a month.

I believe more and more writers are talking about money now because they *can* (no confidentiality clauses when you're an indie author), and because it's pretty exciting that authors don't have to give 80 percent or more of their money to publishers. We get to keep the money our stories earn. How cool is that?

I know writers who happily took a $1,000 advance and 6 to 8 percent royalties. Less than two short years ago, I would have taken a deal like that, too. And no, I'm *not* bashing traditional publishers. I would have taken that deal and I would have been happy because there weren't too many choices back then. If taking that deal was the only way to get my foot in the door, I would have signed on the dotted line.

I recently signed a contract with Thomas & Mercer. I might never know if it was financially the best move for me, but no matter what, I have zero regrets. I'm having a blast. I will have maximum exposure on the Amazon site and I love working with my editor and I have a whole team of people available to help me at T&M.

I don't know about you, but now when I'm writing, I love knowing that all of my hard work might actually pay off in the end. It's just *one* more way to motivate myself to sit in my chair and write. And I don't think it's a bad thing to be motivated by money. If an author is making money, that means people are buying her book, and if her book keeps selling, it probably means that her book is being recommended by readers. Word of mouth is powerful advertising. Nothing is more important than readers.

And for those of you who are curious like me and like to see real numbers, here are a few real numbers from the Indie Voice authors:

THERESA RAGAN

"Having My Baby," an 80,000-word contemporary romance, earned over $60,000 in four months.

$523.76 is how much Theresa earned after her first month as a self-published author. (March 2011)

$124,523.91 is what she earned in her best month. (January 2013)

Theresa made her first million within two years of self-publishing. (February 2013)

JASINDA WILDER

Jasinda Wilder started publishing in April 2012 because of financial crises. She started publishing in several genres under several pen names, and by June 2012 she had earned enough to pay her $1,200-per-month mortgage payment. By April 2013, Jasinda earned over $550,000 dollars from just one year of self-publishing. To date she has sold more than a million e-books, and her translation rights have been sold in 15 countries, including Brazil, France, Germany, Hungary, Italy and Serbia.

TINA FOLSOM

In her first month of self-publishing, Tina earned $20. Six months later, she made $32,000 in one month. In three years of self-publishing, Tina has earned over $2 million.

COLLEEN GLEASON

After seven years in which she wrote 19 novels for traditional New York publishers, Colleen is just beginning to focus on the indie side of her career. In the last two years, she's published six books that had been rejected by New York publishers for years because they were too different, and the publishers didn't know how to market them. (Literally.) Unfortunately, the six books are in completely different genres and pretty much unrelated to one another, thus Colleen is still working on developing a branding strategy. (Read her chapter on "Pimping Yourself Out" — she knows what to do, just has to do it now that she has the time!)

Still, these are six books that would be languishing in a computer file somewhere if she hadn't made them available, and they've made her more than six figures in the last 18 months. In addition, she's begun to translate some of her traditionally published *and* indie-published books into other languages. In the last year, she's seen a growing revenue stream from her books in Germany in particular. Soon, the sales from Germany will equal or surpass her domestic sales simply because she has more titles available there.

DENISE GROVER SWANK

Denise had never published before she released her first book in July 2011. She made $102 that first month. Her best month she made $72,000 from January 2013 sales. Denise has made approximately $500,000 in two years.

JANA DELEON

When Jana DeLeon's New York publisher went thumping down the drain in 2010, she knew that as soon as she got rights to her backlist, she'd self-publish them. She hoped to make some purse money, and by that, she quite literally meant money for purses, as she has a slight Coach Factory online addiction. Until the end of 2012, Jana still worked full-time and was under contract with Harlequin Intrigue, so the backlist books were all she had to work with until a new indie release in mid-2012.

She released the five backlist books in late 2010 and made $427 that first month. Whoohoo! A purse.

Despite a lack of marketing and the author's slight aversion to social media, those backlist books made her a little over $100,000 in 2011, and she realized that this was so much bigger than purses.

In 2012, Jana began making an effort with social media and played with pricing, sales and other marketing devices. The additional hours and complete lack of personal life paid off and Jana made $290,000.

At the end of 2012, Jana quit her day job to write fiction full-time — living the dream! She's released two novels and one novella in a little over five months and hit the USA Today and New York Times best-seller lists. She hopes to close in on the million-dollar mark by year-end.

LILIANA HART

Liliana Hart had never been traditionally published when she started self-publishing back in June 2011. She picked a pen name and told her husband — no one else — because self-publishing still had such a bad stigma attached to it. So she literally started from zero. Zero fan base and zero money.

In her first month of self-publishing, Liliana sold 444 books and made $827.11. Exactly one year later she was making $60,000 a month. A year after that she was making $120,000 a month. She's now sold a million e-books and has made almost $2 million in two years of self-publishing.

Liliana Hart earnings

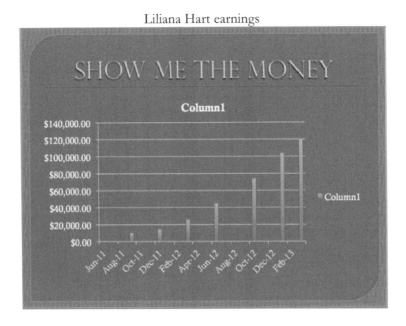

DORIEN KELLY

Dorien is new to the indie world after traditionally publishing for over a decade. In her first full month of self-publishing backlist (September 2012), Dorien made $93.24 on three books, with one offered for free. Three months later she was making over $5,000 a month on books that hadn't made her a penny in several years. Now that she's getting ready to publish new works, she figures things will really get interesting!

JANE GRAVES

After traditionally publishing for 13 years, Jane began self-publishing in October 2012. Still under contractual obligations with her publisher, she was able to self-publish only one book — a romantic comedy from 2001 she got the rights back to. In its first month as an indie book, it earned $827.65. Over the next eight months, it averaged over $1,700 per month, selling enough copies one month to land on the USA Today best-seller list.

Compared with her Indie Voice colleagues, you may think Jane's earnings don't seem like much. But that single backlist book from over a decade ago is on track to net her $20,000 in one year. She has more indie books coming and is looking forward to compounding that $20,000 several times over.

DEBRA HOLLAND

Debra was an unknown, unpublished author when she first self-published. Her first month was only two days long because she launched "Wild Montana Sky" on April 28, 2011, and "Starry Montana Sky" the next day. She sold 16 books and made $13.06. In her first full month, she sold 570 books and made $377.12. The second full month was $2,132.80. In July and August, she self-published "Sower of Dreams" and "Reaper of Dreams," and in December, she launched "Lywin's Quest." In the first year (mostly from the three Montana Sky series books) Debra had almost 97,000 downloads and made about $88,000 in royalties.

HOW WE DO (DID) IT

BAD BOYS AND HORRIBLE WARNINGS

DORIEN KELLY'S STORY

British mystery writer Catherine Aird wrote, "If you can't be a good example, you'll just have to be a horrible warning." As I look at my writing and marital choices, there's a strong case to be made that I am your horrible warning.

Once upon a time, I was a lawyer. I had three children under the age of 8, I was working endlessly and I was missing most of my children's life events. I knew I needed a change, but I wasn't sure what I wanted to do. Then inspiration was delivered to me by a staff paralegal named Anna, who insisted on not doing her work and reading at her desk instead. One night, after a heart-to-heart with Anna about her future, I came home with her reading material: a worn copy of Jude Deveraux's "A Knight in Shining Armor." Three months later, neither Anna nor I were working in the same place. Anna had quit before she could be fired, and I had decided to go home to write.

I gave myself a deadline of three years to sell my first book. After all, I had become a lawyer in three years. Becoming a published author couldn't take more time than that, right?

In my case, dead wrong.

Like any good recovering attorney, I did my research and found out about Romance Writers of America. I joined my local chapter and learned from anyone and everyone who would take the time to listen to my newbie questions. A year later, I was on to my second complete manuscript. (Let's not talk about that ugly first one.)

No. 2 was a lot like me: flip and sassy and not at all sure what it wanted to be when it grew up. But that manuscript won the Romance Writers of America's Golden Heart Award for Single Title Romance in 1998. The title of that manuscript was "Millennium Man." And I was sure it had the hottest marketing hook, *ever*. It was an action-adventure story with love and dead bodies and a kidnapping or two, set on the supersonic Concorde, with a group of lucky contest winners being zipped around the world to ring in the new millennium, over and over. With a hook like that, I saw nothing but sunshine ahead.

I was so naive. The traditional publishing industry is slow now, but it was glacially slow back in 1998. I was ultimately told by an interested publisher that even if I could successfully make the revisions they wanted, the book wouldn't fit into their publishing schedule until the year 2000, which wouldn't work at all. The book that needed to party like it was 1999 was dead on arrival.

Horrible Warning No. 1: It is not wise for an author to make a book's marketing hook center on something that happens only once every thousand years. If you miss it the first time around, odds are pretty good you're not going to be there for the second.

At that point, my self-imposed three-year "success" deadline had passed. While I had another full manuscript sitting at Harlequin, it had been ages since I'd heard anything about it, and I was sure that that it was going to be rejected. My husband had been encouraging me to end this craziness. To him it seemed that the writing was making me unhappier than practicing law. And he was sure that my sizable stack of agent and publisher rejections meant I was doing something very wrong.

He thought that instead of writing, which by then he considered to be my hobby (that word made me wince), I should take up golf. I am the least athletic person you'll ever meet. And I hate golf. But I told him I was done. I had given writing my best shot and I would learn to golf. However, I was saved from that horrible fate. Only a few days later, a lovely woman from Harlequin called me, and I never bought a set of golf clubs. I also learned to stop torturing myself.

And that's **Horrible Warning No. 2: Being a writer is tough. This industry is brutal. Don't punish yourself more by creating self-imposed, nonsensical deadlines for "success." And don't necessarily listen to your husband, either. Unless he's like the other TIV spouses. They, to a man, are amazing.**

After that first sale, things moved quickly. I had worked hard at my craft, and it paid off. In addition to writing short contemporary romance for Harlequin, I landed the agent of my dreams and sold three Irish-set single-title romances at auction to another publishing house. I was sure the years of struggle had passed.

As it turned out, they were just beginning.

After my first Ballymuir novel had been published, had respectable sales, and had placed as a finalist in RWA's Rita contest (it's like the Academy

Awards but without the big budget), my editor called me. She said, "I've been reading your romantic comedies for Harlequin and I think the second book in your series for us should be more like them."

I got off that call and cried. My rom-coms were short and snappy. The novels this publisher had contracted to buy were dark and emotional, with flawed characters. These books were about redemption and forgiveness. They were the books of my heart.

My agent told me to buy back the last two books. She said that it made no sense to do what was being asked of me. After a sleepless night, I decided to gut it out, to do what the editor wanted and move on. This was business, after all. But every word I wrote on those next two books felt like a betrayal of my abilities and of my commitment to the characters in those stories.

Therein is **Horrible Warning No. 3: Trust your instincts. Once you have learned your craft, if it feels wrong, don't do it. No one cares more about your words and your stories than you do.**

Not long after I completed the final Ballymuir book, I returned home from a business trip to find a typed, unsigned note from my husband on our bed. He had left me. He'd packed and walked out of the house without saying anything to our children, who were home with him. I'll give you three phrases and let you put together your own vision of what floated my ex's boat: *Internet hookers, amateur porn actress* and *yaks*. But there was a consolation prize: I knew that one day — after my children were grown — I was going to get a hell of a book out of all of this.

And while I can laugh about it now, I don't want you to think that I wasn't terrified and devastated, because I was. I had two teenagers, a 12-year-old and no steady income. I was making money from writing, but not enough. And while I had once been a busy attorney, a few years earlier in a moment of sheer lunacy, I had turned in my license so that I'd never be tempted to practice law again.

Horrible Warning No. 4: Don't quit your day job until you have a major wad of cash all of your own sitting in the bank.

Two days after the ex had made himself perma-scarce, I marched myself to a psychiatrist, who wrote me a prescription for Xanax. And for nearly a month, other than going to see my shrink, all I did was sit on the sofa in a Xanax haze and cruise match.com. Yes, it was a little soon for dating, but being brutally dumped can do funny things to a girl.

After that month, I flushed the Xanax and allowed myself to be angry. In fact, I created a form of gardening therapy. While the kids were at school, I'd go out in the yard and use a rusty old butcher knife to slice open mulch bags as I refreshed the flower beds for spring. There might have even been a little stabbing going on. I called the game "Die, Bastard, Die." Lucky for me, I have no nearby neighbors who could see me, or I'm sure

THE NAKED TRUTH ABOUT SELF-PUBLISHING

there would have been a police intervention.

During this time, among other projects, I was writing a book for NEXT, which was Harlequin's ill-fated women's fiction line. The story was called "Marriage as a Second Language," and was about a middle-aged couple with communication problems. Every day, when I wasn't stabbing mulch bags, I would stare at the blinking cursor on my computer screen and feel like a complete failure at both life and writing. I finally called my editor and told her unless Harlequin was comfortable with my story involving butcher knives and blood, I couldn't write it. My editor was very understanding, and at that point, a little scared of me. But that was okay. I scared myself.

NEXT eventually folded, which didn't surprise me since I had also written for Duets, Temptation, Flipside and Signature Select. For a while there, I was pretty sure I was the kiss of death to series romance lines. But I came away with **Horrible Warning No. 5: Sometimes the smart thing to do is set aside a failing project. Harlequin clearly understood that concept, but I was a little slow on the uptake.**

Life wasn't done with me, though. In a matter of weeks, my father died and my beloved Harlequin editor was let go. Through it all, I kept writing, though anything resembling a career plan had gone through the shredder.

In the summer of 2009, Janet Evanovich spoke at the RWA conference in Washington, D.C. Toward the end of her talk, she mentioned that she was looking for a romance novel collaborator. I was feeling a little poorly that day. As it turns out, I was actually coming down with swine flu. But when Janet said she was looking for a co-author, the hair on my arms rose. I was sure that meant it was going to be me, and this feeling wasn't the result of the fever and chills that were setting in. I emailed my agent on my BlackBerry while Janet was still talking and told her to get the ball rolling. Later, when I was leaving the room, I listened to the chatter around me. I heard more than one person say they didn't have the nerve to send their work to Janet. And I sometimes wonder but for swine flu delirium, whether I would have, either.

But as it turned out, I had been right to be ballsy and put my work out there. Janet and I wrote two books together. It was an interesting process since the two of us are both quite set in our ways. Our collaboration wrapped up in the summer of 2012, and suddenly I realized that I had been in survival mode for so many years that I still had no actual career plan.

Horrible Warning No. 6: Write a business plan. Update it every six months. Do all the things I would tell my clients to do back when I was a lawyer, but never did for myself.

I felt as though I was back at Square 1 in my writing career.

During the 2012 RWA Conference, Jane Graves introduced me to Liliana Hart and her husband. The four of us sat at the hotel's outdoor bar and drank and talked for hours. I do mean *hours*. People came and went, we drank more and more, and I sat there in shock (the good kind) as Liliana told me what she had learned and how life-changing self-publishing had been for her and her family. I write to feed myself and my family. It's. A. Business. I took Liliana's generously given advice.

While I'd had the rights to my Ballymuir trilogy since mid-2011, on the advice of my former collaborator, I hadn't yet self-published it. In the space of four weeks, I revised that trilogy, got it formatted, had covers made, and put those babies up for sale by the end of August 2012. My bank account is very happy with me, as is the university where my youngest is now attending college. I can actually afford to pay it!

Since I'd also listened to my instincts a little bit back in 2011, I have a day job. It helps pay the bills even if it means I can't yet devote all of my hours to writing. And I'm not quite ready to let go of that "don't quit your day job" advice. Still, I have resurrected "Marriage as a Second Language" and am letting my heroine have her divorce and her freedom. "All Good Things" (I have retitled the book) will be out in July 2013 to launch a series of novels and novellas about divorce craziness called The Divorcee Chronicles. I'm also releasing a new Ballymuir novella as the first step in continuing that series. Readers enjoy it, and I love writing it. I'm even working with my beloved ex-Harlequin editor again, having hired her to edit my work.

I have come full circle — and in a very short time — all thanks to self-publishing and the kindness of Jane Graves and Liliana Hart. But I'm sure both Jane and Liliana would say that I'm here because I chose to listen and actually get to work.

I'm sure I'll make tons more mistakes and will have to update my list of Horrible Warnings very soon. But what I have learned and embraced is that as writers, we need to be brave, we need to be flexible, we need to be positive and we need to work like fiends. It's a tall order, but I'm game!

P.S. I now have the most incredibly kind, sexy and wonderful significant other, ever. I'll save those Bad Boys for my writing.

Visit Dorien at www.dorienkelly.com.

TRADING UP

JANE GRAVES' STORY

I grew up one of those kids with her nose in a book. By age 5, I wasn't only reading books, I was writing them. When I was in grade school, I used to ask my mother to drop me off at the local library and leave me there for hours so I could bask in my own little heaven. In high school, I took every English, literature and composition class I could. But I was a horse nut, too, and I wanted to become a veterinarian.

Then my high school counselor told me veterinary medicine was "a difficult field for a woman" (can you imagine?) and maybe I should think about another career. She suggested that because I'd shown some talent for writing, maybe I'd like to pursue that. My assertiveness didn't come until later in life, so I did as she said. I went to the University of Oklahoma School of Journalism in the sequence of professional writing, learning how to write popular fiction from professors who'd actually been working novelists.

Then life intervened. I got married. Had a baby. Then in the mid-1990s, I was really feeling the urge to write again. But doing it on my old Selectric typewriter? God, no. Back then we were so broke we couldn't pay attention, but my husband did the first of about a million things to support my writing career. He found a guy who had a used PC-XT he sold us out of his garage for $200. It had no hard drive, only floppy disks, and this was back when floppy disks were actually *floppy*. But all I cared about was that I could save words, and I was off to the races.

I wrote a romantic suspense novel that *almost* got published. That near miss encouraged me, but at the same time I realized my inclination was to write light, not dark. I wrote a short romantic comedy, and it became a finalist for the Romance Writers of America's Golden Heart Award for the best unpublished manuscripts of the year. An editor from Harlequin judged the final round. I didn't win the award, but I got something better. She bought the book. In the next few months, I sold four more. To date, I've written 10 books for Harlequin and 10 books for a couple of the big New York publishers.

I'm one of those authors who did everything "right." I've never had any trouble getting contracts. I've won a gob of writing awards. I've been a RITA award finalist so many times (without winning!) that Susan Lucci and I are soul sisters. But while I was getting decent advances and my books were selling relatively well, I wasn't feeling the surge in my career that I'd always imagined.

Then one day at an RWA chapter meeting, Liliana Hart mentioned to me that she was indie publishing. Then she mentioned how much money she was making indie publishing, and I about fell out of my chair. The more I heard about authors bypassing publishers and going straight to readers and making a lot of money doing it, the more I wanted a piece of that action.

I began slowly down the self-publishing path, because I was still under contract to my publisher, and I held the rights to only one of my backlist books, "I Got You, Babe." It's a romantic comedy that was originally published in 2001 that was making me less than $400 every royalty period. In 2012, I put a new cover on it and launched it on four platforms. One month that book sold enough copies to make the USA Today best-seller list, and it's on track to make over $20,000 its first year as an indie book.

Now, $20,000 a year is a laughable amount of money for my fellow Indie Voice authors. Most of them make way more than that in a single month. But it's been a real eye-opener for me, making me understand once and for all that the only thing standing between me and making a whole lot of money self-publishing is *more content*.

The next thing that profoundly changed things for me was joining with nine other authors to form The Indie Voice. Our group began with four of us coming together at a Novelists Inc. conference, and then we added six other members later. I consider myself fortunate to have been in the right place at the right time to be included in this group of authors when, in comparison, I'm just getting started. They're all so high-energy and so successful that for me, just sitting around talking with them about self-publishing is like trying to drink from a fire hose. I just lap up whatever I can and hope I don't drown.

I've recently gotten the rights back to another book — that first little romantic comedy I sold to Harlequin, "Stray Hearts" — and I'll be publishing that one, too. I still have a book in the works from my publisher, but I'm also writing a series of romantic comedy novellas I'll be self-publishing soon. Beyond that? More books. A *lot* more. When I take $20,000 times *a lot more*, I like the numbers I come up with.

Do I still make money traditionally publishing? Yes. Some people might even say it's a lot of money. But is it where I thought I'd be after 13 years in the business? Not even close. My husband and I talk all the time about what we want, where we're going, and how much fun we're going to have when we get there. But I gotta say that the journey itself is a blast, too. Self-publishing has reinvigorated my outlook on this business in ways I can't even describe, and I can't wait to see what tomorrow brings!

Visit Jane at her website, www.janegraves.com.

MY BIG BANG

JANA DELEON'S STORY

In the beginning, God created the heavens and the earth. And God said, "Let Jana write ..."

Okay, so maybe it didn't start exactly like that. And I probably don't need to take my story back to Genesis, but I'm going to do it anyway. Hell, it's not like anyone's forcing you to read it.

The real start:

In the beginning (i.e., before kindergarten), my mom got me a subscription to Dr. Seuss books, and I fell in love with reading. One night, my mom did what a lot of exhausted parents do when their child yells for "one more book" before bed, and she tried to skip some pages. I corrected her, and that's when she realized that I'd memorized every book and could darn well read them myself.

In elementary school, I started writing my own stories and continued into junior high. I stopped sometime in high school and didn't write during college. When I first finished college and started my accounting career, I tried to write, but I sucked. The Internet wasn't around so information wasn't readily available like it is now. Eventually, I put writing aside and concentrated on becoming a CFO.

I made CFO at 32 and thought, "What the hell do I do now?" I wasn't particularly impressed with the job, although the pay was good. The one thing I was certain of was that I did not want to be an accountant when I grew up. So I started researching other professions. About that time, a friend turned me on to Janet Evanovich and I loved the books. The characters were outlandish and quirky and they were mysteries — my favorite genre.

Shortly after I started reading Janet, my grandmother passed away, and I went home to Louisiana for the funeral. It had probably been a decade since I'd been with all my extended family and friends in one place, and it was eye-opening. I stood in the cemetery, watching everyone around me, and thought, "These people are not normal." And then an idea struck me — if Janet could do it in New Jersey, then I could do it in Louisiana.

So I went home and started writing.

My first book was really bad, as most first books are, but it proved a couple of things: I could tell a story, I was funny and I could finish a book. So I joined RWA and started learning all the things I didn't know. That was 11 years ago. I sold my fourth book three years later to Dorchester Publishing and it used it (and four other authors) to launch a new line.

Shortly after that sale, I jumped off the corporate ladder, giving up huge pay and even more stress and overtime to take a job as a technical writer. I sat in a cubicle all day, with minimal interruptions, and designed software training for financial software. It was the perfect balance of salary/insurance/work hours and allowed me to focus my energy on fiction.

I was starting my fourth book with Dorchester when I started seeing the signs of a business in trouble. Given my accounting experience, I knew what failure looked like. When I signed the contract for the last book in my series, I knew I'd never see another dime for it. I told my agent (the incredible Kristin Nelson) to watch for the first sign of breach of contract and get my rights back.

It was a bit of a fight, but she got my rights back in late 2010, and I put my self-publishing plan into action. In 2010, self-publishing wasn't the huge business it is now, but I figured anything I made off the books was more than I had. And I'd already accepted a contract with Harlequin Intrigue, so I wasn't "out of the game." When things took off with my backlist sales in 2011, I couldn't believe it. When they got even better in 2012, I started to think this might last. I might actually be able to quit my day job and write full time.

At the end of 2012, I did just that. With all my debt paid and two years of salary in the bank, my conservative side was finally ready to free my inner artist. I couldn't be happier.

Now, I spend all my time working for myself, and it's a *ton* of hours, but I don't mind. I no longer have to answer to narrow-minded New York opinions of what sells and what readers want. I don't have to wait so long to see my book published that I've forgotten most of it. And although I was fortunate with all my covers, I don't ever have to worry about being handed the Awful Cover of Death.

My background in accounting, finance and IT has been an incredible asset to running my own business, and I thank God every day that I have those skills in my back pocket. But what I love most about my life now is waking up every day and knowing that the one thing I get to care about the most is the story.

Visit Jana at her website, www.janadeleon.com.

THE LONG HARD ROAD TO SUCCESS

THERESA RAGAN'S STORY

In 1991, I was pregnant with my fourth and last child. On leave of absence from work and bored out of my mind, my sister handed me my first romance novel, "A Knight in Shining Armor" by Jude Deveraux. For a few hours I was taken to another world. The escapism and joy I felt while reading "AKISA" was something I had never experienced before. I was so connected with the characters, Douglass and Nicholas. I cried and I laughed and the moment I read the last page, I knew I wanted to be a writer.

I was raising four kids and I had a full-time job. It wasn't easy trying to find time to write, but I knew I was a "real" writer when nothing could stop me from getting words to the page. I wrote in the car, in bed, in any quiet room I could find. I had found my passion and I decided right from the beginning that I was not ever going to give up. I was going to prove to my children and to myself that hard work and perseverance really do pay off.

Having always been fascinated by knights and castles, I knew I wanted to write a story set in medieval times. Because I loved the idea of being thrown into another world, I decided to start with a medieval time travel. I made weekly trips to the library since there wasn't Google or Internet at the time (at least not in my house) and I began to research the medieval era. Years later, I knew I had only hit the tip of the iceberg when it came to 15th century England and I still hadn't written a book. It was time to stop researching and *write*. I had a lot of notes by then, character's names and many scattered scenes, which I began to put together like a puzzle. Sometime in 1997, when my fourth child was entering kindergarten, I finished that book. Assuming a query letter was really a cover letter, I sent off a letter to a few literary agents telling them about my wonderful story. I

even got a response from an agent asking to see the first three chapters.
I thought I had done it. I figured all that hard work had done the trick. I was jumping up and down and I even had my sisters crying for me. Less than two weeks later, I had my first rejection and I was bummed. *Very* bummed. Because, the truth of the matter is, when you get that high, it's a long way back to solid ground. Oh, well, like I said, I had read a lot of books, including "how to" books, and I knew rejection was part of the deal. I guess I was sort of hoping I could skip that part. No such luck.

I joined Romance Writers of America and my local RWA chapter in Sacramento in December 1997. I learned more in that next year than I had in the last five years put together. My advice to any new romance writer would be to join RWA and your local chapter as soon as possible. If you want to learn your craft, that's the place to start. I found a critique partner, met some invaluable writer friends and attended as many RWA National Conferences as I could manage.

I did *everything* I possibly could to learn my craft: I drove hours each week to critique with published authors I had met at my local RWA chapter. Many times I shared a room and a bed with writers I hardly knew, so I could afford to attend writer's conferences. I ran from workshop to workshop, soaking it all in. I also read countless romance novels and I wrote late at night and early in the morning to get the writing done. As I said before, nothing was going to stop me.

After writing for six or seven years, I signed with my first agent. Once again, I was at the top of the world, figuring it was only a matter of time. By 2008 I had signed with my second agent. I had also finaled in RWA's prestigious Golden Heart competition six times, but I still couldn't get an editor at a publishing house to take a chance on me.

In 2009 my husband suggested I self-publish, but I wasn't ready to give up the dream of being traditionally published. Self-publishing was considered off-limits if you wanted respect in the industry. Plus, I wanted to see my books on the shelves at Borders and Barnes & Noble.

Beyond frustrated, I said to hell with writing romantic comedy and decided to write my first thriller. I titled the book "Kidnapped" and ultimately "Abducted." I killed off any character that couldn't spit out intriguing dialogue or make the scene work. I also started to research real-life serial killers and quickly began having nightmares. I couldn't walk into my kitchen without looking at the knives in a whole new light. My husband began to sleep with one eye open. I am only half-kidding. I set the book aside for at least six months. When I came back to the story, I loved what I had written and I quickly finished writing "Abducted." Suddenly, writing thrillers became fun and therapeutic. I loved writing about strong heroines who had been to hell and back and yet still found a way to go on living and even find some joy in life.

In 2011, my youngest daughter, the one I was pregnant with at the beginning of my journey, was going off to college. The economy was the pits and I knew it was time for me to look for a real job that pays. While reading the want ads for a job outside of the home, I read a blog about other author friends of mine who were self-publishing and actually making money doing it. I knew I had to give it a try. I had absolutely nothing to lose at this point. I emailed my agent, making sure it was okay to publish my time-travel romances since I knew she wasn't interested in those stories. I was hoping to sell 10 books. Within months I had sold thousands of books. I couldn't believe it! Tired of waiting for agents and editors to read my newest book, "Abducted," I decided to take my career into my own hands. I parted ways with my agent and then proceeded to publish six books in nine months.

In less than two years as an indie author, I sold half a million e-books and made more money than I ever dreamed. If you put in the work and the time, if you believe in yourself and your books, if you work hard to learn your craft, I believe it can happen to you, too!

You can visit Theresa at www.theresaragan.com.

WRITING MAKES YOU PREGNANT

LILIANA HART'S STORY

Seriously. If you stay home and write all day you'll be knocked up before you can type "The End." I totally know this from experience. At least, that's *my* experience. But I do have a tendency to write very steamy sex scenes, so maybe that has something to do with it.

I should probably start my story before the knocking-up. I've always been one of those people considered a jack-of-all-trades, but like most people who are considered as such, I was a master of nothing. I was *good* at a lot of things. But not great. So when I got to college, I wandered aimlessly, looking for something that would make me love the thought of spending the next 60 years doing it. After six majors and five years of school, I still hadn't found that thing. So I ended up majoring in music because that's what I knew better than anything else. I minored in art history just for the hell of it because I figured I might as well be good at two unemployable things.

I loved to read. I mean, I skipped a whole week of school so I could finish Diana Gabaldon's "Outlander." I read all the time, two and sometimes three books a day. And I thought … I could do that. I could write a book. So at 18 I sat down at the computer and started writing my first novel. All I remember is that there was a blizzard and a stranger knocking on the door. By Page 4 they were both naked and steaming up the pages — maybe some things haven't changed so much.

By Page 20, I decided that writing was hard. It was too hard when I had so many other things to do, like decide what the hell I was going to do with my life. Seriously, you guys, I was a lighting major for a brief amount of time for God's sake. I also dabbled in interior design, art history, Italian, business and education ... it was ridiculous. So I went back to reading books all the time and occasionally I'd start another book and get enough words written for it to be too hard.

Then I got married and started teaching school, and real life came crashing down. Did I mention my husband and I both went to a private university? When we got married we had more than $100,000 in student loan debt. That's not a great way to start a marriage. Talk about numbers (check out Jasinda Wilder's chapter)! The numbers didn't compute. We went to a private university so we could both become teachers. In 2002, the monthly teacher take-home pay was $2,200 per month in the state of Texas. Take out rent, car payments, insurance, student loan payments and bills and we were left with about $12 to last the other 29 days of the month. Things like student loans and the ridiculous interest they charge isn't something any student thinks of while she's in school. It doesn't really hit you until you get that first bill.

I know that's a situation almost every other person can relate to. Living from month to month, racking up credit card debt and shuffling bills around to figure out how long you could wait to pay before there were fees applied or they'd turn the water or electricity off. We had a $300 overdraft coverage at our bank and we'd use it to squeeze by until the end of the month, trying to add the overdraft fees in our head to add to the next month's paycheck. We'd search for spare change, or if things got really bad, we'd ask our parents if they had anything extra.

I should mention I got pregnant very quickly after we got married — like honeymoon quick. Apparently I'm very fertile. And I'm a great example of that tiny percentage of women that birth control doesn't work on. Not kidding. All my husband had to do was walk by me and I'd get pregnant. Very. Fertile.

So we were in debt up to our eyeballs right out of school, newly married, with a baby on the way. And you all know how it goes when you're in debt, it just keeps getting deeper and deeper, and you just keep shoveling like crazy, but the shit and mud end up falling back on top of you. We weren't spenders. We didn't take out credit cards to go on vacation or buy awesome things. We took out credit cards to eat and buy formula and diapers.

Our first daughter arrived and we had a decision to make: I could either go back to work and put her in day care, which was at minimum $800 per month. Or I could quit work and stay home with her. We compromised a bit. I stayed home with her and taught private lessons out of my house. Then I got pregnant with baby No. 2, and I knew I'd have to go back to work.

I don't know if you guys are familiar with the world of band directing, but it is an intense job that is at a norm 70 hours per week — most of the time closer to 80 hours per week. It's as time-consuming as coaching, if not more so. So my second daughter was born and I immediately went back to work (marching band camp in the heat of summer) when she was just a couple of weeks old. I cried for two solid years because I never saw my children. I was miserable. And I felt guilty for being miserable because through it all, my marriage was good and my children were amazing.

What I did discover during those two years was that I needed to find something for myself that made *me* happy. I loved my husband and my children very much, but I needed an escape from what was happening in my life. So during spring break of 2005 I started another book. This time I swore to myself I'd finish it — even when it got hard. I wrote every day of the time I had off — all day long and well into the night. And six months later I had a finished manuscript in my hands.

The thought of going back to another school year and being away from my children again was heartbreaking. I *hated* the thought of going back. I'd already missed first steps and first words, and I knew I'd miss a lot more before it was over.

But my husband came to my rescue. Did I mention he was my real-life hero? He told me I should stay home with the girls and be with them. He also told me I'd have more time to continue writing. You see, I'd finally found that thing I'd been looking for that I could see myself doing for the next 60 years, and I wanted to give it a shot and see if I could get published.

He didn't tell me that because we'd won the lottery or because we'd gotten a windfall of money from somewhere. He did it because he wanted me to be happy. A hero, right? The solution for my newfound freedom was for him to find a second, and maybe a third, job to supplement my income. So my husband would leave school every afternoon at 3:45 and he'd drive directly to the restaurant where he'd wait tables until 10 o'clock at night. On the weekends he took on extra private-lesson students.

He made the sacrifices so I could follow my dream. We were still poor and in debt, but I felt as though a load had been lifted from my shoulders. I was able to spend time with my girls and write at the same time. And writing made me very happy.

I wrote three books during my first year of writing full time, and after months of querying I finally found my first agent. She was a reputable agent at a small boutique agency and she loved my voice. She was the first person, besides a relative, who'd ever told me I was any good at writing. You know how we are — writers are needy. We need the pats on the back and the accolades. We need to be reassured that what we're doing isn't complete crap or an utter failure.

We polished up the manuscript until it sparkled and then she sent it out on submission. Several weeks into the submission process I got an email from her saying her husband had gotten cancer and she had to focus on that. She still wanted to be my agent, but she had to put her clients on hold for a little while. She pulled the book from submission and I had to think long and hard about what I was going to do. I ultimately decided to part ways with her and look for another agent. I felt bad for her and the situation, but I still needed to do what was best for me. Even then I understood this was a business.

So I queried more agents with a different manuscript, and this time I had two offers. I went with one of the top agencies in the country. We polished up the manuscript and it went out on submission. Several weeks later I got a call from my agent. She was leaving for maternity. And she wasn't sure she was going to come back.

Sigh ... I was more discouraged than ever. My husband was still working three jobs, and I could tell it was taking its toll on him. I was pregnant again myself — remember the birth control thing? Yeah, it failed more than once. I'd written six books by that point and none of them had sold. In all fairness, only two of them had been shopped because I had horrific agent luck.

I wished my agent well and we parted ways. I knew my writing had improved by leaps and bounds. I knew in my soul at this point that I was good enough that I would sell eventually if I just kept at it. But I was also extremely discouraged. At the time, there was no self-publishing. You had to go through an agent, and you had to wait months, sometimes a year, for anyone to get back to you about your book.

I knew if I didn't sell soon I was going to have to go back to work. I couldn't keep letting my husband work himself to the bone. I decided if I didn't find an agent and I was unable to sell that I'd go back to work and put my dream of writing aside forever.

I made a list of 10 agents who were the best of the best. Dream agents. And I numbered them from first choice to last and then I sent out queries. Nine out of the 10 of them requested the full manuscript. Three of them offered me representation. Two of those three were agents from the top two agencies in the country. I had conversations with both of them and felt like I clicked immediately with one of them, so I signed on with her and started to have hope that my dream wasn't as dead as I thought it was.

A couple of things happened about this time: The state of Texas decided $27,000 a year should no longer be the minimum salary for a teacher. It raised it to $40,000 a year. The school called me and asked if I'd be willing to teach part time. And my husband and I started taking a financial class by a man named Dave Ramsey. Maybe you've heard of him? It seemed as if there was light at the end of the tunnel after all. We'd never be rich, barely middle class, but we could maybe pay off our debt and be comfortable.

A year went by and that manuscript all of those agents were excited about didn't sell. Then there was another that didn't sell. And another. The acquiring editors loved my voice. They wanted the books. But each book was shot down in marketing because they couldn't figure out how to shelve my work. I was too cross-genre. I've decided that's a marketer's way of saying they're too lazy to figure out how to sell your books. After all, I've figured out how to market those same books quite well.

This happened to me *four* times. I'd get an email from an editor saying they loved it and then I'd get another email telling me marketing didn't want it. *Four times.* By this time I was pregnant again with baby No. 4. I'm telling you, I had to do something with all that free time I had. My agent emailed me one afternoon and told me I should consider self-publishing. She said a lot of her clients were doing it very successfully and that I should give it a go. I promptly told her, "I don't think so."

This was at the end of March 2011, and self-publishing still had such a horrid reputation. It was for writers who'd decided to sell out. For those who had given up on being a *real* author.

But she'd planted the seed, and I couldn't stop thinking about it. I had a drawer of 10 novels that would never see the light of day, and all but the first couple were good books. I thought about it some more, and then I started reading blogs and watching the other clients of my agent to see how it was going. I finally talked myself into it and decided to upload five titles in June 2011.

Of course, I was totally embarrassed to have stooped so low. I knew if anyone ever found out I might as well dig a hole in the ground and jump in so I wouldn't have to face the scorn of my peers. So I chose a pen name and told no one except for my husband. I mean *no one*. Not even my own mother, and especially no one in my local RWA chapter.

The books had already been edited by my agent, my husband was computer-savvy enough to learn how to format, and I was just dangerous enough with Photoshop that I could make covers that weren't embarrassing. They weren't amazing, but they were good enough for a start. Remember, we had zero extra money to help start up this self-publishing experiment.

So we loaded the books at Amazon, Barnes & Noble and Smashwords. And then I sat back and wondered what I should do next. I certainly wasn't ready to tell anyone I had books available for sale.

On the personal front, my husband was still waiting tables, I was teaching private lessons to 60 students a week (teaching privately paid more than teaching full time in the classroom), I was writing full time, and I had four small children to raise. Did I mention we bought a house with my parents so we could all afford to live? We figured between their Social Security checks and our teacher's pay we could survive together.

You can imagine my surprise when those first five books went up and I managed to sell 444 copies to people I didn't know. My family didn't know and I hadn't had the guts to tell any friends, so it had to have been strangers buying the books. My husband probably would've bought that many copies if he could have afforded it, but he was too busy paying the medical bills to make sure I couldn't get pregnant without divine intervention anymore.

Four hundred forty-four copies in one month. An extra $827.11. *Holy shit.* That $827.11 was a fortune to us at that time. What could we do with an extra $800? Buy the kids some school clothes? Organic milk? Pay off the house? The possibilities were endless. And I started writing faster. If I had more books out, then maybe even more people would buy them.

June turned to July and I put out another title. My sales that month were more than double the month before. So was the money. I was really starting to see the possibilities of what self-publishing could do for me. It was no longer starting to matter what other people thought about self-publishing. Not as long as those kinds of checks were coming in. Mind you, I still hadn't told a soul what I was doing.

The problem with my books was that they were all first books of a series. I'd had no reason to continue each of those series because the first book didn't sell. I knew I needed to get a continuous series out there quickly that would hook readers in. I made them short, novella length, and more like vignettes that showed a glimpse into one family's life. I knew I wanted the books to be hot and that they'd be contemporary in setting. That's pretty much all I knew when the MacKenzie family was born. It was July, so the kids were home, but I buried myself in an upstairs room and didn't come out for five days. At the end of those five days I'd written 70,000 words and had four complete novellas. I sent them to two carefully selected beta readers I could trust to keep my secret and then I published them on August 1. You can imagine my surprise when I sold more than 20,000 books that month among all of the vendors. I didn't make as much money as I should have because I was pricing everything at 99 cents at that point with the hope of drawing in readers. But still ... I made a few thousand dollars extra instead of a few hundred. It was going to be the first Christmas we'd had where we wouldn't be worrying how we'd get gifts under the tree for four kids, how we'd feed them through the month, or how we'd pay the bills because we'd skimped a little to be able to buy toys. It was *freedom.*

Then the next month and the next month came and sales continued to get better. I bothered to learn more about the business. I did my research. I studied. I figured out algorithms and did experiments to see what worked and what didn't. I tried different promotional techniques. You name it. I've tried it at least once.

I kept writing with every spare second I could find (check out Jasinda Wilder's chapter about finding time) because fresh content gains more readers. And I worked my ass off. I *still* work my ass off, working 12- and 14-hour days because self-publishing isn't a get-rich-quick scheme. It's a business you have to build and cultivate over time. And like anything that matters, you've got to work hard for it.

Small rant: Seriously, I hate to hear excuses from writers about how they never have time to write. If you really want to write, you're going to find the time. Even when I was working 80 hours a week, I somehow managed to do it. I'd get home from school at 9 or 10 o'clock at night and write until midnight. Then I'd get up at 4 and start again before I had to get ready for school. I'd write during my conference period and through my lunch break. You get the picture. If you want to be a successful writer you have to put your butt in the chair and your fingers on the keyboard and put words on the page. Even shitty words are better than no words. You can go back and fix them later.

Anyway … I got off track. Where was I?

Oh, yeah. *Money*. The sales kept increasing and the money kept growing. Eventually the sales increased to the point that I started telling people what I was doing. Fellow TIV member Jane Graves was one of those first people. All I had to do was show her my KDP report and she looked at me and said she wanted to hear more about it. Because it's not about the *how* or with *whom* you get published. It's about the how much you're being paid. It's all about the money. Not about what publisher's name is on the spine of your book or what bookstore is putting you on the shelves. Nothing will gain you credibility faster than showing a New York Times best-selling author that you're making more than five times what they are in a year.

I'm not saying there's anything wrong with being traditionally published. If the price is right. I happen to be a hybrid writer as well, but it's because I got the terms I wanted. This is business. Books are beautiful things that take an amazing amount of creativity, but it's not your art. It's not your baby. You don't have to be a starving artist to gain recognition. It's business. And the point of any business is to make money to support yourself or your family.

It's a business. In January 2013 I realized that what I needed from my agent had changed. I was grateful to her for showing me the path to self-publishing. She was a great agent. But my needs and goals were no longer what they were when I first signed with her. So we parted ways amicably, and I decided I wasn't going to start looking for another. The only reason I would have gotten another was for foreign rights.

Sometimes fate steps in when you're not expecting it. The week after I left my agent, "Dirty Little Secrets" skyrocketed to the top of the charts. It was No. 1 at Barnes & Noble for several days and hung out around No. 13 at Amazon for a while. It was enough to put me on the USA Today list at No. 57 for the first time and garner the attention of a literary scout and several foreign publishers.

I had no idea what a literary scout was or if it was even a legitimate offer, so I did what most authors do when they have questions — I emailed Hugh Howey and asked him. It turns out a literary scout is pretty legitimate. And I needed an agent in a hurry. The problem was I've been in the self-publishing business for a while now. I'd like to think I'm pretty savvy as far as the deals agents are making. There were only two agents I'd even consider for representation for myself: Steve Axelrod and Kristin Nelson. I ultimately ended up going with Steve. I knew he wasn't going to tell me to take a deal just because there was the potential for him to get 15 percent. He'd let me control my own career and make the best choices for me. His foreign rights agent, Lori, is amazing and she handles the foreign deals for me. Film interest is handled by someone else. The arrangement is exactly what I wanted.

As of June 2013, I've been published exactly two years. I've sold more than a million e-books all over the world. My permafree book has also been downloaded more than a million times. I'm making seven figures a year. I'm also paying 40 percent in taxes, investing for retirement and setting up trusts for my kids. I have an accountant, a CFA and an attorney. We've paid off all of our debt and bought two new cars that would fit all six of us comfortably. We also pay private school tuition for all four of our kids.

Self-publishing has made us completely free. We're still the same people and the same family who always loved each other. But we no longer have that financial burden hanging over our heads. We no longer have to worry how the bills will be paid or if we have enough for a birthday present.

I'll be the first to tell you it doesn't work this way for everyone. But if you work your ass off and you listen to the people who give you good advice, you can get pretty damn close. Self-publishing will open numerous doors and give you incredible opportunities. The success will make you work harder. And the journey will make you stronger.

It makes me *happy*. And there's nothing that can top that.

Remember my husband, the hero? He got to have his happily ever after too. (In the first draft of this book I said he got his happy ending, but my mind is dirty and I had to change it to something else.) In July 2012, just a year after I first self-published, he turned in his resignation to the school and came to work for me full time. I think that's the thing that has made me the most proud — not the fact that we can go on luxurious vacations or buy an expensive home if we wanted one. I'm the most proud that I can give him something back after everything he sacrificed so I could make it to this place. He always believed in me and in my writing. He always encouraged me. And even in the hardest of times he always loved me. That's what a true romance hero is.

Visit Liliana at her website, www.lilianahart.com.

YOU'VE GOTTA KISS A LOT OF FROGS

TINA FOLSOM'S STORY

I've done so many different things in my life that I really have to go through my memory in chronological order so that I don't leave anything out.

I apprenticed as an admin assistant in a small knitting factory in Germany, before I became the secretary to a press officer of the Munich Trade Fair. Stints as an *au pair* girl (the fancy word for nanny and household slave) and a cocktail waitress on a Mediterranean cruise ship (the Danae, a ship of the Costa line — remember the Costa Concordia that sank in January 2012?) followed.

Then I moved to London and went from job to job: I was a travel consultant for a Japanese tour operator (and learned to appreciate sushi — free, because my boss always paid for it), went to my first karaoke bar with one of our clients (because he fancied me), and decided that I couldn't sing my way out of a paper bag. I moved on to work as an advertising sales person for a group of German magazines, but couldn't stand the job. Finally I got a job as a secretary with a commercial real estate firm, and promptly fell in love with my boss, a Frenchman. We traveled around the world together for seven months before we called it quits.

I returned to London and went into accounting. While working at the headquarters of a textile manufacturer, I took evening classes and earned my Certified Chartered Accountant license (the equivalent of a CPA). But after eight years in London, I needed a change and decided to go to the U.S.

I moved to New York City, where I attended the American Academy of Dramatic Arts to study drama. I hated it with a passion and left after a year to move cross-country, to Los Angeles, where I enrolled in UCLA

Extension. Screenwriting was what I wanted to do. So I studied for one year, got my certificate, but guess what: In L.A. everybody and their dog wants to be a screenwriter and has a script under their bed. I even worked at a film company (as an accountant) for a while, but in the end, it wasn't to be. Just as well that I'd met my future husband by then!

And off I went, moving to San Francisco. We got married a year later. I had immediately found a job for a CPA firm, and again I went to classes and studied for my CPA license. But I burned out on tax accounting quickly. I got a job at UCSF Medical Center and worked my way up to finance manager. On the side, I ran a small tax preparation business, and then ventured into real estate sales, but I was never satisfied with what I was doing. Because the only reason I was working so hard was so I could save for an early retirement, so that I could finally do what I really wanted to do: write books!

But then, around 2009 everything changed. I realized I didn't have to wait until retirement to write. I could do it now. When I heard about self-publishing in the same year, I nagged my husband long enough until he finally gave in and let me quit my many jobs and write. But we only had enough savings for me to stay home for one year. He had a government job that was safe, but that he didn't enjoy anymore.

I published my first full-length book in May 2010. I made $20 in my first month. Six months later I had replaced my monthly income. In December that same year I made $32,000 — my husband was shocked, and frankly, so was I. By then I had published three short stories and five full-length books (three in my Scanguards series). And I kept writing.

Because that's what I enjoy doing.

Oh, and my husband? He quit that dreaded job and is now helping me with the business of running my little publishing empire.

Visit Tina at her website, www.tinawritesromance.com.

FINDING MY LOST LOVE

DENISE GROVER SWANK'S STORY

My path to publication isn't exciting.

I was a pretty typical pre-writer. I read a lot as a kid. Maybe not so typical is that I created fanfic before I knew what it really was. In fact, it's a wonder I'm not a screenwriter. Most of my early works were re-enactments and embellishments of books I'd read or TV shows I'd seen — "Little House on the Prairie," "Lost in Space," "The Adventures of Tom Sawyer" (don't ask about this one). Back when I was a kid (Lordy, does that make me sound old ...) we played outside all summer long. We left the house in the morning and didn't go home until dinner. Those are long days to fill, so the neighborhood kids and I would "pretend." We'd each be characters from whatever tale we were re-creating and make up our own story.

See? Totally fanfic.

But by the fourth grade, I started writing my stories on paper. By the time I got to high school, I caught the eye of my English teacher. She saw talent and encouraged me to pursue writing. Her impact has been lifelong. In fact, I dedicated my first book to her memory. But once I got out of high school, I tried to write and found that life got in the way. I'd decide to get serious and start to write, then find my characters wandering aimlessly around in pioneer towns. (I read a lot of historical romance, so obviously, that's what I wrote.) Turns out that my books were missing this essential element called a plot. Go figure.

Life got in the way again. Kids. Two marriages. My second husband and I had moved to Franklin, Tenn., and I hadn't gone back to work. I decided that now would be a good time to write a book. So I began to plot one out in my head, some cheesy women's fic book, all dark and gloomy and totally serious.

And then my life turned dark and gloomy and totally serious.

My husband was in a single-engine plane crash.

You hear how life can change in an instant. I can tell you the moment mine fell to pieces. It was warm, sunny January afternoon. I was at home in the middle of a Southern Living party when my son said there was a man on the phone who insisted on talking to me. He told me that Darrell had been in an accident but he was OK, that Darrell insisted he tell me he was OK. He'd probably broken his ankle and he had a few burns. They were life-flighting him to Vanderbilt hospital to make sure he was OK.

It's also moments like this that you realize you'll believe anything other than face reality. It didn't occur to me until over an hour later, as I sat in the E.R. waiting for that damn helicopter to arrive, that they wouldn't have life-flighted him as a precaution.

It was bad.

It turned out to be worse than bad. For five weeks, my life was on hold, waiting for my husband to survive. Darrell had third-degree burns on over 60 percent of his body and had severe smoke inhalation. He'd get better, then he'd get worse. Then he'd lose his skin grafts. And we'd start over again. Thankfully, he was unconscious for about 90 percent of the time. The other 10 percent was hell. I kept thinking when it was all over, we'd have a story to tell. How Darrell shouldn't have been able to crawl away from that burning plane — the FAA official told me so — so of course, he'd survive. Dying wasn't an option.

Only it was.

He died on March 7, 2006, with me holding his hand. I didn't want him to go through it alone, even though he was in a medically induced coma.

For weeks after, I could barely function, although most people around me had no idea. I still did what needed to be done, but I was on autopilot. I got up every morning because I had three kids at home (one was in college), and the youngest was 3 years old. She needed me. She was my reason to get through the day.

After I waded through my own personal hell, my grief eventually lessened. After the first anniversary of his death, it occurred to me that I still had a story to tell. That I could tell other survivors of the death of a spouse that there was hope. That they could still live, even though the person they were before died with their spouse. They could be like a phoenix and rise from the ashes.

Only I didn't know how to write it.

But life moved on for me. I adopted two more children. (My youngest child with Darrell was adopted from China.) During my adoption process, I started a family blog titled There's Always Room for One More. I started writing stories about my life and my kids. It was on my blog that I learned the art of storytelling. Where I learned how to plot. I was active on my blog for two years, and I loved every moment of it. During this time, I began my memoir of Darrell's accident, and frankly, it sucked. I even recognized how bad it was. So I put it aside and soon after I heard about NaNoWriMo. National Novel Writing Month. I decided I was participating in NaNoWriMo 2009. This was my last shot at writing a book. Either I did it or I didn't. Otherwise shut up about it.

I like a challenge.

On Nov. 30, 2009, I had 69,000 words written for my romantic suspense "So Much to Lose." I finished writing it on Dec. 10, coming in at 97,000. Only don't go searching Amazon so you can buy a copy. You won't find it there. You'll have to search my external hard drive for that puppy. It was bad. Worse than bad. Plot holes so big you could drive a semi through them. But it wasn't totally worthless and I have no regrets.

I finished a book.

And with that newfound confidence, I decided to forgo editing the mess I'd just written and begin a new book, an urban fantasy titled "Chosen." My confidence soon waned as I began writing a book I didn't feel qualified to write. I wrote the first 10 chapters in a near panic attack, but a friend kept encouraging me to write one more chapter, then one more chapter, and by the middle of February, I had another completed book.

I was on a roll.

Thus began the mega-round of revisions and edits. By the end of June I began querying agents and started writing the second book in the series, "Hunted." I got many full requests, but ultimately, all rejections. The killer rejection was the agent who told me she loved it, but she didn't think she could sell it. I was devastated. Time to try something else.

The next day I plotted "Twenty-Eight and a Half Wishes," a rom-com Southern mystery. The day after that, I began to write it. Thirty days later, it was complete at 103,000 words. Again, several editing rounds, trimming off 10,000 words, then querying and little interest.

Time to move on to something else. How about YA? So I wrote a young adult science fiction romance that was originally titled "Torn," but eventually became "Here." I began to query it in April. I had an agent who was *very* interested in "Here" and was also considering "Chosen." I knew she was into dark and edgy books, and "Twenty-Eight" wasn't edgy at all. She wouldn't be interested and "Twenty-Eight" would die on my hard drive. While my first book deserved the eternal exile, "Twenty-Eight" didn't. My beta readers loved "Twenty-Eight" and I had tons of them. About 25 to 30 readers.

That was when I first considered the idea of self-publishing.

Still, it was embarrassing. In the spring of 2011, the stigma with self-publishing still lingered, although more and more people in the publishing industry had begun to see it as an acceptable path to publication. The day I first seriously considered it was when then literary agent, Nathan Bransford, said on his blog that he thought it was acceptable and reasonable to self-publish some books.

By the middle of May 2011, I decided to try it. I had no idea if I was committing professional suicide, but I was going to do it anyway. Not long after my decision, the agent who was strongly interested in "Here" called me to reject the manuscript. Thank God I was in the middle of preparing "Twenty-Eight" for release, otherwise I would have been devastated. Instead, I felt oddly relieved.

After a copy edit, a cover created and donated by a friend, and then a professional e-book formatter, I released "Twenty-Eight and a Half Wishes" in July 2011. I'd been told to expect to sell about 20 books my first month. I sold a little over 200. The next month I sold more than 400. When I began my self-publishing journey, my pie-in-the-sky dream was to sell 1,000 books by the end of the year. *That* was my benchmark for success. I hit 1,000 book sales in September and I sobbed for over five minutes.

I had done it.

Encouraged by the success of "Twenty-Eight," I decided to self-publish "Chosen."

I released "Chosen" at the end of September, expecting all of those readers of "Twenty-Eight" to rush over to buy it. Yeah, not so much. See, readers only genre-hop if they really, really love an author. And I hadn't gained that reader trust yet.

In early October, I was in a bit of despair. I was selling three copies a day of "Chosen" while I was selling 50 to 60 of "Twenty-Eight." I wondered if New York was right. Maybe paranormal was dead. But I'd enrolled "Chosen" in two blog tours that ran back to back and by mid-November, I was selling more than 100 books a day of "Chosen."

I released "Hunted," "Chosen's" sequel, at the end of November. I also released my YA science fiction romance, "Here," at the beginning of November.

"Here" also debuted with slow sales and I expected sales to build slowly like the other two. However, other than a few spurts here and there (no pun intended), "Here" was never a big seller until December 2012, when The Indie Voice decided to run a Black Friday sale. For some reason, "Here" caught on in sales on Barnes & Noble, and pushed up to No. 8 on the Nook best-seller list. It was in the top 100 for almost three weeks. It just goes to show you that you never know when a book will be successful.

The important lesson to learn here is that each book is different. The way "Chosen" behaves in the market and after promotions is completely different from "Twenty-Eight's" behavior. "Here" has always sold more books at B&N. Why? I have no idea. And let me add that just because a book isn't selling well now doesn't mean it's a lost cause. (See above.) If your cover is great, your blurb is good and you have excellent reviews, it just might not be that book's time. But that's the beauty of e-books. They are always out there, waiting to be bought. Unlike a traditional book on a bookstore shelf that gets returned in a few months.

So let's look at some numbers.

The first month I had one book available with 209 sales.

By the end of 2011 I had four books available with a total of 26,691 in sales.

My biggest sales month was January 2013, with 33,751.

I hit 100,000 in sales on May 29, 2012 and I hit the 150,000 mark on Saturday, Sept. 15. I hit 200,000 sales in January 2013 and 300,000 sales in April 2013.

My biggest-selling book is "Chosen" with almost 80,000 sales. My second is the sequel to "Chosen," "Hunted," with over 55,000 sales. My next-largest-selling book not in the Chosen series is "Here" with 30,267.

As of June 2013, I have 11 novels available, two box sets, three short stories and four audiobooks. And one short memoir titled "The Death of Me." Remember that memoir I tried to write? I reduced it into a short piece.

If your sales are lagging, the best advice I can give you is make sure you are releasing a quality product. Great cover, *copy editing*, professional formatting. (If you can format it yourself and make it look great, more power to you!) Second, *keep writing and releasing books.*

Let's say I have a book for sale and I sell only 250 copies a month. But then I release three more books and each one is selling 250 copies. In one month, you're joining the 1,000 club! Plus, the more books you release, the more copies you sell.

That's the dirty little secret that a lot of people don't get.

You can make money as a self-published author even if you aren't a best-seller. If you have your books priced so that you make money ($2.99 or more) and you are selling 1,000 books or more a month (with several books available, that's not so inconceivable) you'll make some nice money. Maybe not enough to live off of. Yet. But keep releasing books. Plus, new releases that are received well will spur sales of your other books within the same genre.

My dream was to be a published author. My path wasn't the one I planned, but it's so much better. I'm living my dream and so can you. Now get back to writing!

Visit Denise at her website, www.denisegroverswank.com.

SUCCESS BEGINS WITH A SEXY COWBOY

DEBRA HOLLAND'S STORY

On New Year's Eve in 1998, I was out dancing and met a cowboy (and those are hard to find in Orange County, Calif.!). We shared a New Year's kiss and started dating. Although we had nothing in common, we had a lot of fun together. At some point, I thought, "If we lived 100 years ago in the West, who he is and who I am just might work." And that's how the idea came to me for my first book, "Wild Montana Sky," a sweet historical Western romance. While I was writing the book, I attended a critique/teaching group led by Louella Nelson. Thus, the finished book didn't belong under the bed as often happens with first novels, and I ended up with a professionally edited product.

I entered "Wild Montana Sky" in the 2001 RWA Golden Heart contest. To my surprise and shock, the book became a finalist. It had never even occurred to me that I could final. The book went on to win. Right afterward, I had so many people tell me that a sale must be right around the corner that I believed them. An acquaintance directed me to his agent, who on the strength of the GH win, took me on.

My agent (despite valiant attempts) couldn't sell "Wild Montana Sky" because it was "sweet" instead of sexy and historical instead of contemporary. (This was the time when the historical market tanked.)

While "Wild Montana Sky" made the rounds of the New York publishing houses, I wrote Book 2, "Starry Montana Sky," as well as "Sower of Dreams," the first book in a fantasy romance trilogy. Although "Sower" was a 2003 Golden Heart finalist, the book didn't sell either. It had good feedback from editors, but just wasn't enough to sell.

My agent disappeared, and I moved on to agent No. 2. She loved

"Sower of Dreams" and was sure she could sell it. She did a wonderful job of editing my books. But after a couple of years of no sales (including my two nonfiction book proposals) and a refusal on my part to accept the offer she did receive for "Wild Montana Sky," she dropped me.

I decided to go it alone without an agent and just write nonfiction books. I'd already planned to self-publish them, not because I was psychic and knew that would be the next big thing, but because I figured I could sell the print books at the back of the room when I gave talks.

What I didn't realize (after years of rejections) was that I'd started stifling my creativity. I'd get a story idea and suppress it, thinking, "It's too much effort to write a book and not be able to sell it."

Then an opportunity dropped into my lap. A friend emailed me that an agent (Jessica Faust) whom she followed on a social networking site was looking for an expert to write a book on grief. I contacted Jessica and sent her the information she wanted. She thought I was perfect for the job. She sent my material to the acquiring editor, and a week later, I had a new agent and my first book contract for "The Essential Guide to Grief and Grieving."

I also had the deadline from hell — five months.

Leading up to the deadline, one of my writer friends started posting to our group about how well her self-published books were doing. I didn't pay much attention (being rather absorbed in the grief book at the time) until around the beginning of 2011, when she posted that she was earning $3,000 a month from her self-published books. That made me sit up and take notice. I said to myself, "I WANT TO MAKE $3,000 A MONTH ON MY FICTION BOOKS!" Little did I know that a year later I'd be making far more than $3,000 a month on my self-published books — February 2012, alone, was almost $18,000.

I so wanted to immediately get "Wild Montana Sky" and "Starry Montana Sky" ready to self-publish, but needed to concentrate on finishing "The Essential Guide to Grief and Grieving." I promised myself that as soon as I turned the grief book in, I'd do just that. My eagerness grew as several of my unpublished writing friends started self-publishing and sharing their numbers. If it hadn't been for those women, I might never have attempted self-publishing. I might not even be very aware of the benefits of self-publishing. I was also lucky to have friends climbing the self-publishing ladder just ahead of me, because they passed on their information about what to do and not do, and I could follow what had worked and what didn't work for them. TIV authors Theresa Ragan and Colleen Gleason are two of those friends to whom I've very grateful!

During the month between sending in my last chapters on the grief book and getting back my revisions, I read through both Montana Sky books, making more editing tweaks. I had the covers designed by my friend,

Delle Jacobs, also a self-published author. I tried (for about half an hour) to follow the Smashwords guide and format my books for e-readers, but quickly realized it was going to be beyond my tech-challenged brain, plus a big time sink. I decided I'd rather pay someone else to do the work — definitely worth the money, because formatters charge $40 to $100 per book.

However, many self-published authors do their own formatting. It seems to take about half a day to a day to learn what to do and do it. So just because I chose not to attempt my own formatting doesn't mean you have to make the same decision.

Late on April 28, 2011, I was ready to self-publish "Wild Montana Sky," with "Starry Montana Sky" to follow the next day. I was nervous about uploading my book on Amazon, afraid that my aforementioned tech-challenged brain wouldn't be able to make it work. To my great relief, each step was clear and relatively easy to do. "Wild Montana Sky" took me about a half-hour to upload. The process has since become much faster because I know what to do. Nook Press and Smashwords are similar enough so that once you've done Amazon, you can do those two as well.

As soon as the two books were live on Amazon (it takes six to 24 hours) I notified my friends. I sold about 10 books that day and had fun checking my reports to see my numbers. Checking soon turned into a compulsion. I probably look at my sales numbers 20 times a day.

The book sales began slowly, but they steadily grew. I was so excited and proud of them that I started showing the covers (on my phone) to my local author friends and telling them about self-publishing. At first, I received a lot of skeptical looks, but everyone was supportive. As the months went on and my numbers grew, those looks began to change. I started to blog about my numbers, wanting other writers to know that self-publishing is a viable option.

I cut back on my psychotherapy practice and corporate crisis/grief counseling to write more. The income from self-publishing more than made up for the income I lost from working less.

My numbers for the Montana Sky series grew. August 2011 was fantastic, earning me over $6,000. I thought the sales would continue to go up. But after Labor Day, my sales started dropping, and doing some promotion such as guest blogs didn't make any difference. My drop in sales mirrored what seemed to be happening for most self-published authors. Even though my sales were heading downward, they still were good. My lowest month was November, when I earned $2,600. (Not bad for low sales!)

In July/August, 2011, I self-published the first two books in my fantasy romance trilogy, "Sower of Dreams" and "Reaper of Dreams." To my disappointment, they didn't do as well as the Montana Sky Series —

different genre, thus different readers. They've been steady each month at about 75-500 sales for the first book, 45-300 for the second. I think the sales will improve now that I've finished "Harvest of Dreams," the third book in the trilogy.

I anticipated that the 2011 Christmas sales of Kindles and Amazon gift cards would pop up self-publishing sales, and that certainly was true for me. My sales doubled. I let out a sigh of relief that sales were heading up and not down, and hoped the wave would last for a long while.

At that time, I also self-published the first book of my space opera: Twinborne Trilogy. "Lywin's Quest" is an epic book at 140,000 words, and I priced it high ($7.99) both to match the word count and because I'm not going to get around to writing the rest of the trilogy for a while. I also almost never mention it exists. So I only have a trickle of sales from this book.

I'd written the first 50 pages of "Stormy Montana Sky" back in 2003 or - 4. But when "Wild Montana Sky" didn't sell, I didn't write more of "Stormy." After I finished the revisions for the grief book, I began to work on "Stormy," which I self-published in mid-January 2012. "Stormy" immediately began doing well, selling 30 books the first day and heading up from there. Surprising to me, the sales of the other two books also increased.

In January 2012, I had my self-publishing goals for the year all mapped out. I planned to finish the third book in my fantasy romance trilogy, and write two novellas and a collection of Christmas stories for my Montana Sky series. Given enough writing time, I also planned to work on the next big book in the series, as well as continue to outline and jot down ideas for the next books. I had firm ideas for three novellas and two books in the Montana Sky series, plus the short stories. (Obviously, my creativity had returned!)

Then I received an email from Lindsay Guzzardo, an editor at Amazon Montlake, which changed everything. She wrote me that she'd read "Wild Montana Sky," loved the book, and wanted to acquire the series.

Luckily it was an email, not a call, so I had a chance to think about her offer. My first reaction to an editor calling out of the blue and wanting to acquire my books was *not* the expected jubilation. Instead, I felt ambivalent. I was thrilled to be asked, but my plans were deeply engrained in my mind, and I wasn't sure I wanted to give up control of that series, nor risk losing the money I was making.

I took the rest of that day to research Montlake. I knew some authors who'd already signed with them, and contacted them to learn about their experience. (All positive.) I also read several author blogs that talked about the Amazon experience. (Also positive.)

I was particularly concerned about giving up creative control of my series. I knew what I intended to do with these books, and I didn't want an editor telling me no. That didn't mean I wouldn't take editorial direction. I just didn't want anyone telling me that this wasn't my next hero or heroine or next book.

The next day, I spoke with Lindsay. I asked her a lot of questions. Talking to an editor as a successful self-published author versus as an unpublished author was totally different. I felt much more in control, and she had to sell the idea of Montlake to me. Lindsay was so enthusiastic about the Montana Sky series, *and* Amazon's vision for its publishing company, that I became excited too. She told me I could keep my titles, my covers (although polished up a bit) and the control over which books I planned to write next. Then she said the magic words: "We know where the historical romance readers are." So I said, "I'm in."

As soon as the contract arrived, I contacted a literary attorney and began the negotiation process. (My agent was out on maternity leave, and she had never represented these books.) I wanted to make sure I could continue to self-publish novellas and short stories in the Montana Sky series, while Montlake published the big books.

One of my favorite self-publishing moments happened the day I had the final version of the Montlake contract sitting unsigned on my desk. I received an email from an editor at one of the big six publishing houses, asking to acquire the Montana Sky series. I emailed her back that I had a contract from Montlake, but since I hadn't yet signed it, I'd be willing to speak with her. She called me, but the terms weren't as favorable as Montlake's. When I declined the offer, she said, "Oh, I'm so disappointed. And my senior editor will be too. She told me she really wanted your books."

I politely said, "Well ... you had your chance. My agent submitted these books to your house several years ago, and she rejected them."

Hah! Even now I get a kick of out of how wonderful it was to say that to her!

In February, Amazon sent a big batch of historical romance readers an email with several "best-selling historical romances" on it. One was "Wild Montana Sky" (at that time still a self-published book.) My sales went through the roof — 843 that day. The next day, they targeted another group of historical readers. Again, "Wild Montana Sky" was on the list. Seven hundred twenty-five that day. I watched the sales rank creep lower until I hit the top 100 Kindle list, and moved as low as No. 73. "Wild Montana Sky" stayed on the list for three days.

My April 2012 Amazon sales were lower than February and March, and May was lower yet. And this seemed to be true for many self-published authors. Some attributed it to the unseasonably nice weather, when people are active outside; others blamed the release of the Harry Potter series on e-book for taking readers' book buying money for the month. Still others blame income tax payments. I think was probably a combination of various factors.

The vast majority of my book sales have occurred on Amazon. Barnes & Noble and Smashwords sales have been negligible in comparison. This is not the case for every self-published author. Some do very well on B&N and Apple (Smashwords also puts my books on Apple), perhaps even better than Amazon.

This changed for me in the second week of April 2012. For no reason that I can discern (although that doesn't mean there wasn't a reason), "Wild Montana Sky" started to sell well on B&N, growing to the point that it more than doubled compared with my sales on Amazon. The next two books in the series didn't outsell the ones on Amazon, but those sales slowly increased as Nook readers finished Book 1, and moved on to buy Books 2 and 3. "Wild Montana Sky" made the B&N Nook top 100 list, moving as low as No. 20. I stayed on the top 100 list for about a month.

A few weeks later, my Barnes & Noble and Amazon sales combined catapulted me onto the USA Today best-seller list. I was No. 137 for a week. It was a huge (and emotional) surprise, and from now on, I can label myself as a USA Today best-selling author!

I reached my one-year mark at the end of April 2012 selling almost 97,000 e-books. In April 2013, I crossed the 200,000 sales mark.

In June 2012, RT Reviews magazine selected "Wild Montana Sky" as a Hot Pick For July in its "What's Hot This Month in Self-Publishing" column. It didn't really impact sales, probably because I didn't have print books (they came out on August 28, 2012), but it was still a nice surprise.

My sales held steady over that summer, which wasn't the case for a lot of other self-published authors. I had a nice three-day boost when Ereader News Today showcased "Wild Montana Sky." (A nice surprise because I hadn't submitted to them, nor paid for an ad.)

Over the summer of 2012, while I weathered a breakup with my boyfriend and a move, I worked on the short stories for "Montana Sky Christmas." I wanted to have the book ready to coincide with the Montlake release of "Wild Montana Sky" and "Starry Montana Sky." I self-published "Montana Sky Christmas" on August 28.

Right before the Montlake versions launched, I had to take "Wild Montana Sky" and "Starry Montana Sky" down from Barnes & Noble, something I didn't like doing. When I'd made the decision to go with Montlake, I'd known that B&N wouldn't carry the Amazon imprint e-books. (But they do the print and audio books.) In January 2012, with negligible B&N sales, I couldn't foresee the April boom that would catapult me onto the USA Today list. Although the B&N sales steadily declined from May, they were enough in August that I hated to give them up. And, indeed, without the first two e-books available on B&N, the sales of my other books returned to being small.

However, Montlake's push of the books more than made up for it. By November, I had 50,000 sales of "Wild Montana Sky" alone. In January, "Starry Montana Sky" was a Kindle Daily Deal, and I sold about 5,000 books that day. Six weeks later, "Wild Montana Sky" was a Kindle Daily Deal, at about 3,000 books sold. The Montlake sales did what I wanted, which was drive sales of my other self-published Montana Sky books, and also sent some to The Gods' Dream Trilogy.

Left alone without an Amazon push, the Montlake books tend to sell about the same as they did as self-published versions.

In December 2012, I self-published my first novella, "Painted Montana Sky." At first I priced it at 99 cents, then at the end of December, I experimented with $1.99 and found it sold just as well. So I've kept it at $1.99.

In February, Amazon selected "Starry Montana Sky" as a Top 50 Greatest Love Story pick. Wow. I was amazed. Who would have thought two books that no traditional publisher would buy would have the journey "Wild Montana Sky" and "Starry Montana Sky" have had in their first two years? It's been an *amazing* experience, and I'm so very grateful I chose to self-publish!

Visit Debra at her website, www.drdebraholland.com.

TRYING EVERYTHING AT LEAST ONCE

COLLEEN GLEASON'S STORY

I began writing when I was in sixth grade. I spent a lot of my free time, when I wasn't reading or hanging out with friends, working on various stories — most of which starred my friends and me having adventures. At that early age, I had visions of being like Laura Ingalls Wilder or John-Boy Walton (two of my childhood heroes, for obvious reasons).

However, being a practical Type A sort of person and enjoying my creature comforts, as I got older, though I continued to write all through high school, I put that dream aside for real life. I wasn't about to take the starving artist route. Instead, I went to college, got married, got a good job, got my MBA, had three children, and continued to work in a sales, marketing and management position ... but all the while I continued to write my stories.

I was trying to break in somewhere in the romance or mystery genre, and so I wrote many different stories: two historical romances, two gothic-sort of romantic suspense novels, an action-adventure novel with a female lead and another humorous mystery-adventure series lead-in with a female lead (à la Stephanie Plum), and finally began working on a novel about a vampire hunter who lived during the time of Jane Austen.

Through the years, I'd submitted my novels and partials to agents and publishers alike. I'd studied the market, watched who was acquiring what, networked, attended conferences, and continued to receive positive and encouraging feedback from agents and editors. I signed with a well-known, reputable agent in late 2003, and although she submitted a variety of my novels, none of them sold (though I got a lot of "We really love her voice/the story/the premise/the writing," but they couldn't buy it for a number of reasons).

Then in the spring of 2005 I finished the historical vampire hunter novel, and I *loved* it. My agent loved it. She said she could definitely sell it. (I'd heard that before. …) But it was summer, and she wasn't going to do anything about submitting until after Labor Day because everyone was out of the office in the summer. So while I waited, I started working on an erotic novel just for the fun of it. I had no other ideas, and I'd always wanted to know what happened down in the lair of the Phantom of the Opera during the "Music of the Night" scene, so I played around with it just for fun.

In the meantime, I was unemployed (because the startup company I'd been working for was sold, and they didn't need another sales manager), and I didn't have any ideas for a new book. I was halfheartedly looking for a job, doing some consulting, and trying to think of a new project to work on — all the while, the practical side of me knew that being a writer, making a *living* as a writer, was such a pie-in-the-sky proposition, I really had no business spending time and effort on it. (Remember, I am a Type A personality. I'd never been unemployed in my life — since I got my first job at 15.)

I remember walking into dinner with my two writing buddies, utterly dejected and frustrated and ready to give up. I had no new ideas, my agent had had my best book for three months and hadn't sent it out yet (the "timing wasn't right") and I had no new projects in mind. I needed to get serious about finding a real job. There were tears and low-grade shrieks involved. I was a hot mess.

About three weeks later, my agent called me (that in itself is a story — but too long to share here). She said, "Colleen, are you sitting down?"

I promptly sat and she proceeded to tell me we'd sold the first (and a second) vampire hunter novel in a pre-empt to NAL for a very nice sum of money. I was, as one can imagine, ecstatic.

That was the beginning of seven years of ups and downs in the traditional publishing world. I am the poster child for having opportunity after opportunity being squandered — not on my part, but in the realm of bad timing and market shifting and editorial issues.

Less than six months after I sold my first vampire hunter book (which eventually became "The Rest Falls Away," the first book in the international best-selling Gardella Vampire Chronicles), I sold the erotic novel about "The Phantom of the Opera" that I'd been messing around with — to my same editor at NAL. Over the next four years, I wrote a total of eight novels for that editor at NAL: five Gardellas and three erotic novels based on classic literature under a pseudonym.

While I was finishing up the last two books on my NAL contract (one erotica, one Gardella), through a friend I met an editor at Avon. She loved my writing (she was not the first editor at a different house from where I was contracted who'd expressed interest in my work), and she wanted a proposal from me for a contemporary paranormal.

I willingly and excitedly put something together for her, especially since I'd seen the writing on the wall with NAL: The first Gardella did quite well, but for a variety of reasons (lack of distribution and visibility, plus a truly awful second-book cover, and minimal communication between my agent and editor), the last four books in the series weren't what we call "well-published." My editor at NAL, whom I love to this day, fought for me to be able to finish the series and write the fifth book — which I did, and they probably printed a total of 15,000 copies — and then despite its success overseas, the series was forgotten and allowed to go out of print.

The three eroticas did quite well, but this was long before "Fifty Shades of Grey," so they didn't explode. NAL was more than willing to do a fourth (or more) erotica, but I chose not to go that route, because in the meantime, I had sold on proposal three books to Avon — that contemporary series.

Except the contemporary series turned out to be a dystopian romantic suspense series that everyone was absolutely stoked about. Avon wanted me to write under a different name than Colleen Gleason because they wanted to launch the series as a debut author with three books back-to-back-to-back (three months in a row), which is generally a perfect recipe for success. Everything was aligned, and Avon even came back to me for a re-up for the next three books in the series, and for more money — before the first book was even released.

But then things went terribly wrong.

Two things happened that I believe kept those first three books from exploding as everyone believed they had the potential to do: The covers looked more like erotic romance novels than dystopian romantic suspense (or even romantic suspense, period — see my chapter on "Pimping Yourself" where I talk about genre cues and packaging), and the distribution broke.

The first two books did very well, selling thousands of copies in the first couple of weeks after each release. They were everywhere: Target, Meijer, Wal-Mart, B&N, etc. But the third book somehow went from selling thousands of copies in Wal-Mart (which at the time accounted for a good 30-50 percent of sales for mass market paperbacks) in the first week for the prior two books to selling 30 copies. In *all* of Wal-Mart.

That was my first clue something really bad was happening. I thought maybe the books just didn't make it to Wal-Mart on the shelves in time for the "official" release of the third book, and that the next week, we'd see the thousands of copies of sales — which had increased for each of the other books.

But it never happened. The sales at Wal-Mart were a mere trickle of what they'd been before, and elsewhere as well. I was getting emails from people asking why they couldn't find the third book. The sales never picked up in Wal-Mart, which turned out to be the kiss of death. This was 2010, so this was before the e-book revolution — so if you didn't see the book in the stores, it pretty much didn't exist.

No one ever investigated (as least as far as I know) what happened, and I was given no explanation. That third book shouldn't have tanked — and I suspect the reason was, as I said above, the distribution broke.

By the time the fourth book came out, in early 2011, we were in the midst of the Borders debacle and the Anderson Merchandisers mess, and the Kindle had been released. The entire industry was in a state of flux, and when "Night Betrayed" was released the last week of January, it *tanked*. There was no distribution or placement, no one was shipping to Borders, the book was nowhere and had no support, no placement, no co-op. Six weeks later, I got a call from my agent (a new agent, by the way), who informed me Avon was suspending the release of the fifth book.

"Until when?" I asked.

"They don't know. They want to regroup, repackage the book so it has a new sort of cover, etc., try to figure out how to breathe new life into the series."

OK. I guessed I could handle that — mainly because I'd already been paid my advance for that book. I was actually waiting for the approval on the proposal for the sixth and final book at that time, so I realized at that point, the sixth book might never be published.

However, once again, opportunity smiled down on me, because about a year earlier, a very influential editor at MIRA Books (part of Harlequin) had contacted me out of the blue and asked me to write a proposal for a historical vampire series. She'd loved my Gardellas, thought I was an amazing writer and just heard from the B&N buyer that they wanted Regency-set vampire novels. I did the proposal (although it was a series I never would have proposed had I not been invited) and the editor bought a trilogy from me based on a two-page proposal.

Talk about an opportunity! MIRA was going to release these books in trade paper format and the covers were going to be fantastic. Everyone was very excited about them. (I'd heard that before. …) The first book was due to be released in April 2011 — just a couple of months after the fourth book for Avon. (Yes, the one that tanked. But remember, I was writing under a different name for Avon — Joss Ware — and I went back to Colleen Gleason for MIRA.)

So I turned in the first vampire book and my editor raved to me — and others — about how wonderful it was, what a great writer I was, how much she loved my work. She had a few tweaks for me to make, nothing major, very minor — which I did. She thought it was great. She paid me for the book.

And then she turned the book over to her assistant to read.

And her assistant began to suggest changes ... changes that didn't work for me, or the way I wanted to write the story. Changes that *changed* characters and their relationships and were, quite frankly, cliché and boring suggestions. And I politely disagreed and made my case, and didn't make any of the changes the assistant suggested (mind you, this is after my editor had accepted and *paid* me for the book) ... and then I got a phone call from my agent.

My editor was going to cancel the contract for all three books if I didn't make these changes.

I felt as if I'd been shoved into a time warp or something. WTF??

Long story short, we came to an uneasy agreement about some tweaks that I would make, and some that just didn't work for me. I turned in the book. But by then, the damage was done.

The books were basically demoted from being a hot thing MIRA wanted, and B&N wanted, and everyone was behind, to ... nonentities.

My editor passed me off to her assistant for the second and third books (oh joy!) — and although the assistant was fine to work with on those books, and absolutely was blown away by the third book in particular, again, the damage was done. The covers weren't quite right (go look at "The Vampire Voss" — even the reviewers on Amazon made comments about it), and there was *no distribution*, no placement, no nothing for these books. Which, might I remind you, were trade paperback (and had been *requested* by B&N) ... right during the early days of the e-book revolution and the worst part of the recession. No one could find them, first of all, and secondly, they were overpriced, and third ... the covers. Just not *quite* right.

Yeah. They tanked too.

So all of a sudden, after selling **17** books to major New York publishers, I found myself at a complete loss. My career was at a standstill. I didn't know when or if Avon was going to publish Book 5 (it finally did in August 2012), or whether I was ever going to write Book 6, and I had three names I wrote under (not good for branding!), and it was kind of a disaster.

But I picked myself up, dusted myself off, and listened to some very wise women writers I knew and put together a proposal for a really fun, high-concept YA steampunk novel. My agent sold it in mid-2011 to a mid-size publisher, and "The Clockwork Scarab: A Stoker & Holmes Book" will be released in September 2013. (Depending when you are reading this, it could already be released.)

Once I realized I wasn't going anywhere fast with New York, it was early 2011. I had heard people talking about self-publishing on Amazon and elsewhere, and at first I didn't see how that would apply to me. But then I started thinking about those six books I'd written previously — the ones that no one wanted to buy in New York. I slowly began to edit, rewrite, format, etc., those books, and put my first one up in March 2011. It took another few months to get the next four books up and available. (During that time I also wrote the steampunk novel I'd sold.)

From the beginning, those five random books sold steadily, although not in crazy numbers like Liliana's. The problem I had was that they were — and still are — all different genres.

There's nothing that ties them together but my name, and while that works to some extent, I'm here to tell you that readers don't always move easily from genre to genre. That is one lesson I've learned about publishing in general — it does help to have a three- or four-book series in one genre to hook the readers before moving on.

My other problem was that six of my books were written under a different name (Joss Ware) that no one associated with Colleen Gleason — so that was a failed branding effort, in my opinion, and really did nothing to help my career. Joss Ware is a nonentity at this point.

I did end up writing the sixth book for Avon in early 2012 in about two months because my editor never told me to actually write it. (She'd never approved the synopsis, then one day asked when she was going to get that book because they had it slated for release in early 2013!) Then I wrote a second YA steampunk and a novella for a collection with three other writers.

By the end of 2012, I was fully a hybrid author: I was out of contract with Avon, NAL and Harlequin, and I had just finished my initial contract with the YA publisher.

I am currently working on tightening up my branding by writing more books for my most well-known and popular series (The Gardella Vampire Chronicles) as well as continuing the series I've self-published. Having so many books in different genres was a detriment to me when I launched my indie career, and although I'm making over six figures a year, I realize I could be more well-established if I had a smoother, more cohesive brand. So that is my new focus.

In the meantime, I have the traditionally published young adult book being released with an amazing amount of support from the publisher (who, after some of the difficulties I've had with prior publishers, has been utterly wonderful to work with), and I have a writing schedule planned for the next year with a variety of projects I'm *dying* to write — and books my fans are waiting for.

I couldn't be happier, knowing that I can continue to work with any traditional publisher with which I see eye-to-eye, but at the same time, I can still have a career that will *never* be completely controlled by someone else again.

Visit Colleen at her website, www.colleengleason.com.

FINAL THOUGHTS

DON'T neglect craft. All the marketing in the world cannot disguise a shoddy product.

DON'T write one book, then spend all your time marketing it. The first rule of marketing is that product sells product. Release a book, then write another. And another. And another.

DON'T do your own book cover unless you have professional-level skills. Nothing screams "this book sucks" more than an amateurish cover. Why prejudice readers so that they never read the first sentence? (The same goes for your website.)

DON'T go free too soon. Patience is the name of the game. If you have only one book available, why make it free? If it's a successful free run, you just drew a lot of attention to yourself but have no additional product to capitalize on. Have at least three books available (preferably in a series), then go free with the first.

DON'T limit yourself to one revenue stream. Expand your business interests to every revenue stream possible in order to maximize profit.

DON'T spam people. You won't like the results.

DON'T compare your career with another author's. While all indie careers will share things in common, every indie journey is unique to that author. It's like comparing apples to oranges.

DON'T talk smack about other authors. It only makes you look bitter.

DON'T neglect your physical and mental health. It will come back to bite you in the ass.

DON'T ignore social media. Readers want to interact with writers they love. Word of mouth is a big portion of book sales.

DON'T assume you can edit your own work. Hire a professional editor.

DO study craft. A writer should never stop improving their technique.

DO establish a professional-looking presence on the Internet.
DO interact with readers within your comfort level.
DO create a work schedule so that things don't fall through the cracks.
DO surround yourself with other writers who have positive attitudes and similar career goals.

Visit The Indie Voice at their website, www.theindievoice.com.

ABOUT THE AUTHORS

Eight writers met, many for the first time, on a windy day at an all-inclusive hotel in Cancun, Mexico on February 22, 2013 in a big ass hot tub. What began as a mere spark of an idea to join together to promote and market literally exploded into plans for yearly meetings in faraway lands, including a castle in Ireland. The possibilities were almost as limitless as the Mimosas consumed by Jane Graves.

Every writer in attendance, successful in their own right, had an opinion. Ideas were flowing and excitement building even before Denise Grover Swank talked Theresa Ragan into doing endless shots of tequila. Bonds were made and notes recorded while Colleen Gleason dropped to the floor and performed backbends, inversions, and restorative poses, in hopes that she could get this passionate group of writers to connect with their deeper selves.

Debra Holland was the only one who had her shit together, focusing on both body and mind and doing her best to help others attempt to glimpse the glass half full at any given moment. Liliana Hart, wearing colorful sundress, big sunglasses and giant hats, was the hostess with the mostess, inviting us all to her massive suite with its sprawling bathtub and endless food and drink. Poor sick Dorien Kelly coughed out legal advice over our five days of tropical bliss while Jana DeLeon became the leader in note taking, accountability, and snarky remarks.

Just as the Declaration of Independence was conceived in liberty and justice for all, so was The Indie Voice created in a group effort formed without ego and with unparalleled team spirit.

Discussions about swag and anthologies abounded, and what could have easily become pandemonium amongst a sea of estrogen became instead a perfect blend of wit and intellectual genius. Our mission statement began as "a seamless, effective marketing group that adapts rapidly to change" and by the end of the week became a statement of principles that made much more sense: "Reaching Readers, Travel and Drinks."

Needless to say, bonds were made, friendships were forged, and the moment everyone got home, big ideas did not disappear within hectic work schedules, but instead became reality amongst a deluge of Facebook comments and emails. In hopes of realizing widespread results, two more writers, Jasinda Wilder and Tina Folsom, were suckered into joining The Indie Voice, completing this unique partnership.

Crazy does not begin to describe this wild group of clever and passionate women, but it's a great start.

Made in the USA
San Bernardino, CA
11 September 2013